FIELDS IN THE
ENGLISH LANDSCAPE

FIELDS IN THE
ENGLISH LANDSCAPE

by Christopher Taylor

with 8 pages of plates, and 30 figures in text

J M DENT & SONS LTD   LONDON

First published 1975
© Text, Christopher Taylor, 1975
© Line illustrations, J. M. Dent & Sons Ltd, 1975

Made in Great Britain
at the
Aldine Press · Letchworth · Herts
for
J. M. DENT & SONS LTD
Aldine House · Albemarle Street · London

This book is set in 11 on 13 pt Garamond 156

ISBN 0 460 04159 2

Preface

For the last fifteen years I have roamed the English countryside, trying to explain its history to myself and to my students. In doing this I have been made aware that little, except at a rarefied academic level, has been written about the most obvious features of the English landscape, its fields.

There are books by the score on archaeological sites, houses, castles, railways and much else, but nothing that tells people in reasonably general terms about fields. This book is an attempt to fill that gap. It is not meant for scholarly experts, though I have relied heavily on their researches, but for the general reader with an inquiring mind and an interest in the environment.

Many of the plans which illustrate the work are based on photographs held by the National Monuments Record, and I am conscious of the debt that I owe to the staff of that organization who have helped me over many years. Not for the first time my wife has read, amended and typed this book and once again my grateful thanks go to her.

Whittlesford, Cambridgeshire   CHRISTOPHER TAYLOR

Contents

List of Plates

List of Maps and Plans

Acknowledgments

The author would like to thank the following for permission to reproduce plans and photographs:

H. C. Bowen, Figs. 3a and 9b

P. J. Fowler, Figs. 1a and 7b

Cambridgeshire County Council, Plates IX and XI

Cambridge University Committee for Aerial Photography, Plates III and V

Ministry of Defence, Plate II

Royal Commission on Historical Monuments (England), Figs. 2a and b, 4b, 5a and b, 11a, 28b; Plates I, IV, VI, VII, VIII, X and XII

Introduction

In spite of modern urban expansion and changing industrial and agricultural techniques, fields are still perhaps the most familiar feature of the English landscape. Everywhere, except in the most rugged uplands of northern England, fields of one form or another can be seen. Indeed, they are so commonplace that most people take them for granted and notice them only when the hedges are grubbed up, or walls bulldozed away to make the new prairie-like fields for modern agriculture, or when they disappear for good under the bricks and concrete of our twentieth-century urban civilization.

Yet it is the fields of this country that give it much of its variety of scenery and characterize every part of it. All regions of England have their own types of fields that can be recognized as typical of the area. In Devon we find small irregularly shaped fields bounded by large banks, which are often surmounted by huge thick hedges. In Sussex the rolling downlands are a sea of arable land, divided occasionally by wire mesh fences. Over much of the English Midlands the most common types of fields are those of rigidly geometrical form defined by hedges, largely of hawthorn, with occasional trees. Over the fenlands of eastern England there is an infinite variety of field shapes and sizes, each bounded by narrow and usually straight drainage ditches. Farther north in Westmorland and Cumberland the small stone-walled paddocks, or strip-shaped fields on the sides of the dales, give way to vast areas delimited by apparently endless walls. Elsewhere there are other types of fields and field shapes, for in every area one can find particular fields of unusual form or with unlikely boundaries.

In addition to these fields proper are the remains of other land-forms resulting from agriculture of all periods. Small embanked square paddocks on the downlands of Wessex are where pre-historic farmers ploughed. Similar ones, though more elongated, are found in the same areas or in parts of northern England and these date from the Roman period. Great flights or staircase-like sets of terraces rising up the limestone escarpment in Gloucester-shire or on the hill slopes of Wiltshire, as well as in many other places, are the results of contour ploughing during the medieval period. The common ridge-and-furrow, typical of much of the English Midlands as well as elsewhere, are the still visible remains of the medieval common field systems there. The superficially similar ridges and furrows in the valleys of Wessex are seven-teenth- and eighteenth-century water meadows that formed the basis of really large-scale sheep farming at that time.

All these and many other features remain in our countryside today, and can be recognized and understood by the observant and intelligent traveller. By looking at fields and field shapes, as well as at other agricultural remains, it is possible to understand much of the history of our country. In addition most fields have names, many of which are now being rapidly forgotten. These are of infinite variety, sometimes dating back more than a thousand years. They can tell us much about the owners of the fields, their origins and usage, as well as many other aspects of their history.

Fields, and more especially the hedges that bound many of them, are also of enormous interest to natural historians. They not only provide shelter and food for birds but are valuable and important habitats for all kinds of communities, such as insect and molluscan life. They may also by their very composition contain rare and interesting species of plants and shrubs that can no longer exist elsewhere.

Finally, of whatever form or size, and whether bounded by hedges, stone walls or fences, fields have a visual value which in our overpopulated island is becoming increasingly important. As our houses, shops and roads all take on the same general appear-ance, regardless of which part of the country we live in, the varied pattern of our fields, built up gradually over five thousand years, becomes indispensable to the landscape. Without fields much of our rural landscape would look as bare and depressing as many of our newer urban areas. For, though nature has produced and moulded the underlying rocks into various forms of natural scenery which we rightly admire, the clothing of that scenery by hedges, walls and fences achieved by man over the centuries provides it with charm and interest. The rolling landscape of Suffolk, which gives so much joy to countless thousands of its inhabitants and visitors, would be little more than a dull prairie without its tree-lined hedges and varied field shapes. And how bare and unexciting would the limestone hills of Derbyshire be without the runs of stone walls which break up the views and produce constant changes of patterns and forms. Even in the mountainous areas of our country the scene would lose much without the long fingers of stone which carry the eye across valley and hillside.

In this book we shall be looking at the fields and other agricultural remains which cover our country. Though it is a largely chronological history from remote prehistoric times to the present day, the emphasis is on what remains for us to see at this moment. In this way it is hoped that the interested reader will learn to appreciate some of the complexities of the history of the English landscape as seen through fields, and will become aware of the part played by fields in the past and the value that they hold for the future.

The problems of trying to write a history of English fields are many. One is the dichotomy between the prehistoric, Roman and Dark Ages on one hand and the medieval and later periods on the other. In the former, one relies on the physical remains entirely, and many important details that are basic to the understanding of field development in terms of social, economic and tenurial events and organization are largely unknown and unknowable. In the latter periods there is a gradually increasing amount of written documentation which can be used to explain the context of the physical remains. In a book of this length it is impossible to deal with all aspects of fields and their development and I am well aware that certain important features have been ignored, or passed over too briefly. Certain ploughs and ploughing techniques, and soils, as well as much about farmsteads and other settlements, have been treated in a cavalier fashion or not at all. However, it seemed to me better to concentrate on the fields themselves as visual evidence of the past rather than on anything else. These are the most threatened today, and if their meaning and history are not recognized, the history of agriculture in its widest sense is lost.

Chapter 1

Prehistoric Fields

Though man certainly lived in this country in the latter part of the Ice Age, the beginnings of agriculture did not emerge until a relatively late date in his history. When the last retreat of the ice sheets from the British Isles took place around 12000 B.C., they left behind a bare, ravaged landscape. As the climate slowly improved this countryside was gradually colonized by vegetation. At first little more than lichens and mosses appeared, then birch trees and pines of various types slowly invaded the landscape. Gradually much of England became covered with pine, birch and hazel forests. These in turn were slowly replaced by a mixed oak forest in which elm, lime and alder trees, the latter especially along the rivers and streams, were common.

It was to this landscape that modern men came, probably around 8000 B.C. Archaeologists call them Mesolithic people, and from the numerous occupation sites which have been discovered and excavated it is certain that they were basically nomadic, organized in small family groups who relied for their existence on what the forest around them could provide. They hunted wild animals such as deer, wild cattle and pig, fished in the sea, rivers and streams, and gathered nuts and berries.

Compared with later people, very little is known of these Mesolithic groups. This is partly because as nomadic people they have left little for us to find, partly because, apart from their minute flint tools, little has survived, and partly because it is very difficult for archaeologists to discover these fragmentary traces. Nevertheless, the evidence that has been discovered indicates that these people did not cultivate plants of any kind and therefore would not have had arable land. However, while as yet there is no firm evidence, it may be that these people did gradually learn how to live with animals in a closer relationship than merely that of hunters to hunted. Certainly they did hunt most of the available wild animals, but as time went on they may have learnt how to make better use of these. They had domesticated dogs which they used in hunting, and it is possible that they may have learnt how to herd, protect and manage, in a primitive way, some of the animals in the forests around them. At the moment this is speculation and all that can really be said about these peoples is that they contributed little or nothing towards the history of fields in this country. However, they did begin to interfere with the natural environment around them, which later people were to continue to do, and to develop it for agricultural purposes. The evidence for this comes from the detailed analysis of pollen grains dated to the Mesolithic period. This analysis has revealed that there was a marked increase in the amount of hazel and a decrease in birch within the forests of this time. While this might have been the result of purely natural changes, it has been suggested that it could in part be a reflection of fire, resulting from deliberate human activity; the hazel, being able to withstand forest fires, would have increased while species such as birch would have been killed.

Around 4000 B.C. there is evidence of more definite changes in the archaeological record and in the natural environment which reflect the impact of new and radical ideas as well as perhaps new people. In purely archaeological terms these changes mark the beginning of the Neolithic period, when a quite different material culture is recognizable on archaeological sites. This is usually said to be the result of entirely new and technically more advanced groups of people arriving in this country. While this may be so, there is no absolute evidence for this and it may be that new ideas and methods were acquired from people across the Channel in western Europe by the existing Mesolithic groups without any major influx of invaders. The most likely explanation is that new people arrived here, and new methods and tools were passed on to some of the existing people.

Excavations by archaeologists of the remains of these Neolithic people provide us with information about them and their agriculture in a variety of ways. There are the purely material remains, or objects, found on Neolithic sites, such as pieces of pottery, stone axes, flint arrowheads and so on. These indicate a new and advanced technology—for example the pottery is the first to be found in this country—but they also show something of agriculture. Objects such as saddle-querns imply that grain was collected from either cultivated or wild cereals, and ground to produce flour. More important, some of the stone axes appear to have been used as hoes for breaking up the ground. The pottery found on these sites is also of interest, for occasional sherds contain impressions of seeds which were presumably picked up accidentally during the making of the pots. Examination of these seed impressions has revealed at least three varieties of cultivated cereals: Emmer wheat, Einkorn wheat and barley. The stone axes themselves also imply an ability to clear forest. Excavations on Neolithic sites have also produced animal bones, mainly cattle and sheep, which show that these people kept domesticated herds and flocks while continuing to hunt deer and other wild animals. Also of interest is the relatively common occurrence on Neolithic habitation sites of so-called 'rubbish pits', which on close examination have proved to have been dug originally for the storage of grain and only later abandoned and back-filled with refuse.

The evidence of this kind of material from Neolithic sites is supported by the results of palaeobotanical examination of pollen, work on snails, and the chemical and physical examination of contemporary soils, all buried under banks and mounds built by Neolithic people, or hidden in marsh and bog deposits. This work, when supplemented by dating evidence obtained by Carbon 14 analysis, has revealed a sequence of development of the landscape in agricultural terms.

At a number of places in the north of England, for example at Storrs Moss in Lancashire, there is evidence that around 4000 B.C., when the first Neolithic people or ideas were arriving in this country, there were small local clearances in the all-pervading woodland. This kind of work shows that, as time went on, these clearings were enlarged so that by about 3500 B.C. there is not only evidence for considerable areas of open land within the forests, but also a marked decline in the number of elm trees. It has been suggested that this latter feature is possibly the result of large-scale gathering of elm leaves as fodder for tethered animals.

Later still, around 3000 B.C., there is a countrywide marked drop in the amount of all tree pollen and the appearance of ribwort and cereal pollens. Ribwort pollen is of particular interest, because the plant is a weed found in arable land, which the cereal pollen implies was increasing. Studies of snails and soils of this time also show an increase in the amount of open land as opposed to forest, and charcoal, perhaps the result of large-scale burning of woodland, becomes common. In addition there is a considerable increase in the amount of birch, alder and hazel pollen.

What does all this mean in terms of the earliest agriculture of England during the centuries from 4000 to 3000 B.C.? Though by no means all the questions can be answered at the moment, the work to date suggests that between 4000 and 3500 B.C. small groups of nomadic Neolithic farmers were moving across England and clearing small areas of woodland to provide themselves with habitation sites, grazing grounds and small temporary plots of land in which to cultivate crops. Then, after 3500 B.C., probably because of increasing population, there is a massive attack on the forests by axe and fire. As yet the actual areas cleared are not known with certainty, but the major river valleys, the chalk and limestone areas of southern England, the heaths of East Anglia as well as large areas of the uplands and moors of northern England, were changed at this time to the open land that we often assume was original.

These and other areas were cleared, grazed and farmed, perhaps briefly, and then regenerated to birch and hazel scrubland as the nomadic farmers moved on. The excavations of the settlement sites of these people support this theory. Such settlements that have been examined seem to indicate fairly short-lived occupation and fit in well with the idea of a nomadic people. In addition there is a class of monument built by these people, called the causewayed camp, which still remains in the modern landscape and further supports this suggestion of mobility. These 'camps' exist today in the higher areas of the southern English chalklands, as at Windmill Hill and Knapp Hill in Wiltshire, at Hambledon Hill in Dorset and at Maiden Bower in Bedfordshire. Others, now destroyed by later activities, are known to have existed in lower-lying areas. These curious structures usually take the form of one or more concentric rings of ditches with inner banks, through which are numerous causeways or gaps. Excavations on these sites have revealed no permanent occupation or any large-scale ritual activities. They have been best explained as fairgrounds or meeting places to which the nomadic farming groups returned at regular intervals to come together and exchange crops, cattle, axes and other goods.

However, while these sites and other archaeological and botanical evidence indicate a nomadic people, there are places which show that the Neolithic society was not made up entirely of wandering farmers. There still remain for us to see today other structures of this period, apparently associated with the ritual or religious side of the society. These include massive 'temples', or henge monuments as they are known. The biggest are Durrington Walls, Avebury Circle and the Marden Circle in Wiltshire, and Mount Pleasant in Dorset, but there are many smaller ones such as Arbour Low in Derbyshire. There is also a strange feature called a cursus, which consists of parallel banks and ditches, sometimes running for hundreds of metres across the countryside. The largest cursus of all, in Dorset, is over twenty kilometres long. Whatever the actual rituals carried out at these places, and these are largely unknown, as works of engineering and organization they suggest a highly complex society made up of more than just groups of wandering farmers. The earthen structures themselves and the evidence of massive timber buildings associated with the henges imply some degree of permanent occupation in certain areas, together with perhaps permanent agriculture. The numerous burial mounds of these Neolithic peoples, the long barrows, both earthen and chambered, would also seem in part to reflect a society much more stable in habitation and agricultural terms than the other evidence suggests.

It is from one of these burial mounds that the earliest evidence for fields, as opposed to ill-defined plots of land, has come. The burial mound in question lies near Avebury in Wiltshire, and is called from its location the South Street Long Barrow. There, after the excavation of the mound itself had been completed, careful work on the soil beneath it revealed a series of minute grooves running at right angles to one another and so forming a criss-cross pattern. These have been interpreted as the grooves cut by a 'crook-ard' type of plough as it was dragged through the soil (Fig. 1a).

The crook-ard was the most primitive type of plough found in Europe. Basically this implement is merely a hoe or mattock, formed perhaps in the first instance from a forked tree branch. Instead of the operator facing the tool and pulling it towards him, as with a mattock or hoe, he simply turns round and drags it through the soil and so 'ploughs' it. A larger model pulled by an ox, and perhaps fitted with a stone 'axe' to protect and strengthen the 'share' or tip, is a true plough. While as yet no ploughs of this type have been found in England, the grooves or 'ard-marks' under the South Street Long Barrow are likely to be the result of ploughing the land there with such an implement. The criss-cross effect is due to the land being ploughed in two directions, one at right angles to the other, presumably in order to break up the soil thoroughly. The date of this ploughing was established by Carbon 14 methods at about 3000 B.C. or a little after.

The importance of the South Street plough marks is that there, for the first time in man's long occupation of this country, we have evidence of an actual field. We do not know what boundaries the field had, if any, or what size it was, but there can be little doubt of its purpose. Thus the evidence, slim as it is, suggests that by at least 3000 B.C. the Neolithic farmers of this country, nomadic or otherwise, were ploughing and cultivating small areas of land in a recognizable field system.

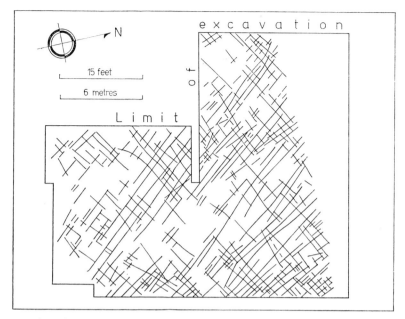

1a   Plan of Neolithic plough marks.

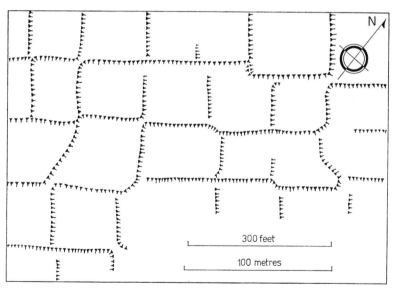

1b   Diagram of prehistoric fields.

The value of this South Street evidence is that it shows this situation as existing in Neolithic times, whereas similar evidence is otherwise found only in later prehistoric contexts. For elsewhere in England similar plough marks have been discovered showing that the same technique of breaking up the soil was practised in the succeeding centuries. At the South Street Barrow itself later, but similar, plough marks were discovered and dated to around 2000 B.C., while others have been discovered under a later round burial mound of the early Bronze Age at Amesbury, Wiltshire, dated to about 1800 B.C. In Cornwall, at Gwithian, excavations have led to the dicovery of almost identical plough marks of two periods. The first were also of the early Bronze Age, while the later dated from around 1500 B.C. Similar marks have been found in even later contexts; at Overton Down, Wiltshire, of the late Iron Age or early Roman period, at Walker, Northumberland, dating from early Roman times, and at Fritham, Hampshire, belonging to the late Roman period.

All these show that a simple and basic form of plough and ploughing method were in use for perhaps four thousand years regardless of technical, social and economic advances elsewhere, a remarkable example of the conservatism of agriculture which will reappear later on. There may, however, have been an improvement in plough type during this long period. Although, as was noted earlier, no actual plough has been found in this country, examples have been discovered on the Continent and one, from Donneruplund in Denmark, which is termed a beam-ard, is a marked advance on the crook-ard. The most important feature of this plough is an arrow-shaped share which could not only cut a deep and wide furrow but also move soil to one side. However, it was not able actually to turn the sod as could later heavy ploughs. In any case, regardless of the evidence (or lack of it) of ploughs, there is much better evidence for the fields and field systems of the prehistoric farmers of England—that of the fields themselves, and it is to these we must now turn.

These fields are the, perhaps unfortunately termed, 'Celtic' fields, a nomenclature now enshrined in all works on fields though totally misleading and meaningless. The most characteristic feature of these prehistoric fields is that they are small in size and usually approximately rectangular, varying from 0.2 to 0.5 hectare in extent and from virtually square to markedly rectangular in shape (Fig. 1b, Plate I). Such fields are—or were before the destruction of the last fifty years removed many of them—widespread over certain parts of the country. These included all the downlands of Wessex and Sussex with examples in Surrey, small areas on the limestones of the Mendip Hills in Somerset, Gloucestershire, Oxfordshire and Derbyshire, and larger areas on the uplands of Dartmoor, Yorkshire, Westmorland, Durham and Northumberland.

This distribution helps towards an understanding of prehistoric field systems. On the whole these fields lie or lay on land which, certainly during the medieval period and later, was marginal. Therefore the fields that remain for us to study have survived only because they lay on land which later people did not use intensively. Other, and perhaps very different, fields elsewhere have been totally destroyed by later activity and thus we have no evidence of them. In addition, the fact that the areas where prehistoric fields now lie were marginal land in later times, might mean that they were also marginal land in the prehistoric period. Therefore the fields that remain may not be representative, and by studying them we may produce only a distorted picture of what prehistoric fields actually looked like. We cannot solve this problem, but we must not forget that it exists.

With these reservations in mind, we can examine the prehistoric fields which remain and draw some tentative conclusions. First of all, why are these fields so small? The reasons are not of course known with certainty and we can only guess. An obvious explanation is a technical one, involving the method of ploughing. If, as has been suggested, cross-ploughing was necessary in order to break up the soils in preparing a seed-bed, given the limited traction power available, either by human beings in the first instance, or by small oxen later on, it was probably more sensible and convenient to keep each individual plot fairly small. In addition, both recent experiments of ploughing with a primitive beam-ard, and the documented ploughing methods of the Roman period as described by the classical writer Columella, suggest that fields might have had to be ploughed twice, once with the ard upright and once with it sloping in order to deepen the furrow and throw the soil sideways. This too would have tended to keep the fields small. On the other hand, the explanation could be the result of the actual ownership or tenure of the fields, or the way in which the land was farmed; that is, if the fields were collectively or individually owned, or if they were ploughed, sown or reaped in common or individually. For the prehistoric period such factors are unknown and unknowable and consequently we are thrown back on purely technical reasons which we can assess though they may not provide the correct explanation.

The boundaries of these prehistoric fields are important. Most often these fields survive today on slopes of varying steepness, a reason for their survival. They are thus delimited, particularly at their upper and lower sides, by scarps or 'lynchets' (Plate I). These lynchets can vary from a few centimetres to 8 metres or more in height. Indeed when these fields have been destroyed by modern ploughing, very often their existence can be recognized by the surviving lynchets on their up and downhill sides. However, these lynchets are a secondary feature of the fields resulting from their cultivation, and not part of their original form. Any type of ploughing on a slope causes movement of the soil downhill, either by gravity or by rainwash. If a field is tilled, the plough will cut a sharp line along its uphill side. The disturbed soil will tend to slip downhill and so leave a well-marked scarp along the edge of the ploughing which is termed a *negative lynchet*. Downhill, on the other side of the field, there will be a corresponding build-up of soil where the ploughing stops and another scarp will form. This is called a *positive lynchet*. Where one field is directly below another, the scarp dividing them will thus be a composite lynchet made by cutting down from below and accumulation from above (Fig. 3a).

The speed at which a lynchet forms and its ultimate height

obviously depend on the slope of the ground, the nature and depth of soil, climate, particularly rainfall, and the method and length of time involved in ploughing the field. These factors are all so variable and little understood that it is impossible to give any single reason for the size of lynchets in prehistoric fields.

Though lynchets build up mainly on the up- and downhill sides of prehistoric fields, they also occur on the other sides. Strictly speaking, if the field is laid out squarely across the contours this should not occur, but in practice these fields are more often set askew to the contours and as a result lynchets may form on all the boundaries.

Where prehistoric fields occur on flat or only gently sloping land other forms of boundaries are to be seen. Sometimes these are small banks, often only a few centimetres high (Plate X). Without excavation it is not always clear what these originally were. Some may be the remains of deliberately constructed stone walls or earthen banks, some just scraped-up ridges of even lines of stones originally used to mark out the area to be ploughed, and subsequently sharpened by ploughing on either side. In other cases, especially on Dartmoor for example, these fields can be edged with upright slabs of stone. Other apparent banks may be the result of clearing the fields of stone and flints by hand and the subsequent dumping of these along the edges. Excavation through lynchets of prehistoric fields has often led to the discovery of the original boundary, now buried deep under the accumulated plough soil. These boundaries include low stone walls and wooden fences, both found in the fields on Fyfield Down, Wiltshire. Elsewhere, as at Gwithian in Cornwall, shallow ditches have been found surrounding fields. On the other hand, there is also evidence from excavations that, before the development of lynchets, some fields were apparently not bounded by any line at all. Exactly how these fields were defined is not clear. Perhaps just the corners were marked, either by stones or by posts, and then the land ploughed within these limits.

This then is broadly what prehistoric fields looked like and how they were laid out and ploughed. But what date are they? Here we have a problem which is difficult to solve. It is clear that arable fields, by their very purpose, involve the continual disturbance of the soil. Also, once in existence, and hedged by banks or clearly defined and ever-growing lynchets, they would tend to remain in use for long periods of time, and perhaps for centuries. Therefore archaeologists who excavate them are not going to find an undisturbed and sealed deposit of datable pottery or other objects which can tell them exactly when and for how long the fields were in use.

Nevertheless prehistoric fields can be dated in two principal ways. Firstly the walls, banks and lynchets can be excavated and pottery incorporated beneath or within them found. Very often large quantities of pottery occur, not as a result of any occupation there, but because the fields were apparently kept fertile by spreading manure on them. It seems that this manure was brought to the fields from the farmsteads and villages where animals were impounded, and before its arrival on the fields acquired a large proportion of domestic rubbish including broken pottery. In this way the fields tend to have scatters of pottery on them, sometimes dating from the period of use, and such pottery is often incorporated with, in or beneath banks or walls, or stratified through the lynchets. A variant of this method is the discovery of datable objects deliberately buried in lynchets and subsequently discovered by chance.

The other method of dating prehistoric fields is by observing their relationships, either by visual examination of the present landscape or by excavation of datable sites or features associated with, overlying or buried and destroyed by them. Supporting evidence of date can also be achieved by botanical or molluscan examination, which gives an idea of the prevailing environmental conditions.

These methods of dating prehistoric fields have enabled archaeologists to establish general periods in which certain of these fields or groups of fields were in use. The results of excavating through lynchets have shown that some were in use during the Iron Age, that is, in the three or four centuries before the Roman conquest, as at Fyfield Down, Wiltshire. Others at Horridge in Devon, Ebsborne Wake in Wiltshire, Lulworth in Dorset and Tawedrach in Cornwall, where hoards or single objects of Bronze Age date had been discovered within the fields, were perhaps already in use by about 1000 B.C. or even earlier.

Relations between various datable features and the fields themselves have revealed similar or even earlier dates for some of them. At Shearplace Hill in Dorset and Itford Hill in Sussex, excavation of settlement areas which were contemporary with adjacent fields has produced dates of around 1200 B.C., while at Ogborne Mazey, Wiltshire, an even earlier settlement has been discovered actually built over and through a pre-existing field lynchet. In Cornwall, the general correlation between the distribution of Bronze Age burial mounds or barrows and areas of fields is such that a broad degree of contemporaneity is suggested, while at Gwithian in the same county a date of around 1600 B.C. for the fields there has been established. Just as important is the number of cases where, by careful examination, it has been established that early Bronze Age burial mounds are situated in such relationships to prehistoric fields as to leave no doubt that they are later than the fields. Examples of these are known from Pentridge Hill, Dorset, Winterbourne Abbas in the same county (Fig. 2a) and on Fyfield Down, Wiltshire.

From this it emerges that 'Celtic' or prehistoric fields were already in existence over large areas of England by at least 2000 B.C., and, if the evidence of the South Street Long Barrow plough marks is accepted as showing similar fields, by just after 3000 B.C. There is very little difference in the overall size and shape of these fields throughout this long period of time, indicating that either ploughing or other agricultural methods remained reasonably static, and/or that the basic tenurial and social organization which lay behind these fields stayed the same.

So far we have examined these prehistoric fields as if they were nothing but isolated groups scattered over the countryside, and, as a result of modern destruction, this is unfortunately often true of what remains to be seen on the ground. However, in a few

31

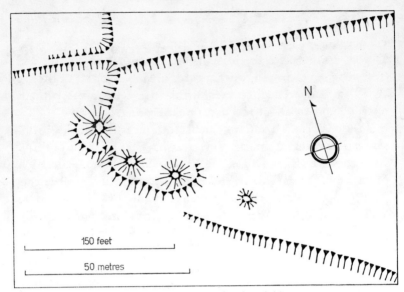

150 feet

50 metres

2a   Bronze Age barrow lying on corner of earlier field.

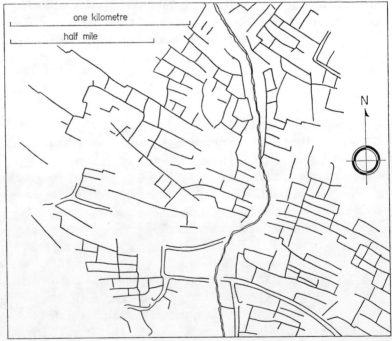

one kilometre

half mile

2b   Prehistoric field system, Piddletrenthide, Dorset. Bounded by earthen banks and scarps.

places, where recent activity has been restricted, large areas of fields survive, often covering hundreds of hectares. These may be seen in south Dorset, Wiltshire, on Dartmoor and in parts of Yorkshire. More important, air photography has revealed traces of these fields extending over vast areas, sometimes three or four kilometres across, associated with contemporary roads or trackways. Nothing at all can be seen on the ground today and the air photographs are the only evidence, but these photographs greatly extend our understanding of the prehistoric fields in a number of ways.

First, because they show that larger areas were cultivated in prehistoric times, they widen our knowledge of the range of farming activity in these periods. It is now clear that over much of prehistoric England the picture was not one of small groups of people living in isolation and cultivating a few fields, but of large numbers of farmers living fairly closely together and cultivating huge tracts of land. The occurrence of prehistoric fields, not only on level ground or gently rolling countryside, but on steep hillsides which have not been ploughed since, indicates that in some areas there was considerable pressure on land. Thus we can be sure that at various times during the prehistoric period large parts of England were under almost continuous cultivation. This is especially important when we realize that most of the surviving fields lie in what was perhaps marginal land. Our view of what the so-called primitive prehistoric farmers could and did do is radically altered by this picture of large areas of arable land (Fig. 2b).

Even more striking in terms of organization and farming ability is the evidence revealed by close examination of some of these large tracts of fields, not as individual plots but as whole systems. It might be assumed that these systems were gradually evolved as individual farmers brought one field after another into existence when the demand for arable land increased, but the plans of many of the larger areas of prehistoric fields suggest a different form of development. There is a clear indication of long, often straight, parallel and continuous boundaries forming huge land units of several hundred hectares, within which the actual fields are fitted. That is, it appears that far from fields being made piecemeal one at a time, huge swaths of land were cleared, defined by boundaries and then subdivided into the small fields. This shows an ability to plan and execute large-scale agricultural alterations to the prehistoric landscape which has hitherto been thought of as beyond the capacity of the contemporary people. Where such boundaries are not identifiable, huge blocks of fields, all orientated in the same direction, even when divided by valley and streams, point to a degree of forward planning (Fig. 2b).

Though once again, as with much of prehistoric archaeology, it is impossible to interpret these changes in terms of social or tenurial organization and, more important, the actual way the fields were organized and cropped by individuals, the implications are that this work involved enormous communal effort and technical expertise rather than individual work. It suggests some form of overall control of certain aspects of prehistoric agriculture, either by lords, or by 'estate managers' of some kind.

Just as disconcerting, with regard to preconceived ideas, is another aspect of large-scale agricultural land use in prehistoric times. Until now we have concentrated almost entirely on arable fields, made and formed for the sole purpose of growing crops. But, as was noted above, the early Neolithic farmers were also involved in stock raising. The importance of cattle and sheep in the farming economy continued throughout prehistoric times as the bones of these animals found on all Neolithic, Bronze Age and Iron Age occupation sites reveal. In the earlier prehistoric periods, stock was perhaps grazed on the newly cleared land beyond the arable fields, but as the landscape filled up and less and less land was available for indiscriminate herding of stock, definite areas of pasture land had to be defined and bounded. This was presumably necessary not only to control physically the stock itself for grazing conservation and protection from outsiders, but also to prevent damage to adjacent arable land.

The legacy of these 'pastoral areas' survives in the modern

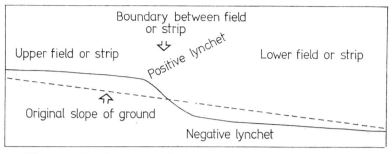

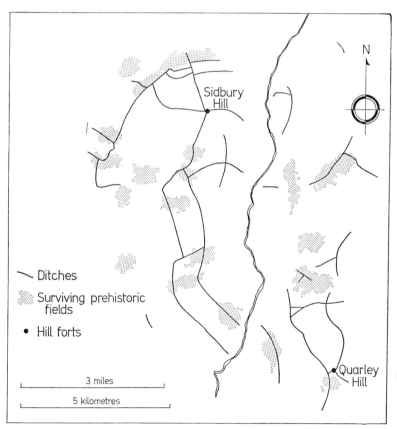

Ditches

Surviving prehistoric fields

• Hill forts

Sidbury Hill

Quarley Hill

N

3 miles

5 kilometres

landscape today, or can be distinguished on air photographs in certain parts of England, notably Wessex. Long continuous banks and/or ditches of considerable size can be traced often for many kilometres across the countryside, and these appear to divide up the land into huge blocks, each covering as much as ten square kilometres (Fig. 3b). These are generally termed 'ranch boundaries' and, though not accurately dated in most cases, can be shown to originate certainly from before the Iron Age (*i.e.* 500 to 600 B.C.) and probably from around 1500 to 1600 B.C. They may in fact start even earlier though as yet absolute proof is not forthcoming. Again these boundaries suggest an ability to conceive of land division on a large scale, to carry out considerable physical work in purely engineering terms and to operate complex pastoral organizations.

So far much of the evidence of prehistoric fields and pastoral enclosures has been taken from the lowland areas of England, and especially southern England. It is in these areas that the most remarkable achievements of prehistoric farmers can be seen today. In other and less favourable areas of the country, however, we also have evidence of fields and field systems that is to some extent different from that of lowland England and may be interpreted as a response to the difficult environment of these uplands. Nevertheless there may be another explanation. While the fields that remain to be studied in these areas have their own intrinsic interest in any case, they may show us an earlier stage of development in the history of fields that is irrecoverable from lowland England. This is because of the destruction that is a result, not of medieval or later ploughing in these areas, but of prehistoric activity as the complex pattern of fields evolved during these periods.

For example, on Dartmoor there is extensive evidence that the earliest fields which remain today were irregular and curvilinear walled plots, often associated with piles of stones or clearance cairns as well as with contemporary hut circles (Fig. 4a). These are probably to be dated to somewhere between 1000 and 3000 B.C. It seems, however, that these plots were gradually replaced

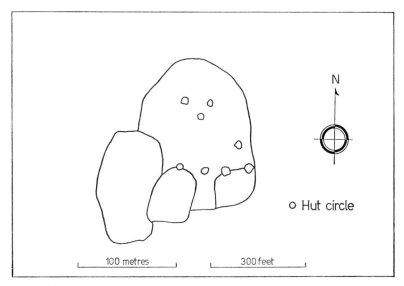

4a   Prehistoric fields and hut circles, Sheepstor, Devon. Stone wall boundaries.

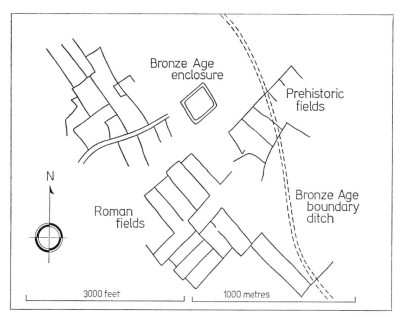

4b   Prehistoric and Roman fields, Martin Down, Hampshire. Bounded by earthen banks and scarps.

by fields of a more rectangular character, more like the normal prehistoric fields, though still bounded by stone walls. These fields appeared shortly after 1000 B.C. Similar circular plots being replaced by more rectangular fields are known from Yorkshire. It may be that here we have some of the evidence of field development which is lost to us elsewhere in England. With it, it is perhaps possible to draw up a tentative development sequence of fields during prehistoric times. This starts with the initial small-scale clearances of the woodland by the early Neolithic peoples around 4000 B.C., with such agriculture as there was being mainly in the form of hand-dug plots. As time went on and the population expanded, continued land clearance took place and the increase in stock rearing prevented regeneration of the forest. By 3000 B.C. the plough had certainly appeared, and arable land took the form of small irregular or curvilinear fields. In the more populated lowland areas, these plots were gradually replaced by the more familiar rectangular fields by 2000 B.C., and by 1500 B.C. at the latest the massive exploitation of the landscape with organized clearance and field layouts was already in being. By 1000 B.C. there was a fully developed agricultural landscape in lowland England, while in the uplands the older circular plots continued in existence until that time when they were gradually replaced by small groups of rectangular fields.

So far the development of prehistoric fields has been discussed largely in terms of farming alone; however, the fields did not stand by themselves. They were only one part of the rural landscape, of which a major aspect was the settlements of the people who made and worked these fields. We have already noted that in the Neolithic period before 2000 B.C., while some evidence suggests a basically nomadic people, there are indications that some parts at least of that society occupied permanent living sites. From the evidence of the fields alone, after 2000 B.C. it seems that some semi-permanent settlements would have been required, and by 1500 B.C. the appearance of the carefully organized and laid out countryside indicates a reasonably fixed pattern of settlement. And indeed this is so, for few of the known field systems are totally without evidence of associated farmsteads and hamlets by 1500 B.C. Where large areas of prehistoric fields survive, or can be seen on air photographs, the whereabouts of settlements are often clearly indicated by the appearance of small irregular paddocks or curved enclosures, bounded by banks or walls. Close examination of these may produce evidence of slight depressions or raised platforms where the sites still exist, or scatters of pottery, bone and other material where they have been destroyed by modern ploughing. Both are indications of the sites of huts and other structures used by the inhabitants. Some of these settlements have been excavated with remarkable results.

One such is Shearplace Hill in Dorset, where a group of em-banked circular enclosures situated within a large area of pre-historic fields was examined. The excavation revealed remains of two circular buildings, basically timber huts, associated with a 'courtyard', an outer farmyard, as well as evidence of stock rearing including cattle, sheep and pigs. The whole farmstead was dated to around 1200 B.C.

There are other examples of this kind of settlement connected with fields of both earlier and later dates. Even more common are the almost countless excavations of Bronze Age and Iron Age settlements from all over England which, because of their situa-tion in areas that have been cultivated ever since, have no trace of their fields around them. Though these settlements, of what-ever date, vary somewhat in detail and especially in terms of size, type of house and archaeological material, they all consistently reveal evidence of the agricultural activities that went on in the surrounding and now untraceable fields. Bones of sheep, cattle and pigs are common. Quern stones for grinding cereals, pits for storing grain and even timber granaries are all known. Cultivated seed impressions on pottery are also a common occurrence. Thus even when no fields can now be recognized, we can be sure from the evidence found within the farmsteads that they did once surround these settlements. The widespread occurrence of, for example, Iron Age farmsteads on chalk uplands, barren heath-lands, river terraces and heavy clayland in every part of England,

all having evidence of intensive agricultural activity, shows just
how much of the country was being farmed in later prehistoric
times.

Where the fields do remain there is other evidence of farming
activity than the farmsteads. This takes the form of trackways or
lanes running through the fields. These may be terraced ways or
slightly hollowed ways. They can often be seen entering or leaving
settlements, passing through the fields and sometimes opening
out into areas which were apparently pasture (Figs 2b and 4b).
Such features once again not only show the complexity of the
countryside in later prehistoric times, but greatly add to our
knowledge of the way in which it was run.

Thus, after a fairly slow start in the Neolithic period, the development of fields and the rural landscape in general went on apace
during later prehistoric times. Even before 1000 B.C. much of
England was occupied and farmed on a large scale and in a well-
organized pattern. Perhaps most of the country, the higher uplands and the marshy valleys and fenlands excepted, was being
used by either arable or pastoral farmers or by both. Even by this
apparently early date there can have been few places where the
imprint of the farmers' labour was not obvious or relatively close
at hand. The countryside as a whole was being widely utilized
and, in some places, perhaps over-utilized by a sophisticated, far-
sighted and technically competent farming community.

Yet the reality is even more complex than this. In spite of the
simple sequence outlined above, in the later prehistoric period
at least the situation was not one of steady development and
expansion. Within it constant changes took place about which
we know little and understand less. We can see some of these
changes by studying the fields that remain, or by excavating contemporary settlement sites, but exactly what was their cause is
often still a mystery.

First of all, even after the fields were established, the basic layout was not necessarily permanent. Subsequent farming could
and did either ignore or deliberately obliterate existing fields to
produce new ones on top. Thus the South Street Long Barrow

excavation revealed that, while the barrow itself was built over the first plough marks, some time after the construction of the barrow the area was again ploughed. The latter plough marks clearly belong to a different field system and were dated to around 2000 B.C., nearly a thousand years later than the first.

Much more common is the evidence for alteration of the existing field shapes by later farmers. One of the most characteristic features of the square or rectangular prehistoric field is the occurrence of larger ones which are clearly the result of the breaking down of the field bank or lynchet between two pre-existing fields to make one (Plate I). In some cases slight traces of the former bank or lynchet survive. The vast majority of these breaks or enlargements are undated and many are certainly of Roman date (see p. 51 below). Nevertheless some appear to be of prehistoric origin, and probably reflect a constantly changing land-use pattern, perhaps resulting from differences in ploughing methods, crops, ownership or other causes. Nor must it be assumed that once in existence fields were continuously cultivated. Evidence from excavations suggests that at times certain prehistoric fields were abandoned for long periods. For example at Fyfield Down, Wiltshire, an excavation through a lynchet, though it showed that the adjoining field was cultivated for many centuries, indicated that this cultivation was intermittent; this was not just in the sense of occasional fallowing, though there is clear evidence that this took place. While the field was originally cultivated probably in the later Bronze Age and certainly in the early Iron Age (*i.e.* 700–200 B.C.), it was then apparently abandoned and not re-ploughed until early in the Roman period (A.D. 100–150). This particular gap is an extremely long one, but the existence of such periods of non-cultivation is really important in terms of the working of such systems. They suggest that some fields were abandoned after fairly intensive cultivation in order to allow natural recovery of fertility, a feature to which we will return (pp. 62 and 68 below).

Even more interesting perhaps is the evidence from the upland areas of England where it seems that there might have been a complete secession of arable cultivation around 500 B.C. in some places. Elsewhere, while no widespread break in agricultural practices is obvious, there were certainly local changes in land use, often on a considerable scale. One of the pieces of evidence for this is the occurrence of areas of prehistoric fields that are divided by later ranch-boundary ditches. Thus at both Martin Down, Hampshire (Fig. 4b), and Bulford Down, south of Sidbury Hill, Wiltshire (Fig. 3b), as well as at many other places, a boundary ditch cleaves the earlier arrangement of fields in such a way as to prevent their use. This indicates that there was a reversion from arable farming to stock breeding at some time. And, of course, the reverse situation occurs where a ranch boundary was later used as the edge of a block of new fields, suggesting a turnover from pastoral to arable farming.

At what exact period these changes and alterations occurred is usually not known and, more important, why they took place at all is beyond our knowledge. Sometimes there are possibilities, such as climatic deterioration. For example, it is known that between 900 B.C. and 400 B.C. England had a generally wetter and colder climate than in the preceding and succeeding centuries. This may have caused the abandonment of arable fields on the uplands when it became no longer possible to grow crops in the wetter conditions. Most of the other changes observable in lowland England are not, however, so easily explicable in simple climatic terms. Nor can they be interpreted in terms of changing population or advances in technology, neither of which seems to have happened to any great extent. The real explanation of these changes, especially those involving stock raising to arable farming or vice versa, is more likely to be in the effect of complex economic and social movements which, archaeologically, are impossible to recover. We can only catalogue the results, which show that prehistoric farmers, like their successors, reacted to economic and social pressures and accordingly changed their ways of obtaining a living from the land.

In the last four or five centuries of the prehistoric period, during the so-called Iron Age, the various pressures on prehistoric

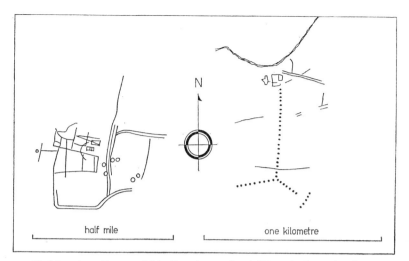

5a   Prehistoric or Roman fields, Peterborough, visible only from the air.

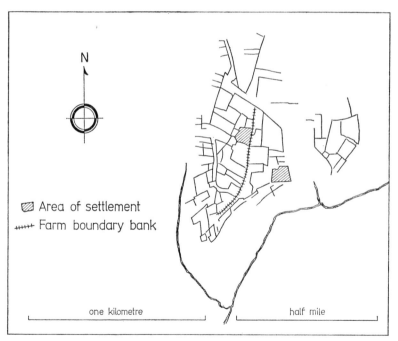

5b   Prehistoric or Roman settlements, fields and farm boundary, Corfe Castle, Dorset. Stone wall boundaries, now grass covered and only a few centimetres high.

farmers and thus on the landscape increased, and the results can still be seen in some parts of England. Undoubtedly the most important factor here was a considerable increase in population. Iron Age settlement sites are known in almost all parts of the country, sometimes in considerable numbers, and often on seemingly unsuitable land. For example, in south-east Northamptonshire, in an area mainly covered by glacially derived clays and certainly well forested in medieval times, the density of known Iron Age settlements, mainly small farmsteads, is about one to every square kilometre. Other parts of the country, with a similar density of settlement, saw at this time the appearance of great fortresses crowning hilltops. Some of these, though by no means all, were permanently occupied by large numbers of people. These forts reflect not only the increasing population but also the need for these people to organize themselves into groups for protection. There is certainly evidence in this period of tribal groups organized and led by warrior chiefs. These seem to have controlled, perhaps by force of arms, the regions around their forts.

As a result of this increased population, more and more land had to be taken into cultivation or used for stock raising. The landscape filled up, and most of it must have been carefully divided between tribes and family groups and demarcated by some form of observable boundary either artificial or natural. Some of these divisions, at different levels of society, may still be seen in some places in southern England. At the upper levels there exist what may be termed estate boundaries: those banks and ditches that radiate from some high focal point and carefully delimit vast tracts of land containing hundreds of hectares of fields, large zones of pasture and many settlements. One such can be seen around Quarley Hill, Hampshire, and another around Sidbury Hill, Wiltshire (Fig. 3b), though here all the boundaries appear to be earlier than the final stage of the hill forts that seem to be their foci. At the bottom level of the social scale we can sometimes see the boundaries around and between individual farms. Thus at Kingston Down, Dorset (Fig. 5b), there still exist two small

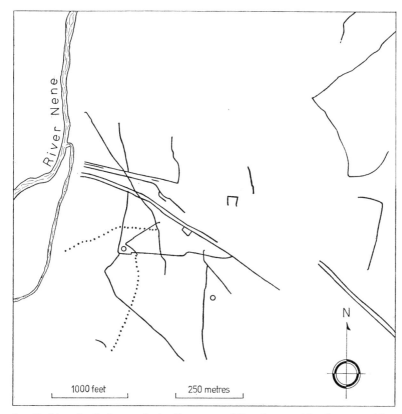

6a Prehistoric ditches and pit alignments, Warmington, Northamptonshire, and Elton, Huntingdonshire, visible only from the air.

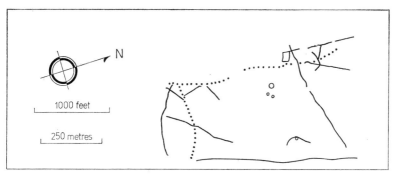

6b Prehistoric ditches and pit alignments, Collyweston, Northamptonshire, visible only from the air.

settlements, each with its surrounding fields, and with a clearly defined low boundary bank dividing them. Air photography of the gravel areas of the major rivers of England, as well as of light limestone and chalky soils, has also revealed curious rows of pits often up to two or three kilometres long, known as pit alignments. Their exact date is unknown, though they appear to be of the later prehistoric period. Their purpose is also unknown but they must represent some form of boundary, perhaps of estates or farmsteads. In the Welland Valley in Lincolnshire attempts have been made to see them as the boundaries of farms, though this is not proven (Fig. 5a). In the same areas, air photographs also show lengths of often discontinuous ditches which join, cross and ignore these pit alignments (Figs. 6a and b). These are rarely in a form that indicates size of fields, and though they may be fragments of once complete fields, their original form, shape and date are unknown.

By the end of the prehistoric period then, when the Roman armies arrived in A.D. 43 much of England was not only settled, but extensively cultivated and grazed in a complex agricultural system which had developed over the previous four thousand years.

Chapter 2

Roman Fields

Before discussing in detail the form of agriculture and the resulting fields which were the basis of rural life in the Roman period, it is important to take note of two fundamental and perhaps contradictory facts. First of all, the arrival of the Roman army, with the subsequent conquest of Britain and its absorption into the Roman Empire, did not result in a marked break in the agricultural development of this country. The impact of Roman civilization was considerable in many aspects of British life, but agriculture may not, in the first instance, have been one of these. Perhaps the most important point to note is that there was no alteration of the basic population of the country. The Roman army came, conquered and occupied, and was followed by relatively few administrators and traders whose job was to rule and exploit the newly acquired territory. But the existing Iron Age peoples lived on and merely passed under the control of the Roman Empire. The soldiers, officials and the merchants introduced new methods of government, new fashions of house construction, new types of pottery, and these and much else were eagerly, or reluctantly, accepted by the conquered tribes. However, the basic structure of society remained the same. Local Iron Age chiefs, living in circular wooden huts and ruling their followers from the heights of a hill fort, merely descended to the newly laid out town, built a stone house with all its veneer of civilization, accepted the job of local magistrate and continued to rule their followers, who mostly remained to farm their old land.

As time went on all levels of society accepted various aspects of Roman civilization. The outcome was that the upper classes acquired town houses, large villas and perhaps the rudiments of Roman education and religion, while some of the humbler farmers replaced their circular wooden huts with rectangular stone ones, painted their plastered walls in the approved manner and bought their pottery from the nearest market or itinerant trader instead of making their own. Yet beneath this veneer of 'civilization', throughout most of England the agricultural basis of society was largely unchanged. The Iron Age estates became Roman estates, though still owned or controlled by the descendants of their prehistoric owners, while the individual fields continued to be cultivated by the children of Iron Age peasants. With this background in mind, therefore, we should not expect any massive or sudden change in the methods of agriculture.

However, the second point which must be taken into consideration, and might change this picture, is the one already mentioned in the previous chapter concerning prehistoric fields. That is, that most of the surviving fields definitely dated to the Roman period, and from which we can draw our conclusions, are mainly in areas that have been little used since that time. For this reason the appearance of these fields on what has been marginal land since the Roman period, and was perhaps marginal land even then, has to be very carefully assessed. To take them as typical of what existed over the greater part of Roman Britain may seriously distort our picture of Roman agriculture and its development. One may only be looking at the most conservative and backward areas of Roman farming and thus, because they cannot be seen, ignore the results of the advanced agricultural techniques which the Romans introduced.

Certainly we do have clear indications that during Roman times new tools and, in particular, a new type of plough became available to those farmers who wanted them and could afford them. Iron hoes, scythes and spades have all been found in Roman excavations, but more important is the discovery of the iron parts of heavy ploughs of a very different type from the light prehistoric ard. From these parts it is possible to see that there was in the Roman period a kind of plough which could actually cut, lift and turn over the soil. This was achieved by having attached to the basic plough frame a *coulter*, shaped like a knife, which cut into the sod vertically. Immediately behind it was a *share* to cut horizontally under the sod and behind that a curved *mould-board*, usually of wood, which actually turned the sod over.

The advantage of such a plough over the older ard-type plough of prehistoric times was twofold. First, it enabled the soil to be completely turned over and broken up, so providing a better seed bed and obviating cross-ploughing. Secondly, as it was far more robust than its predecessor, it could be used to break up heavy land, particularly that on clay, which the ard plough could do only with great difficulty or not at all. Thus the existence of such a plough during the Roman period would have enabled the farmers, in theory at least, to increase their production by both improving their ground preparation methods and extending their activities into previously uncultivable areas. Certainly both these features were to become desperately needed as the Roman period advanced, to cope with the demands from a rising population and the export market. While the latter is known to have existed and must have played its part, the increase in the population of the country was probably the more important factor.

The number of Roman settlements found by field walking, air photography and excavation, especially over the last twenty years, is staggering. Literally thousands of sites are now known, ranging from towns through large villages to hamlets, villas and single farmsteads. They have been discovered on every type of soil, in every conceivable situation, on highland and lowland alike. In some places, as in eastern Northamptonshire, the density of settlement can rise to as much as two per square kilometre and even then many more settlements still remain to be discovered (Fig. 7a). While obviously not all these places were continuously occupied throughout the four hundred years of Roman rule, the actual number inhabited at any one time must have been considerable. Just how many people lived in England it is difficult to say, but the estimate of two million for the whole of Britain is probably far too low.

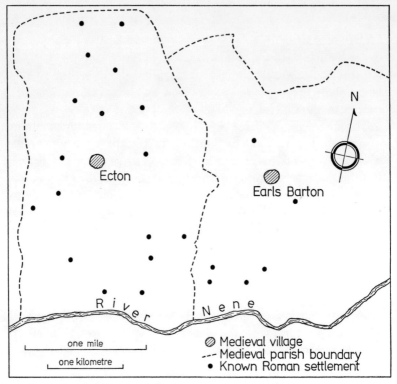

7a Roman settlements near Northampton.

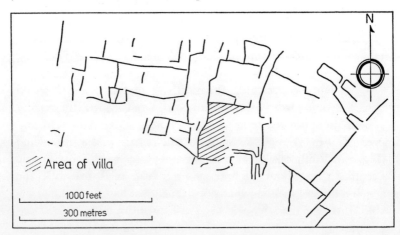

7b Roman villa and fields, Barnsley Park, Gloucestershire. Stone wall boundaries, now grass covered and only a few centimetres high.

In order to provide all these people with even a minimum subsistence diet much more land would have been required to be
farmed than in later prehistoric times. Almost certainly large
areas of the heavier claylands, especially in midland England,
which had perhaps defeated large-scale arable farming up to that
time, must have been brought into cultivation. There is no
remaining evidence of extensive stretches of Roman fields on the
heavier claylands of the Midlands, but the existence of the many
Roman settlements there implies it. More important is that
almost every field in midland England, when carefully walked
over and examined, will provide a few degraded sherds of Roman
pottery, presumably carried there mixed with manure when the
now non-existent fields were cultivated. In addition, there must
have been further intensification of farming on the lighter soils
which had already been cultivated for many centuries.

The most obvious of these latter areas are the chalk and limestone uplands of southern England, parts of Dartmoor and certain regions in northern England where fields still exist. Here,
for the most part, the existing pattern of prehistoric fields continued in use with little obvious change, as did many of the associated farmsteads. Excavations of these fields have revealed that
they were ploughed in the Roman period, apparently in exactly
the same way as they had been in prehistoric times. There is
evidence, however, that the breaking down of field divisions to
make larger blocks, already noted as occurring in the later prehistoric period, not only continued in Roman times but was much
increased. Hundreds of hectares of surviving prehistoric fields
have this feature, indicating a growing demand for larger fields.

Most of the surviving fields of prehistoric type, known to have
been cultivated in the Roman period, seem to belong to small
farmsteads and hamlets. The fields of the large Roman villas,
where more advanced field types might be expected, are largely
unknown. This is because these villas usually lay on good-quality
land which has been under cultivation ever since and thus their
fields have long disappeared. But there are a few examples where
fields associated with a large and important villa do remain

largely intact, and these contradict the assumption that villas had different fields from the humble farmsteads. At Brading on the Isle of Wight there are traces of fields on the hillside behind a villa, and probably contemporary with it, which are no different from those known in prehistoric times. More convincing are the fields at Barnsley Park, Gloucestershire, which are actually attached to the remains of a villa (Fig. 7b). Though the remains are slight, having been much damaged and altered by later activity, enough exists to show that they are little more than a series of small embanked paddocks, very similar to those of earlier centuries.

In addition to the continued use of the old fields in Roman times on the lighter chalk and limestone soils, there are indications of new types of fields altogether. These are the so-called 'long fields'. Except for their shape and size, they are identical to the traditional prehistoric fields, in that they are bounded by banks, or lynchets, the latter formed in the same way as in the older type of field. But they tend to be long and narrow, that is, they are four or five times longer than they are wide, and they are also larger: up to one hectare in area (Fig. 4b). Usually arranged in blocks of parallel fields, they appear at first sight to be similar to medieval strip fields, but they must be clearly distinguished from these. There is no doubt that these long fields are all of Roman date and in some places can be shown to have been actually laid out over the earlier and smaller square prehistoric fields.

These strip fields are not confined to the light soils of the chalk and limestone uplands. They have also been found on lower ground. For example, at St Ives, Huntingdonshire, a small farmstead has been excavated which, though it was first occupied in the late Iron Age, continued in use well into the Roman period. There the fields of the Roman farm that were discovered, though very small, were also in the form of strips, ten metres by thirty metres, bounded by ditches. These may, however, be special plots only and not real fields at all.

Very small irregular fields or plots around Roman settlements are more common than the strip ones, but they may have been used only as paddocks for stock or perhaps as vegetable gardens. Sometimes there are indications of larger irregular fields, as an excavation on a late Iron Age and Roman farmstead at Wyboston in Bedfordshire revealed. These covered an area of about three hectares and apparently were the total arable land of the farm. They consisted of eight irregular paddocks of various sizes, enclosed by ditches. The existence of a corn-drying oven in one of these paddocks has been said to indicate a concentration on cereal crops. But the discovery of cattle, sheep and pig bones showed that stock was also raised, perhaps being grazed in other areas that were not included in the excavation.

In addition to these small paddocks there is, in many lowland areas, evidence of large fields; that is, larger than the early pre-historic fields and indeed bigger than the chalkland and upland long fields, or even the enlarged prehistoric ones. It must be said that, at this moment in time, few of these are accurately dated, and much more work needs to be carried out before the final details can be established. The types of large fields that seem to have existed have been recognized on a Roman farm near North-borough in Lincolnshire. The farmstead appears to have had a minimum of ten hectares of land. Within this land there were at least three fields of about one hectare apiece but, more impor-tant, one of some five hectares (Fig. 5a). Such fields should be carefully distinguished from very large enclosures of sometimes up to twenty hectares in extent—also visible on air photographs and largely undated—which are likely to be late prehistoric or Roman in date. Some are certainly Roman and must be basically for stock and not arable land at all.

Many of these enclosures or large fields are visible from the air in the river valleys of England where the light gravel soils allow us to see them. Usually it is not possible to identify complete field systems or, because of lack of excavation, to date them.

Perhaps the most remarkable area of England in which to see Roman fields is the fenlands of Lincolnshire, north Cambridge-shire and north-west Norfolk. Unfortunately few remain on the ground today, for this area is now amongst the most valuable agricultural land there is, and all but a few isolated sites have long been destroyed. But from the air a very different picture can be seen (Fig. 8a). There, a whole Roman rural landscape is recoverable, in which homesteads, tracks and fields of all types can be identified. The background to this is in itself very remarkable. In the last few centuries before the Roman period, the fenlands were the marshy and inhospitable wilderness of popular legend. At the beginning of Roman times, however, much of the fenlands adjacent to the Wash was emerging from a shallow sea which had deposited a layer of silt over the area. What had been extensive tidal flats became low siltlands situated just above high tide level. Tidal water was then confined to a multitude of winding channels traversing the former estuary, now shrunken seawards.

By this process these rich siltlands became for the first time potential farmland. The result was that within a few years Romano-British people started to move into this region and, between A.D. 100 and 150, a massive settlement of these siltlands took place. Literally hundreds of new villages, hamlets and farmsteads appeared, linked by trackways and surrounded by their fields. There was also a similar spread of settlement along the fenland edges, an area now reasonably dry for the first time in centuries.

Some historians have suggested that this expansion of settlement and agriculture was organized by the Imperial Government. We have no information as to whether in fact this was so, but the pattern of those new settlements and fields suggests that it was not. From evidence elsewhere in the Roman Empire, it appears that when land was newly exploited under government control there was a carefully planned basic layout of roads and boundaries, usually on a grid system, which was called centuriation. However, in the fenlands of eastern England, there is no trace in the surviving pattern of any such overall layout and therefore of control. Nor do the fields themselves, except on rare occasions, display any marked organized plan. In fact they show even less careful and widespread forethought in planning than do many of the prehistoric field patterns (see p. 33 above).

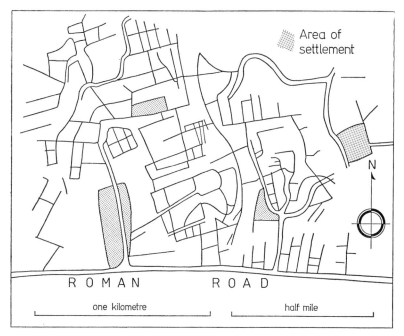

Area of settlement

N

R O M A N   R O A D

one kilometre   half mile

8a   Roman settlements and fields, March, Cambridgeshire. Ditched boundaries.

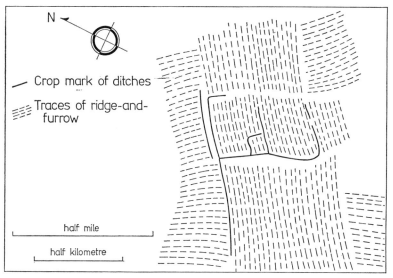

N

— Crop mark of ditches

≡≡ Traces of ridge-and-
    furrow

half mile

half kilometre

8b   Ridge-and-furrow and earlier enclosures, Great Bourton, Oxfordshire.

Most of the fields in the fenlands are indeed of the almost square or roughly rectangular prehistoric form, normally less than 0.25 hectare in area, bounded, because of the physical environment, by drainage ditches. The arrangement of these fields is, for the most part, fairly haphazard and most appear to be the result either of slow piecemeal expansion, or of completely unplanned setting out.

In addition to the square or rectangular fields, there are a number of examples in the fens of long strip-like fields of the type already noted as occurring elsewhere, as much as 200 metres in length while being only 20 metres in width. These are often arranged in blocks, but again there is no indication of any overall layout. In a few places there are indications of a rectilinear layout, but these are very local and do not extend beyond individual settlements and their fields. Thus the fenland field systems as a whole appear to be no different from Roman fields noted elsewhere, despite their formation in a completely new agricultural environment.

The basic question as to the use these new fields were put to is still largely unanswered. Was the opening up of the vast fenland for agriculture intended to be for arable crops or stock? Both ideas have been put forward by archaeologists who have worked on these areas. Certainly there is ample evidence of cattle being the predominant type of animal, but whether it is true, as some workers have said, that the fenlands were mainly a cattle ranching area is more doubtful. On the other hand there is no conclusive evidence that the region was 'the granary of Roman Britain'. The most likely explanation is that it was one of basically mixed farming, although arable is likely to have predominated.

In passing it must be pointed out that these newly colonized lands in the fens did not remain prosperous, whatever the original idea behind the exploitation of the region. In the relatively unstable environment, the constant battle by the fenland farmers was not always successful and many of the settlements and their fields were abandoned around A.D. 200 because of recurrent flooding. Others, however, managed to survive until at least the early fifth century A.D.

Finally, in this discussion of Roman fields we must turn to a type well known in other parts of the Roman Empire: the mathematically surveyed fields. This is the system known as centuriation, which consisted of large-scale delimitation of areas of land within a standard grid, inside which the fields were laid out. As this system of centuriation was widely used elsewhere in the Empire, there is no obvious reason why it should not have been developed in this country, either under government control or by large enterprising landowners. Yet, although many attempts have been made to find such systems of centuriation, on the whole there has been little success. Once again this may be because of the existence, in all the areas where one might expect it, of later fields that have removed all traces. Certainly there is no evidence of centuriation amongst the surviving Roman fields on the chalk downlands, the upland hills or fenlands. Nor is there any definite evidence of it from the multitude of Roman fields revealed by air photography on the light gravel soils of the major river valleys. In the case of the chalk and upland fields, this may well be because we are seeing only the most backward types of fields on the marginal land. However, this does not seem to be the case in the gravel areas, which cannot by any means be considered as marginal in Roman times.

It could be argued that in these areas the existence of an organized landscape of farmsteads and fields, originating well back in the prehistoric period, prevented any large-scale change in the field systems and that only minor alterations could be made. According to this theory, the only places where centuriation could occur would be on land hitherto unused. Yet in the one area where massive primary colonization is known to have occurred—the fenlands—there is no trace of centuriation.

Nevertheless, before completely rejecting any idea of planned field layouts in England during the Roman period, certain features must be taken into account. While many of the older attempts to find signs of centuriation have been rightly rejected, more recent work has produced possible examples. One is at Rochester in Kent, where north of the town a known Roman road and a series of existing lanes, as well as air-photographic evidence of ditches, suggest some form of grid layout with the blocks measuring approximately 700 metres square. This measurement agrees with the official Roman imperial land unit blocks of 400 *actus* or 200 *iugera*. Within this basic unit there should be subdivision into actual fields, but no such definite traces have been found. Another possible example is at West Bletchington in Sussex, where both excavation and air photography indicate a basic grid, and here even some rectangular fields, albeit very small, appear to be laid out along the major grid lines. Since only a limited area has been investigated, however, we cannot be certain that this was true centuriation. A very recent attempt to see centuriation has been made at Great Wymondley, Hertfordshire, where it was apparently correlated with the later arrangement of medieval fields. Once again, though, the results are not altogether convincing.

Nevertheless, the possible relationships between some form of Roman fields and the later medieval open- or strip-field layout may be seen in some places. The implications of this are considered later (see p. 67 below); at this point only the somewhat vague evidence can be noted. On some air photographs taken of areas of later medieval fields, now ploughed out, it is possible to discern traces of large, roughly rectangular closes or fields, bounded by ditches, underlying the medieval fields (Fig. 8b). The boundaries of these ditched fields agree to a marked extent with the 'furlongs' or blocks of strips of the medieval fields, and may be the basic reason for the eventual shape of these furlongs. These large ditched fields are quite different in size from the dated Roman fields known elsewhere. They can be as much as five hectares in area, though they may have been subdivided. None of these fields, if such they are, has been excavated and therefore dated, and thus we cannot be sure whether they are Roman at all. The only certainty is that they are earlier than the medieval field arrangement, and could be prehistoric or even early Saxon. Nor is it possible to say whether they were for stock or for arable crops. Nonetheless they are of a size not completely unknown in Roman times (see p. 53 above) and, although so far not many examples have been identified, are probably far more common than has hitherto been realized. At present such fields must remain an enigma.

To sum up our knowledge of Roman fields, we can say that they exhibited a wider variety of shape and size than those of the pre-historic period. There are fields which are indistinguishable from the small rectangular prehistoric ones; some of these indeed may actually originate in that period but others are probably true Roman fields. There are those resulting from the break up of the earlier fields, producing new ones of 0.25 to one hectare. There are also various forms of long fields of up to one hectare in area, while larger, rectangular ones are known with areas of up to five hectares. In addition, there is the possibility of rectangular fields in the two- to four-hectare range, though these are undated, Finally, there is evidence of very large enclosures, probably for stock raising.

Why is there this range of fields? The first and most obvious explanation is that they result from the introduction of the heavy plough. This, by its ability to turn the sod properly, would have obviated the necessity to cross-plough and, therefore, enabled larger fields and long fields to be produced. However, though the plough type may have played its part, this is perhaps too easy an explanation. The real reason may have been the result of com-plex social and economic changes connected with the impact of the Roman Empire. Most of these we can only guess at, but they are perhaps the most important of all. In the more remote areas, peasant farmers may have continued to cultivate much as their ancestors had always done. But in the regions of better and heavier soils, close to the large population centres, old methods may have been abandoned, and old and new land alike cultivated in different ways under new economic pressures and new landlords, by mak-ing use of the technical advances of ploughs and ditching tools.

The appearance of villas in certain areas, probably in the main the centres of major estates, by the end of the first century A.D. may reflect the new agricultural and economic forces at work. These were perhaps reinforced by governmental pressure aimed at producing food for the military establishments in the north, as well as by capital introduced by overseas merchants and traders. This growth of villa-estates in the late first and second centuries must have produced the necessary food for export and for the army, but as can be seen from the growth of the towns and the innumerable rural settlements, the *Pax Romana* also brought a greatly increased population. Thus there was a constantly growing demand for food, which must have led to more and more land being cultivated by both new and old methods. Certainly in the second century, even in the Pennine Hills, primitive Romanized villages and fields appear. In addition, there was an increasing call for taxation from the Roman government as a result of the ever-rising defence expenditure for the Empire, and this must have forced greater efficiency and expansion in agriculture.

The actual production from these fields is also important. We have already noted that the evidence from the fenlands is not conclusive as to whether arable or stock was the main basis of the agriculture there. Elsewhere in England we can be more certain. There is little doubt that most of the fields in this country were used primarily to grow cereals of various kinds. Wheat, barley and oats are all known from excavations of Roman sites, while millstones are common and even watermills have been found. Many villas as well as forts have revealed traces of granaries, and grain-drying ovens or furnaces are amongst the most common structures found on Roman occupation sites from grand villas down to tiny farmsteads. From this evidence it is quite obvious that the basis of Romano-British agriculture was grain production.

Other crops, however, though less common, were also grown. Amongst these were beans, peas, turnips and flax. It seems likely that some of these were grown with the cereals as parts of three-course rotations, a marked advance on the simple crop-fallow pattern which was probably practised earlier. The appearance of root crops also might imply animal feeding on some scale and this is reflected in the archaeological record. Bones of cattle are very common on most Roman sites, and many villas and farmsteads have produced byres, cattle sheds and stables as well as stockyards around them.

In the more heavily populated and cultivated areas it seems that cattle may have been either grazed within the large enclosures that are known, or stall-fed. On the other hand, in some places they may have been allowed to range fairly freely. At the Roman settlement at Appleton in Norfolk, the association of horse and cattle bones suggested cattle ranching on a considerable scale, while many of the prehistoric ranch enclosures in southern England may have continued in use.

Sheep, too, were important, especially in later Roman times. Indeed, British wool was renowned throughout the Empire and sheep were probably used mainly for their wool rather than for their meat. Almost all parts of the country have revealed evidence for some sheep being kept, though perhaps not in great numbers everywhere. Certain areas may have been primarily sheep-producing ones; the Kent and Essex marshes, the Norfolk brecklands and the Hampshire downlands have all been suggested as possible regions. However, there is no certainty in the matter. In any case, it is doubtful whether fields for sheep as such existed, because the main purpose of keeping sheep, after their wool, was to fold them on the arable fields for manure. Pigs are also well attested to in Roman times, though in relatively small numbers. But they have left no trace in the contemporary field systems.

Thus taken as a whole the fields of England at this time seem to exhibit great variety of form and size, related to complex economic developments as well as purely technical advances. The overall picture is one of generally mixed farming with a concentration on grain, and with stock of secondary importance.

In spite of all this material evidence we have little indication in detail of how these Roman fields were worked and this is important in any attempt to see how they were adapted to new uses in the post-Roman period. We still have no clear idea of what area of land was under cultivation at any one time, or how much land single farmsteads, hamlets or villas needed. Attempts have been made to work out the areas of fields associated with a given villa or farmstead, but all these have been largely based on guesswork, for the archaeological evidence is either doubtful or non-existent. Nor do we know for certain what crop rotations, if any, were practised, or the extent of the crop yields.

On the whole, allowing for very poor yields and a massive surplus for both seeds and market, the general impression of the amount of cultivated land associated with each settlement is surprisingly large. In Hampshire we find a group of settlements made up almost certainly of no more than single farmsteads comprising only two or three family units; each farmstead appears to have had an average of over 200 hectares of land. In Dorset, a series of estates seem to have ranged from 150 to 250 hectares each, while the field area of a villa at Faversham in Kent has been estimated at 120 hectares. Again in Dorset, two small hamlets at Frampton had at least 360 hectares of fields, and in Sussex some minor settlements had between 100 and 120 hectares of arable land apiece. Owing to the difficulties of obtaining such figures, not least because of the destruction by later farmers of much of the evidence, all these areas can be regarded as minimal. But even accepting them at their face value, it seems difficult to believe that all this land or even two-thirds of it (allowing for a third being fallow at any one time), was under cultivation. After all in Saxon and early medieval times, the *virgate*, a unit of around 30 acres (12 hectares), was regarded as the basic requirement for a husbandman and his family. It is more likely that merely a part of the total land of these settlements was permanently cultivated and that much was taken into cultivation at certain times only. It may be that the overall area of fields which can be traced was actually used in two different ways. Part was permanent arable, certainly never fallowed but intensively manured, and part was brought into cultivation in sections at various times, with long periods of fallow between. That is, in agricultural terms, an infield-outfield system was being practised. This suggestion is of vital importance when we look forward to the fields of the Saxon period.

Chapter 3

Saxon Fields

The fields and field systems of Anglo-Saxon England are the most difficult of all not only to explain, but even to find. As we saw in the previous chapter, there is plenty of evidence for Roman fields of various kinds, and by the end of the Saxon period we have evidence of the traditional medieval open- or strip-field system in existence over much of the country. But for the long period from the early fifth century to the tenth century there is little evidence of fields, either on the ground or from the available historical sources. Once again it may be that the later fields have destroyed all the evidence, but even so one might have expected some indications. In fact the fields of the Saxon period are largely unknown. To establish any kind of understanding of how the known Roman fields became the medieval strip-fields we have to tread warily and uncertainly through a few pieces of definite evidence and a mass of guesswork and supposition.

To begin with, it is as well to remove one major and long-held preconception concerning Saxon fields. This is that the Saxons, when they arrived in this country, brought with them a fully fledged strip-field system which they imposed quite arbitrarily on the existing landscape, wiping away all trace of the pre-existing fields. This is now generally regarded as highly unlikely for a number of reasons. First, what little documentary evidence there is concerning Saxon fields seems to indicate that the common strip-field system known from medieval times did not exist in that form in the early Saxon period. Secondly, as we have seen, by the end of the Roman period England was exceptionally well populated and intensively farmed. In spite of the devastating impact of the Saxon invaders, who certainly killed and drove away a large number of people, it seems that a considerable proportion of the existing population remained where they were and, in the first instance at least, were enslaved by the incoming Saxons, who gradually absorbed them. These Romano-British people would probably have continued to farm their holdings in much the same way as they always had, at least for a certain time. Thirdly, as far as we can tell from the available evidence, there were far more Romano-Britons than Saxons, even in the main areas of Saxon settlement in southern and eastern England, and thus it would have been difficult to eliminate these people entirely and take over their land. Lastly, and most important of all, the incoming Saxons were farmers, looking for land. Faced with a countryside covered with fields of various types and under cultivation, as well as with countless settlements of various sizes, it is unlikely that they would have had the time or the inclination to destroy that landscape totally and put something else in its place. It is far more likely that they merely took over what they found there as a going concern, continued to farm it, and then perhaps gradually altered it to their own ideas under the pressures of the changing economic and social conditions.

Modern research is tending to suggest that this actually happened. The incoming Saxons seem initially to have established their new homes close to or within the existing settlements, and individual farms or estates were taken over as working units. In some cases it would appear that the actual difference in agricultural terms between the late Roman and early Saxon farming was minimal. The ownership or control of the estate passed into Saxon hands, but the day-to-day work continued much as before, being carried out by the Roman peasantry.

In any case the actual Saxon settlement of England was a long-drawn-out process and in certain areas was never completed. For while the first Saxon settlers arrived, probably as hired mercenary troops, as early as the late fourth century in eastern England, it was perhaps around 450 before south-east and eastern England became fully Saxon territory. Thereafter the progress of Saxon

I. Prehistoric fields, Smacem Down, Dorset. These fields, edged by low banks and scarps, have been preserved because they were formed on steep slopes which later farmers have never ploughed.

II. Saxon and later fields, Povingdon, Dorset. These heath-edge fields, north of the Purbeck Ridge, are of two very different periods. The irregular ones near the ridge are probably later Saxon or even earlier. Those farther north within the heath are of eighteenth- or nineteenth-century date and represent encroachments of that period.

III. Medieval ridge-and-furrow, Braunston, Northamptonshire. Here many of the characteristic features can be clearly seen. They include reversed 'S' curves, variation in ridge width and the later hedged fields superimposed on it.

IV. Medieval strip lynchets, Sledmere, Yorkshire. An example of the less spectacular but typical form of medieval contour ploughing.

V. Medieval enclosed fields, Middlebere Heath, Dorset. Along the edge of Poole Harbour, visible in the foreground, are a series of small irregular hedged fields. These were carved out of the surrounding heathland by farmer/fishermen, certainly before the fourteenth century.

VI. Stone-walled fields, Castleton, Derbyshire. The characteristic reversed 'S' curved sides to these long fields indicate that they were formed by enclosing pre-existing open strips.

VII. Watermeadows, Woodford, Wiltshire. The channels along the spines of the ridges and in the furrows, along which water flowed, are clearly visible.

VIII. Parliamentary enclosure fields, Barrowden, Rutland. Here the rigid geometry of the layout reveals the hand of the professional surveyor who planned these new hedged fields.

IX. Site of airfield, Bottisham, Cambridgeshire. The perimeter track remains, while part of one of the runways has been planted with trees. The result is a new field pattern, very different from the surrounding one, which dates from 1808.

X. Multiple field systems, Gordale, Yorkshire. Here is a remarkable series of superimposed fields. In the left middle distance are the remains of prehistoric fields, edged by low banks and scarps. Below and to the right are medieval strip lynchets which have cut into the earlier fields. On top of all these are the walled enclosures of the nineteenth century.

XI. Strip fields, Soham, Cambridgeshire. These unhedged strips, still under cultivation, are a rare survival, albeit much altered, of a medieval open-field system.

XII. Modern housing estate, Swaffham Bulbeck, Cambridgeshire. The estate has been fitted into a field formed by parliamentary enclosure of 1801.

settlement westwards was relatively slow, and it was well into the seventh century before even political control passed to the Saxons in south-west England and along the Welsh borders. Throughout these long centuries, regardless of the undoubted political, military and economic troubles and disasters, Romano-British people lived on and farmed their land, which was all they could do in order to live.

Therefore the development of Saxon fields, if such can be said to have existed, must be seen in the context of initial political and tenurial control over a basic and much older agricultural way of life which submitted to change only at a very slow rate. Continental evidence may be considered here, for recent work in Europe has shown that the Saxon peoples, far from having a traditional medieval strip- or open-field system when they set out for Britain, were in fact cultivating small rectangular fields very similar to the English examples dated to the Roman period. There are also examples of strip or long fields in some places on the Continent, again similar to the Roman ones in this country. Thus the development of the open-field arrangement of the typical medieval fields may be seen as occurring both in England and on the Continent well into post-Roman times and quite unrelated to racial factors. Therefore if we wish to see what in fact early Saxon fields looked like, we can, perhaps, merely look back to the Roman fields and suggest that they were much the same.

Nevertheless, this situation certainly did not remain static and changes took place as the Saxon era advanced. We must now look at some of these in detail. It is clear that many of the Roman fields and their associated settlements in the more remote areas, such as the Wessex downlands, the moors of south-west England and the uplands of northern England, were abandoned at some time. Some of these seem to have been deserted late in the Roman period as happened, for example, to the settlement and its fields at Woodcutts in Dorset. But most went on well into the fifth century before they were given up. One reason for this may have been the economic difficulties of the times when these marginal lands were no longer profitable. Another may be that there were climatic changes, while overcropping of the thin soils, some of which had been under cultivation for centuries, may also have been a factor. Probably a combination of all these is behind this abandonment. On the heavier, richer soils, however, the land continued to be farmed.

Certainly the Roman organization may have decayed. There has been much discussion by archaeologists and historians of economic decline and other difficulties at this time, and the abandonment of the great villas as well as other Roman settlements, many of which were the administrative centres of Roman estates, cannot be denied. It seems that the Saxon settlers and their dependent or enslaved British peasants often set up their homes on new sites away from the villas, while the estates themselves usually carried on as basic agricultural units, regardless of the change of ownership. For example, work in Dorset and in Wiltshire, as well as elsewhere, has suggested that many medieval parish boundaries, known to have been the defined limits to estates in later Saxon times, were already established in late Roman times. It seems therefore that the basic unit of late Saxon—and indeed of medieval— farming, the parish, could have originated in estates taken over from the Roman landlords. In any case, not enough is known of the origins of most of our so-called Saxon villages to be sure that they were all founded on new sites. Detailed work on many of these villages has revealed Roman occupation and more will undoubtedly come to light. Inevitably the fact that we still live in these villages makes the archaeologist's work difficult, but there is reason to believe that most medieval villages were occupied in Roman times and their fields subsequently taken over by the Saxons.

However, the basic problem of exactly how the Roman fields described in the last chapter became the medieval or open-strip fields still remains. Can this difficulty be resolved? It must be, for the origin of the medieval field system itself needs to be understood if its history is to be seen clearly. Yet at the moment this cannot be done with any certainty and only suggestions can be made about it.

To begin with we must look at the variety of Roman fields which the Saxons found. These included small rectangular ones, larger but also rectangular fields as well as long or 'strip' fields. However, these fields are distributed unevenly over most of the country owing to later destruction, and we have no precise idea of the overall pattern. Further, and perhaps more important, we have no real idea of exactly how these fields were worked. That is, we do not know whether they were farmed in common or as individual fields, and how much was permanent arable, how much was temporary. Clear indications of rotation systems are also not forthcoming. Then, when we look at the fully developed medieval open-field system as it emerges from the study of documents and the landscape in the later medieval period, we see considerable differences in layout, methods of operation, ownership and crop production. These variations are not confined to differences between, say, the medieval fields of Kent and Leicestershire or those of Norfolk and Lancashire; there are also major differences between adjacent field systems within one locality. In addition there are large areas of England where the open- or strip-field system never developed, or existed in only a few places. In these areas the basic form of field, even in the medieval period, was the hedged or walled plot. Again, this type of field is not solely confined to regions such as south-west England, where the Saxon influence came late and was never dominant; it also occurs in many other regions, well within the areas of relatively early Saxon influence such as Dorset (Plate II). Thus any indication of how and when the various forms of later Saxon or early medieval field types developed is largely unknown and we can only speculate.

One possible way is as follows. In late Roman times the various settlements were perhaps surrounded by an area of intensively cultivated land, either as enclosed fields or as long 'strip' fields. This is demonstrable by the available evidence. Beyond these fields may have lain other plots that were brought into cultivation for only short periods of, say, two, four or eight years and then abandoned for periods of up to, say, twenty-five years. This idea is, of course, unproven at the moment but, as was indicated earlier, there are suggestions that land was abandoned for long periods even in Neolithic times to allow for natural recovery of fertility, and that the same feature occurred in the later prehistoric period when fields were left uncultivated at intervals (p. 41 above). Furthermore, this habit of cropping some land on a temporary basis is also indicated from certain admittedly slender evidence in the Roman period (p. 62 above).

The arrangement of intensively cultivated permanent arable, associated with larger temporarily cropped areas, is technically called an infield-outfield system. In its simplest form it is well known in many parts of the world, and is perhaps one of the most primitive types of agricultural organization. Indeed it existed almost unmodified in parts of the British Isles until relatively recent times, notably in Scotland, but also in northern England. This system may have been the method of working the existing fields that the incoming Saxon settlers found, and which they either took over themselves, or allowed the surviving Romano-British farmers to continue to work for them. There was thus no radical change whatsoever during the first years of the Saxon era to field shape, layout, or method of farming.

Indeed, where there was no pressure to alter such a system in later times, no real change took place. The basic requirement for a lack of change was one or both of two factors. First, no massive increase in population which would have required more land being cultivated, and, secondly, the availability of large amounts of surplus land which could always be used either as temporary arable or extensive grazing. For example, in the county of Dorset on the relatively sparsely inhabited heathlands in the east, there is no indication that there were ever medieval common fields composed of a multitude of strips. Only isolated farmsteads and hamlets existed whose occupants always farmed hedged fields. While much of the present landscape also contains the result of piecemeal enclosure of the wastes over many centuries, around the farmsteads themselves there is a remarkable series of rectangular fields with botanically rich hedges indicating a high antiquity. Beyond, on the farther heathland are other fields, some long abandoned and visible only after fires, which appear to have been temporary enclosures (Plate II). In this kind of environment it seems that there was never any pressure from either increasing population or shortage of land to develop the primitive system any further, so that it remained in existence for centuries. Thus we may have in such places the original form of Saxon fields, based perhaps upon the older Roman or even pre-historic system of infield-outfield.

However, over much of the rest of England and especially in the lowland areas, such a system had to change. With the growth of population as the earlier hamlets developed into villages, more land had to be brought into intensive cultivation. That is to say, the infield was enlarged. In time, this enlargement of the infield would have completely taken over the outfield as well, and sub-sequently would have reduced the available grazing land beyond. This would have had two effects. First, arrangements would have had to be made on a communal basis to allow stock to use even the arable land for grazing purposes, and this led to the develop-ment of common grazing rights—a basic part of the medieval common- or open-field system. Also, and perhaps more important, the existing rectangular fields, or indeed the long 'strip' fields, would have been subdivided either to provide subsistence for everyone or as the result of inheritance laws. If this suggestion of evolution is accepted, we have two of the basic features of the later medieval common fields developing out of the earlier Roman and prehistoric systems. However, the ultimate establishment of this medieval form of agriculture was probably related to many other and varied factors which we will examine in the next chapter.

The methods of ploughing these Saxon fields, whatever form they took, are equally uncertain. No ploughs of definite Saxon date are known, but taking the Roman and later medieval evi-dence, there can be no doubt that the heavy plough existed and was used. The only piece of evidence for such a plough in the Saxon period has come from Gwithian in Cornwall, oddly enough well outside the main area of Saxon settlement, and dated generally to between the sixth and ninth centuries. Here excavations revealed plough marks cut into the underlying soil. As a result of the unusual circumstance of the marks being sealed by wind-blown sand, it was possible to see the traces of the sod which had been inverted by the plough. The obvious implication is that the implement used there had a share, coulter and mould-board. The lines of the marks themselves, lying parallel to one another in one direction only, also indicate that cross-ploughing was not being carried out. Therefore, from this one place only, we have evidence of cultivation by means of a heavy plough in the Saxon period.

The crops of the Saxon fields are better known, for we have information both from excavations on settlement sites and from documents and place names. From the first source, carbonized grain and seed impressions on pottery show that wheat, barley, oats and flax were grown, while palaeo-botanical evidence from pollen analysis has indicated that hemp was being cultivated, at least in East Anglia. Documentary sources also confirm that wheat, oats, barley and rye were grown, and place names such as Ryarch, Banstead, Barton and Linton again display knowledge of rye, beans, barley and flax.

Animals including sheep, cattle, pigs and, rarely, goats are also known from archaeology, place names and documentary sources to have been kept, but there are no traces of fields being used solely for stock.

Chapter 4

Early Medieval Open Fields

Almost the only fact that is generally known about medieval England after the date of the Norman Conquest is that each village was surrounded by two or three large open and unhedged fields, divided into a multitude of strips, all individually owned but farmed in common. Yet, as one might expect, the reality was far more complicated than this. Not only were there great variations in appearance between the common or open fields of any one area and another, and even between those of adjacent villages, but these variations went deeper in terms of the way in which the fields were worked and the cropping rotations carried out. In addition, despite many ideas to the contrary, this open-field system was flexible; it could, and did, change in response to various economic and social factors operating over the centuries. There were also strip fields in many places where there were no true open fields at all.

The real common-field system consisted basically of four elements. First arable land was divided into strips which were owned or tenanted by various people each of whom farmed a number of these scattered about the fields. Then both arable and meadowland were pastured by the stock of the same farmers after the harvest and in fallow years. This meant that on the arable land, strict rules as to what was sown had to be enforced. Thirdly, the pasture and waste, where available, were used by the farmers for grazing their stock, often again with strict control on the numbers of animals allowed. Finally, all these activities had to be organized by a formal meeting of the farmers, either at a manorial court or at a village assembly. It may be noted that this definition of an open- or common-field system does not say anything about cropping in rotation in two or three fields, or describe the physical form of the strips themselves: whether they were bounded by hedges or banks, or were completely bare of any physical limits. Nor does it refer to the necessity for the even distribution of strips throughout the arable fields. This is because none of these things was absolutely necessary in such a system. Finally, this definition tells us, by implication, that the mere existence of strip fields was not a true common-field system unless it was accompanied by the other elements.

In its classic form, the common-field system as defined above was characteristic of the midland counties of England in the medieval period and later, though it is doubtful whether the system had actually evolved sufficiently to reach this state much before the twelfth century. In any case even in this region, recent work has shown that common fields were much more complex and varied in operation than is usually believed. For instance, the existence of two, three or more common fields had no significance at all in agricultural terms. The unit of rotation was not the field, but the furlong, the term given to individual blocks of strips all aligned in the same direction, groups of which made up the field itself. Therefore, not only was a three-course rotation possible in a two-field system, but in fact almost any rotation system could be practised. In addition, under this system, individual strips were left to fallow or used for permanent pasture within the overall fields. This latter point is especially worth remembering when we move on to look at the physical remains of these fields in the present landscape. All this took place in the medieval common fields of the English Midlands.

Elsewhere in England there were marked regional and local variations in the form and working of the common fields and some of these even occurred in the Midlands themselves. The reasons behind these variations can be enumerated as follows. To begin with, the form of the fields existing before the common fields developed could affect their physical layout. If what had been large rectangular Roman fields were subdivided into blocks of strips, the resulting furlongs would be of a different size and shape from those developed from the subdivision of the smaller Roman rectangular fields, or of long fields.

Secondly, and of much more consequence, there was the varied physical environment of England in terms of climate, soils, slope and aspect. All these led to differences in crops, cropping techniques and rotations as well as in general land use with regard to concentration on pastoralism or arable farming. Associated with this physical factor, and indeed stemming from it, was the availability of waste land. In upland areas, land of a kind was always available for expansion of either arable or pastoral farming, all other things being equal. But in certain other regions, especially in parts of the Midlands, waste land was probably in short supply at an early date, and therefore grazing and meadowland became valuable, with the complexities of rights of grazing over arable and fallow and its careful regulation an absolute necessity.

Even more important were the various social factors at work, particularly the way in which land, whether in the form of strips, fields, farms or estates, was passed from one generation to another. For example, the existence of partible inheritance—that is, the procedure of dividing the land equally among all sons—would lead to a constantly changing system, whereas impartible inheritance, when the land passed to the eldest child only, would tend to make the system more stable. As these customs varied from area to area, and from one class of society to another, the complexities of the resulting field systems are almost impossible to define. Marriage settlements, exchanges, buying, selling and leasing were also varied and equally indefinable. The size, form and pattern of settlement, too, related perhaps to both physical and social factors, would obviously affect the size, form and complexity of the associated fields.

In addition to these social influences, economic considerations need to be borne in mind, and basically this means changes in demand for agricultural products. The most obvious of these was alteration in population size. More people meant more land required for crops and, if it was already in short supply, less land

73

for pasture. This would lead to more intensive agriculture and perhaps subdivision of units, whether of farms, fields or strips. Fewer people would mean abandonment of land and perhaps amalgamation of strips or farms. Also, and certainly from the twelfth century onwards, the growth of urban centres producing additional demands for food would lead to the development of market-orientated agriculture and even specialization in certain products, both for human consumption and for industrial use. In the end the development of new methods of cultivation, new crops and new implements, and the speed of their acceptance by individual peasants or lords, would have affected the form of fields.

All these factors and others must have played their part in producing variations in the medieval common fields. We must thus see these fields as having immense variety of form and operation throughout England, as well as being constantly altered and adapted to changing conditions. For this reason it is quite impossible to identify a standard type of medieval common-field system in this country. If one looks in detail at specific areas it is possible to see some of the physical variations that were already in evidence by the fourteenth century.

For example, in the Weald of Kent and Surrey the influences of the physical background, partible inheritance, the dispersed form of settlement—particularly in the form of farmsteads and hamlets—all helped to produce a curious pattern of small blocks of open or strip fields, not always cultivated or grazed in common, mixed up with areas of enclosed fields. Some of the latter were apparently cultivated in strips for cropping purposes and then later sold, leased or inherited as individual strip holdings. In other places a form of infield-outfield seems to have been practised.

In northern England, in the upland valleys of Yorkshire, Northumberland, Durham and elsewhere, the dispersed pattern of farmsteads and limited areas of good soil helped to preserve the presumably original forms of infield-outfield systems; while on the lower, better areas, large villages produced complex common fields more akin to the English Midlands. In East

Anglia too, the original infield-outfield arrangement remained intact, especially on the sandy heaths of the Breckland, though the later importance of sheep resulted in an unusual pattern of rotation and cultivation of crops to accommodate the folding of large flocks on the arable.

Thus although by the early fourteenth century there was over much of England a form of strip-field cultivation, it was extremely varied in both appearance and organization. And of course none of these systems was static. As has already been suggested, they were all perhaps derived from a basic infield-outfield system, possibly founded on an earlier Roman or prehistoric pattern. As time went on, the variations described developed as a result of a multitude of pressures upon them. Of these, it was the continued growth of population from Saxon times to the fourteenth century that proved to be the most important since it meant that in most areas expansion of arable, at the expense of pasture, continued. In this way the strip fields were being continually expanded. Frequently the arable reached the ultimate limits of the villages' or townships' lands at an early date, and the indented pattern of many existing parish boundaries, where the strips of each parish interlocked, still shows this today (Fig. 9a).

This expansion was generally called *assarting*, and it is possible to see exactly how this was carried out. There seem to have been two basic methods. In one it is certain that there were collective efforts by groups of farmers to extend the cultivated land outwards by clearing a new block of waste at the limits of the permanent arable. Once this was done, the newly cleared land was immediately divided into strips and allotted to those people involved in the work. These new strips were then incorporated into the existing system of cultivation practised on the adjoining fields. Even where the newly cleared land lay well away from the existing fields it could be and often was subdivided into strips and thus became a separate open field. There are examples of this occurring, particularly in parts of Hertfordshire and Oxfordshire. In the latter county, the farmers of the village of Islip apparently cleared some 80 hectares of land across the river from their main

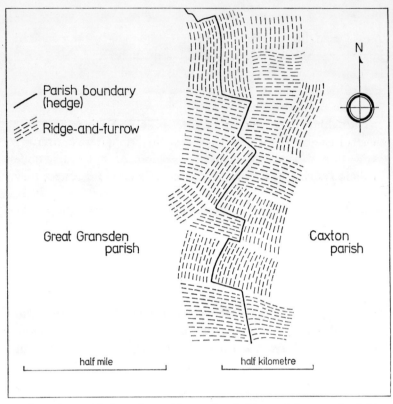

9a Irregular parish boundary with associated ridge-and-furrow, Cambridgeshire.

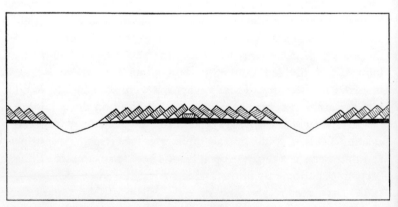

9b Diagram of a plough ridge during formation.

fields some time between 1086 and 1300, and divided it into strips. Its name, Sart (assart) Field, reveals its origin.

In the second place, there was assarting by individuals who cleared land and often enclosed it with a hedge or bank. This was then farmed separately from the rest of the open fields. In many cases these fields remained enclosed and we shall return to them later (see p. 94 below). But these fields, as a result either of inheritance, marriage settlements, sales or leases, were often later broken up into strips, cultivated in common and brought into the existing open-field system. This event can be illustrated from Coleshill in Warwickshire, where a piece of land which originated as an enclosed assart granted to one Simon March in the mid thirteenth century was, by 1300, divided into strips held by eleven separate tenants and called 'Marchesfield'.

In some places whole new common-field systems came into existence in this way. For example, in Yorkshire in the twelfth century, farms made up of enclosed fields taken from the waste were gradually subdivided into strips as a result of continuous partition amongst the heirs as population increased. Thus within two hundred years the farmsteads had become hamlets or even villages and the enclosed fields common open fields.

Within the general strip-field systems, whatever their various forms, a great diversity of crops was grown. The flexibility of these fields in terms of rotations meant that a number of different crops could be grown side by side, given reasonable co-operation. Nor must it be assumed that these fields were totally arable. The same flexibility of cropping enabled certain parts to be taken out of the common arable at times. Especially in areas where there was a dire shortage of pasture, individual strips were left fallow or allowed to revert to pasture to provide grazing in some years. In a number of East Anglian parishes there are frequent references to such strips, called leys, from the thirteenth century onwards, while in Oxfordshire, for example, there are also several thirteenth-century accounts of strips actually being enclosed by temporary fences to allow folding and, therefore, increased manuring for particular purposes.

The crops grown on these common fields were numerous. It must be realized by now that because of the flexibility of the common-field systems it was possible to have very complex rotations and much more than a simple sequence of cereals, peas and fallow could be undertaken. In fact, depending on climatic and soil conditions, the cereals wheat, barley, rye and oats were grown in various places as well as mixtures of all. In addition, peas and beans were cultivated often mixed with cereals, and in certain places flax was grown. All these crops are well documented from medieval records. Field names also help here, though only those which are recorded in early medieval documents are valid. Thus Bean Croft, in the parish of Marston Mortmaine in Bedfordshire, is mentioned in 1232 as Bean Hill. Lincroft, at Kneesall in Nottinghamshire, first mentioned in 1244, means land on which flax was grown, while Wadeacre, recorded in 1312 at Walton in Derbyshire, is the place where woad was cultivated.

So far we have been looking at the medieval field systems in terms of origins, layout and cropping practices. But the remains of these fields survive on the ground today for us to study, and to add to our knowledge of their appearance and methods of cultivation. The most common type of these remains is what is known as ridge-and-furrow. No observant traveller in the Midlands of England can have failed to see this particular feature and it also occurs extensively elsewhere. Ridge-and-furrow consists of long narrow ridges of soil, lying parallel to each other and usually arranged in roughly rectangular blocks, separated by depressions or furrows (Plate III).

The first point which has to be made concerning this ridge-and-furrow is that it is produced solely by the action of ploughing with a 'heavy' plough; that is, a plough capable of turning over the sod and which, therefore, has a share, coulter and mouldboard of some form. Thus in essence, ridge-and-furrow can be of any date after the introduction of such a plough and is not necessarily medieval. Nor, in spite of its elongated form, does it have to be associated with medieval, common or open strip fields. Ridge-and-furrow is produced by first ploughing a normal furrow across the field. Then, on the second or return run, a furrow is cut closely parallel to the first, and the sod turned inwards to meet the one cut from the original furrow. The third run is then made next to the first, with the sod turned over the original one. Thereafter the process is continued back and forth across the field (Fig. 9b).

Obviously such ploughing does not build up earthen ridges by itself. If a whole field was ploughed in this way, nothing more than a flat area with a slight incipient ridge where the sods of the first two runs met would be produced. Only by ploughing a series of relatively narrow strips, individually, will a set of slightly raised ridges, separated by furrows, appear. Even then a single ploughing in this way would not produce marked ridges. It requires constant ploughing over a long period of time, following the exact form of the original strip, to enable the ridges to develop to any height. Therefore the occurrence of ridge-and-furrow means either that the ridges have been deliberately built up for a special reason, or that, given a need to plough in narrow strips with a fixed mould-board plough, the production of ridges is accepted as an inevitable result.

This then is how ridge-and-furrow is formed. As such it can be produced at any time and indeed can be and sometimes is produced in this way today. However, when one looks at many areas of ridge-and-furrow, especially from the air, there appears to be a relationship between the shapes and layout of the ridges and furrows and the known pattern of common or open field strips of the medieval type. The individual blocks of ridges can be seen as equating with the blocks of strips called furlongs, and the varied arrangement of the end-on and interlocked strip furlongs is repeated exactly in the pattern of ridge-and-furrow furlongs. Thus there can be no doubt that at least part of the ridge-and-furrow still preserved over many parts of England is connected in some way with the medieval fields. As we shall see, however, these medieval fields not only existed in many places until the nineteenth century, but were also modified considerably in the late and post-medieval periods to take account of new agri-

79

cultural practices. Because of this the ridge-and-furrow which we can still see today is not necessarily the result of medieval ploughing; it may derive from the form imposed during the last time it was ploughed in that way. Thus much of the existing ridge-and-furrow is, strictly speaking, not medieval at all but relatively modern.

Nevertheless we can be sure that medieval farmers did ridge their fields. As early as the thirteenth century, Walter of Henley advocated the ridging of fields. More definite and earlier proof has come from archaeological evidence. The earliest form of plough ridge has, once again, come from Gwithian in Cornwall where some have been dated to the ninth or tenth century. However, these are curiously narrow ridges and quite unlike normal ridge-and-furrow. But elsewhere ridge-and-furrow of the more usual type has been found in slightly later contexts. Outside England, at Hen Domen in Wales, it has been discovered overlain by the outer bailey of an eleventh-century castle. In this country, at Bentley Grange in Yorkshire, ridge-and-furrow has been broken up by coalpits dated to the twelfth century (Fig. 10a). Therefore we can be certain that ridge-and-furrow was being formed by ploughing as early as the Norman Conquest.

The study of ridge-and-furrow can tell us something about the methods of ploughing practised in the medieval common fields if we proceed with care. First of all, it is important to note that, though the overall pattern of ridge-and-furrow is similar to the groups of strips or furlongs, the individual ridges do not appear to be equated with the actual strips. Admittedly, the evidence for this comes from the comparison of existing ridge-and-furrow with strips as they are shown on seventeenth- or eighteenth-century maps of contemporary open fields. This indicates clearly that, though the ridges and furrows were related, in practice a strip could be made up of any number of ridges. Thus on a late eighteenth-century map of Higham Ferrers in Northamptonshire, we find adjacent strips comprising one, two, four, two, three and nine ridges respectively (Fig. 10b). Many other examples are known.

10a Ridge-and-furrow overlain by twelfth-century coal pits, Bentley Grange, Yorkshire.

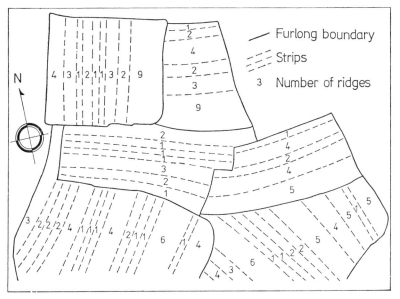

10b Map of the common fields, 1796, Higham Ferrers, Northamptonshire.

The explanation for this is probably that while the ridges were fairly stable, in that they were ploughed every year in the same way, the strips themselves were constantly changing as they were amalgamated with others or split up, following sales, new leases or divided inheritance. Though this is the picture in the post-medieval period, there is no reason to doubt that the same events were taking place before the thirteenth century, for the same evidence of sales, marriage settlements and leasing of land is to be found, and, particularly important in areas where land holdings were divided amongst all the heirs, splitting of strips would certainly occur. Therefore we must see individual ridges merely as the outcome of ploughing techniques, not as units of tenure.

However, we can learn much from ridge-and-furrow, even as the remains of ploughing. For example, a large proportion of the surviving ridge-and-furrow, as well as the strips themselves, takes the form in plan of a reversed 'S' (Plate III). This curious appearance is almost certainly the result of medieval peasant farmers having to solve a basic problem connected with their method of ploughing. On all but the lightest soils, and especially on the heavy clayland, to drag a large plough successfully along the ridges required at least six or eight oxen. These were yoked in pairs to the plough and, when assembled for work, took up a great deal of space. If each ridge or strip had been ploughed exactly straight, such a plough team would have had to start moving forward onto the individual strip by walking over the adjacent strips and ridges. Likewise, when the plough itself had reached the end of the strip, the plough team would again have been stretched across the adjacent fields. But by ploughing in the form of a reversed 'S', the team could commence ploughing by standing on a narrow headland at right angles to the line they were to follow. They then moved forward onto the ridge so that, on reaching the farthest limit, they would have ended at right angles to the ridge on another headland. In this way, damage to the adjacent strips could be avoided. Not all ridge-and-furrow is of reversed 'S' shape; much more is curved to a greater or lesser extent in a gentle 'C' form. This, too, is probably the result of planning to avoid damaging the adjacent land when the strips were ploughed.

The study of ridge-and-furrow also has value when applied over wide areas. It is usually impossible, using sixteenth-century or later maps showing open fields, to know exactly what the maximum extent of the medieval fields was in many places. This is because, as we shall see, in late and post-medieval times there were many changes in the open-field systems all over the country, including their contraction and even abandonment long before the earliest maps were made. Therefore the identification and mapping of ridge-and-furrow can indicate where cultivation took place even if we have no cartographic or documentary evidence.

One particularly good example of this kind of work is the recognition of the very slight ridge-and-furrow which occurs on the chalk downlands of southern England. Until the Second World War this type of ridge-and-furrow was widespread, though modern destruction has now obliterated all but a few fragments. Ridge-and-furrow of this kind is of interest for a number of reasons. First, it is very slight, the ridges often being almost imperceptible and only a few centimetres high. This suggests that the ploughing that formed it was of relatively short duration, for ploughing over any length of time tends to build up considerable ridge height. Secondly, this ridge-and-furrow often lies on top of older prehistoric and Roman fields, which can be identified under the ridges (Fig. 11a). This in turn means that this type of ploughing was relatively short-lived, for a long period of cultivation would have destroyed all traces of the underlying fields. In fact, in many cases the earlier fields are still almost complete, with only their sides slightly ploughed down. Therefore this ridge-and-furrow represents downland taken into cultivation for a very short period, at a time of acute land shortage. Most of this ridge-and-furrow is undated and undatable, though in some places the fact that it is overlain by even later ploughing of the eighteenth or nineteenth centuries proves that it is of some antiquity. One area of such ridge-and-furrow, on Fyfield Down, Wiltshire, has been dated because of its association with a small

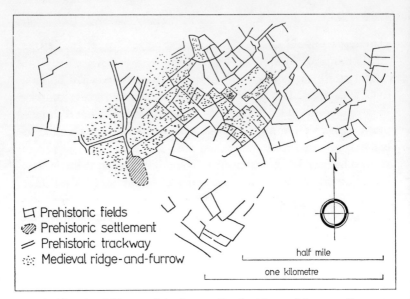

11a Prehistoric fields overlain by medieval ridge-and-furrow, Frampton, Dorset.

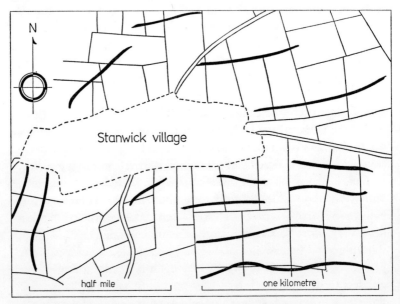

11b Headlands of strip fields overlain by hedged fields of 1838, Stanwick, Northamptonshire. The headlands are visible as low ridges.

farmstead. This indicated that the temporary ploughing here was of late thirteenth- or early fourteenth-century date. This is not unexpected for it falls into the period of the known maximum extent of arable land all over the country, when the population was probably higher than it was to be for the next four hundred years. If the date for the Fyfield Down fields is accepted for much of the rest, then this ridge-and-furrow represents the final push of the medieval farmers into the marginal lands at a time of desperate land hunger. However, it was obviously soon abandoned and without the recognition of this ridge-and-furrow, which is not depicted on any maps, an important part of the medieval agricultural history of the area would have been lost.

Finally, in this examination of the ridge-and-furrow of medieval open fields it is worth noting another physical manifestation of this system of agriculture. In many places in England, modern ploughing has now completely removed all trace of ridge-and-furrow not only from the ground, but also from the lens of the aerial camera. In such places it would seem that there is no way of seeing either the former extent or the layout of these medieval fields. However, this is not the case, for there are features of these fields which even the modern farmer finds it difficult to remove. These appear in the present landscape as long, slightly sinuous ridges (Fig. 11b). They can be of almost any length up to around 700 metres and they range from 10 to 20 metres wide. As they are now usually ploughed over they are rarely more than 0.5 metre high and usually considerably less. Although not easily visible, with practice they can be recognized in the right light or crop conditions. It is difficult to assess just how widespread these ridges are as it is only in the last few years that they have been recognized. They certainly exist over much of the east Midlands, south Lincolnshire, East Anglia and parts of the Home Counties. In fact these ridges are the headlands between the furlongs of the open fields, where the strips terminated and the ridge-and-furrow ran out. They served two purposes; they provided a long narrow strip at each end of the furlongs on which the plough and plough team were turned round, and were also used as access ways to reach the individual strips. After the ploughing of the strips, the headlands themselves were sometimes ploughed, and sometimes left as access roads.

The reason why these headlands were higher than the adjacent ridges, and therefore have survived when the ridges themselves have disappeared, is probably a combination of two factors. One is that these headlands were either never or only rarely ploughed, so that they remained as broad, grassy tracks while the surrounding land was gradually lowered by centuries of cultivation. The other is that the ridges increased in height simply because of the accumulation of earth cleaned off the plough as it turned on the headland.

These headlands, or broad banks, are in fact constantly mentioned in medieval documents referring to the operation of open fields. The documents usually call them baulks or balks and describe them as separating the land of various farmers. Before the recognition of these headlands this description led to the unfortunate and still widely held idea that these baulks actually separated the strips themselves so that each individual strip was divided from its neighbour by a low bank. It is clear from even a superficial examination of surviving ridge-and-furrow that no such banks existed, for the ridges are separated only by the intermediate furrows. The actual strips, therefore, were not defined by anything at all except a furrow, which of course also existed within the strips themselves. This accounts for the many cases in medieval manorial documents where people were accused of encroaching on their neighbours' strips. In the well-known medieval work *Piers Plowman*, the dishonest peasant confesses 'if I went to the plough I pinched so narrowly that I would steal a foot of land or a furrow . . . and if I reaped I would over reap'. When looking at ridge-and-furrow, we see how easily this could be done, whether deliberately or accidentally. On the great majority of open fields in England, the strips were completely undivided and, except for a furrow, there was no way of telling where one strip ended and another began. This lack of set boundaries must have eased the problems of division or enlargement of the land holdings in the medieval fields.

However, it must be pointed out that in a few places, and mainly now on what is marginal land, there are flat strips bounded by low earthen banks, almost indistinguishable at first sight from the much older prehistoric and Roman fields. For example, some 50 hectares of them exist around the village of Kingston, near Corfe Castle in Dorset. These are up to almost 300 metres long and 10–30 metres wide, edged by clearly defined grass banks, about 0.25 metre high. Neither these fields nor other examples known elsewhere can be dated at all. The general impression is that they are not medieval but a later development in post-medieval times. They therefore need not be considered in terms of the appearance of medieval open fields.

Even so ridge-and-furrow, despite its widespread occurrence, was not apparently universal, and documentary evidence points to the fact that ridge-and-furrow was rarely formed in areas such as south Devon and the East Anglian Brecklands. There it seems that strips were ploughed flat, without furrows, in order to retain the moisture. In these areas, grass baulks or strip divisions may have occurred in order to define the strip. Certainly such baulks exist on the still remaining open fields at Braunton in Devon, so that it is possible that the flat strips in Dorset, as noted above, may be of medieval origin. In most parts of England, however, ridge-and-furrow was a normal method of ploughing.

It is still necessary to consider the problem of why ridge-and-furrow appears at all. Farmers rarely carry out complex agricultural works without good reason, yet no really satisfactory explanation has been offered to account for the purpose and widespread use of this technique of ploughing in ridges. The most usual explanation is that it is a response to drainage problems on heavy soils. Without the aid of land drains, a relatively recent innovation, it has been suggested that medieval farmers used the technique of ridged ploughing to provide a way of removing water from the fields by allowing it to run along the furrows. Support for this argument may be seen in the actual arrangement of ridge-and-furrow. For example, an examination of all the ridge-and-furrow in thirty-seven parishes of western Cambridgeshire and 120

parishes in Northamptonshire has shown that on almost all slopes
of more than 5 degrees the ridge-and-furrow runs at right angles,
or nearly so, to the contours. In addition, where there are natural
water courses such as streams and rivers, the ridge-and-furrow
nearly always runs at right angles to them. Detailed examination
of ridge-and-furrow produces additional evidence. Where it nears
a water course, it is characterized by small humps or rises at the
end of the ridges. These have been interpreted as being the result
of removing silt and soil from the adjacent furrows when the
ploughing had blocked them; so that surface water could run
freely into the nearby stream.

On the other hand, the existence of ridge-and-furrow on chalk
downland, limestone hills and dry gravel terraces where no drainage problem exists, has cast doubt on the drainage theory. An
alternative theory put forward to explain this is that ridging
increases the surface area of the field, and so enlarges, by a small
proportion, the amount of land available. This idea has not met
with wide approval. The real answer may be that the technique
of ridging was originally developed as a way of draining heavy
land, but that it subsequently became the normal way of ploughing, regardless of the environment.

Apart from ridge-and-furrow, there are also other remains of
medieval ploughing still visible in the modern landscape. These
are *strip lynchets*, a confusing name that has been given to the long
parallel terraces which are commonly seen on steep hillsides
(Plates IV and X; Fig. 12a). They occur widely in southern and
south-eastern England, Gloucestershire and the uplands of
northern England, but also appear less obviously in areas such
as Essex, Hertfordshire, Cambridgeshire, Staffordshire, Cornwall,
Herefordshire, and in many other places. They have excited much
interest in the past because they are often of considerable size and
complexity. Explanations for their occurrence have ranged from
describing them as terraces cut by river action to medieval vine-
yards, but in fact they are nothing more than the extension of the
normal medieval open fields onto steep ground, at a time when
flatter, more easily worked land was in short supply or non-

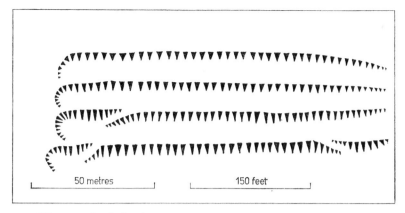

12a   Diagram of strip lynchets.

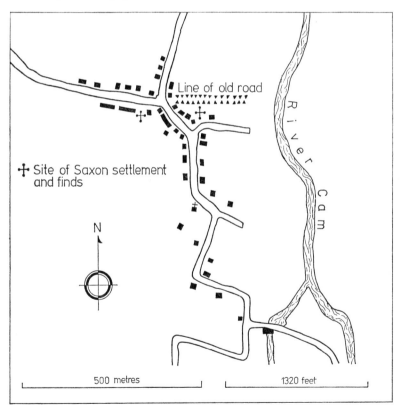

12b   Village plan, Grantchester, Cambridgeshire.

existent. As such, they probably do not deserve all the attention they have received from scholars.

Strip lynchets are made up of two parts. The flat strip itself is usually called the tread, and the steep scarped edge or lynchet, the riser. The great majority of strip lynchets are of contour type, *i.e.* running approximately parallel to the contours, and these often produce the most prominent and dramatic examples. However, there are other examples, usually less prominent, which run diagonally across the contours.

The most characteristic features of strip lynchets are usually their steep risers, sometimes of considerable height. This height is normally a combination of the duration of ploughing and the steepness of the original slope for they were, in most cases, formed merely by the action of the plough moving across the hillside in order to cultivate a strip. As was noted earlier in the case of prehistoric and Roman fields (p. 28), the disturbed soil tends to slide down the hillside and build up on the edge of the strip, and is in turn replaced by soil from the uphill side as the plough cuts back into the slope. Thus the riser is a positive lynchet, with the sharp slope at the back of the strip as a negative lynchet. The other main characteristic of strip lynchets is their length, and this clearly distinguishes them from prehistoric and Roman long fields in particular with which they are sometimes associated, especially on the marginal downlands of Wessex. Strip lynchets are often as much as 200 metres and rarely less than 70 metres in length; that is, they look like the strips of the open fields in plan. Another feature possessed by these fields, which again should prevent their being mistaken for Roman long fields, is the way in which they terminate. Instead of being squared off as were the Roman fields, they either run out onto unploughed land, or end in a sharp curved negative lynchet, formed as the plough was pulled round. Where whole flights of strip lynchets lie together on a hillside they are often linked by ramps which give access to the treads.

Even though these strip lynchets are now universally accepted as being the result of ploughing, there are still doubts in certain quarters as to their medieval date, and some people consistently confuse them with prehistoric or Roman fields, thereby assuming that they originated in that period. The difficulty has been that, as they are the result of ploughing, excavation can tell us little of their date, for pottery of all periods is to be found mixed up in the soil. However, detailed examination of strip lynchets all over England has shown that they often overlie and, therefore, post-date Roman features. In Northumberland they have been found lying across the civilian settlement outside the Roman fort at Housesteads. At Horton in Wiltshire, some strip lynchets were ploughed long after an underlying Roman ditch had been abandoned, while at Plush in Dorset, strip lynchets can be seen to cut across and destroy a Roman farmstead. This proves that strip lynchets must be medieval or later.

They could in fact have been formed at any date when strip ploughing was being undertaken, so that many strip lynchets may not be medieval and, consequently, are strictly outside the limits of this chapter. Certainly many were still in use in the nineteenth century, to judge from contemporary maps, and indeed some remain so even today. At Coombe Bissett in Wiltshire, an exceptionally fine series on a steep valley side is still regularly ploughed, sown with cereals and harvested by combines.

In fact it is extremely difficult to establish a date at which strip lynchets were formed. On general grounds, because they represent ploughing on land not normally regarded as worth cultivating, except at times of extreme shortage, we might expect that many were developed in the twelfth and thirteenth centuries under the pressure of rising population. Much depends, however, on the actual topography of the area in which they occur, as well as the density of population there at various times. Detailed studies by this writer have suggested very different dates for some strip lynchets. Thus at Mere in Wiltshire, where population pressure and the ensuing land hunger became serious only in the thirteenth century, the remarkable flights of strip lynchets there probably date from that time. On the other hand, at Bincombe in Dorset, where the population was always relatively static, but almost all the available land in the parish was on steep slopes, the strip lynchets probably date from the eleventh century at the latest.

The fact that strip lynchets also represent shortage of land can be realized where they are examined in detail. For example, at Worth Matravers in Dorset, a dire lack of land forced the medieval farmers to plough very steep slopes immediately above the vertical sea cliffs where wind and salt spray must have had a devastating effect on the crops. Here also we can see further proof of the site's unsuitability in that at two places, after the strip lynchets had been formed, land slips occurred on the unstable limestone hillside and tore out sections of the fields. Undeterred, the farmers returned and forced their ploughs over the slips to form new strip lynchets.

As with ridge-and-furrow the recognition of strip lynchets can greatly aid our knowledge of the total areas of land that medieval farmers had under cultivation at certain times. There are innumerable examples of strip lynchets occurring in such places as the remote corners of the uplands of Yorkshire and high valleys of Shropshire, far beyond the limits of the permanent medieval arable fields. These remains are, therefore, the only evidence of just how far medieval farmers were prepared to extend their strip cultivation under pressure.

Before leaving this discussion of the visible remains of the medieval strip fields, it is worth noting another aspect that can still be seen in a few places in the modern landscape and illustrates vividly just how flexible these fields could be. This arises from the evidence we have for movement of villages over their own fields as a result of various pressures on those villages. Three different examples, all taken from Cambridgeshire, may be cited here. The first is the village of Caxton, where the early Saxon village grew up along a narrow lane, about a quarter of a mile west of the old Roman road between London and the north, which was known as Ermine Street. By the eleventh century the village had acquired the normal strip fields all around it. But during the twelfth century, as traffic developed along Ermine

Street, the village either migrated gradually or was deliberately moved away from its original site to establish itself along each side of the main road. However, as the land there was divided into strip fields, the new houses were erected on the ends, while the rest of the strips were turned into gardens. The result was that garden boundaries were curved following the edges of the former strips. These narrow, curving gardens exist today, while at the original village site only the church, two farms and abandoned house platforms remain. The actual date of the migration of the village is unknown, but it had certainly taken place by 1247 when the lord of the manor was granted a charter to hold a market in the new village.

At Grantchester the picture is similar in general terms but different in detail (Fig. 12b). There, excavations have proved that the original Saxon village lay at a crossroads at the northern end of the present village. Subsequent growth led to the village spreading across at least three or four of the adjacent rectangular open-field furlongs, with the new main street being laid along the headlands between them. The result of this can be seen in the curious line of the present village street as it turns through six sharp angles, and in the generally rectangular form of the house and garden plots. Again this movement cannot be accurately dated, but it had certainly occurred by 1100, for the parish church, which actually stands on one of the former furlongs, has structural remains of that time.

Finally, at Burwell in eastern Cambridgeshire, the northward extension of the village from its Saxon centre took place along an existing headland between two lines of end-on furlongs. The result is that the present North Street of the village has a long sinuous form lying parallel to other old headlands which remained in use until the early nineteenth century. Once more this extension is undated, and in this case one can only say that it had taken place by 1351 when North Street was first recorded. These examples clearly illustrate how it was possible for large sections of the medieval common fields to be abandoned and used for the extension of settlement, often at very early dates.

Chapter 5

Medieval Enclosed Fields

Though by 1300 there were various forms of open- or strip-field farming over much of England, this type of cultivation was not employed everywhere. There were large parts of the country where no strip fields existed, and agriculture was based entirely on enclosed fields, bounded by permanent hedges, walls or banks. These fields varied greatly in shape, size and purpose, but by and large they developed mainly in localities with a relatively low population, where the people lived more often in isolated farmsteads or hamlets than in villages. In addition, such fields appeared at the limits of the normal open fields on land which had earlier been woodland or waste. It is difficult, owing to the lack of early documents, to be sure when this process started. It was probably continuous from early Saxon times and even then may have been a survival of Roman enclosure. It is best documented in the twelfth and thirteenth centuries when there are innumerable records which tell us what was happening at that time, and this has led to the belief that these fields appeared mainly during these two centuries. In fact this may not be so at all. The documents may merely be reporting the final stages of a long-drawn-out process which is largely unrecorded.

The basic reasons behind this massive development of newly enclosed fields on the fens, in the forests and over the wastes of early medieval England, were a continuing rise in population and a demand for new land. We have already observed that the same expansion occurred in the common or strip fields and, indeed, how some enclosed fields were split up and incorporated within the existing strip systems. In addition, thousands of hectares were reclaimed by individual farmers, enclosed with boundaries and farmed separately.

The most notable regions for this form of reclamation were the remaining forests of England. Here farmers moved out from the villages, set up farmsteads in the woods and cleared areas around them. Other people merely cleared woodland at the edges of the parish, and worked their new fields in association with their strips in the adjacent open fields. All levels of society from small peasants, through local lords to great barons and monastic houses, were involved in this clearance, or assarting as it was known. Only a few examples can be given here.

The first is in the forested area of the Vale of Blackmoor, Dorset. The extensive thirteenth- and fourteenth-century records of the forest tell how various people were reclaiming land at that time. In 1269, the Abbot of Abbotsbury was said to be holding 30 acres of land in Hilton 'which a predecessor of his, who is dead, enclosed', while in 1257 'Adam de Warner, the reeve of Marnhull, occupied in Todber one acre of land enclosed by a hedge'. In the same area in 1302–3 'Walter atte Wodeseyned gives to the Lady Queen 12 pence for a perch and a half encroachment opposite his gate'. Ingelram de Bereger, who held large estates in the region, was granted permission in 1314 to 'reduce to cultivation' two separate areas of land of $76\frac{1}{2}$ acres and 108 acres in the parish of Hermitage. In every area where there was forest there are records of clearance. On the woodland slopes of the Cotswolds near Cheltenham, in 1310, John de Wycombe had a parcel of land 'newly assarted, lying within his enclosures'. Likewise in the wooded lowlands of Shropshire at Botwood 40 acres (*c.* 16 hectares) of land were assarted by the Knights Templars in 1199.

The evidence of these forest clearances is still marked on the present landscape in the former woodland areas. In spite of much later alteration, the modern pattern of irregularly shaped fields, often bounded by thick and botanically rich hedges perched on large banks, shows how and where medieval farmers encroached on the forests. Sometimes it is possible to deduce from the landscape together with the help of documents how this was done. For example, in the parish of Whiteparish in south Wiltshire, in a relatively small area of old forest the fields are highly irregular and have obviously been cut out of the former woodland, but the actual farm boundaries are still visible as relatively straight lines. From this one can see exactly how each farmstead was set up on the forest edge, and the land behind it cleared piecemeal into long strips up to the cleared land of adjacent farms (Fig. 13a). Some of the actual clearances here are recorded in documents, as in one of 1270 where 14 acres (*c.* 6 hectares) of assarts, enclosed by 'a dyke and a hedge', are listed. This example is a complex one showing many farmers at work in the same area.

Elsewhere the work of individual farmers is recoverable. At Knapwell in Cambridgeshire there is an isolated single farmstead on the edge of a small wood surrounded by a group of irregular fields. This farm is first recorded in 1278, and we can, perhaps, rightly assume that the fields are the original ones. That this is so, is suggested by the botanical content of the wood and the field hedges, both of which contain species of plants, such as dog's mercury and herb paris, which are regarded by botanists as indicators of very old woodland. Here, then, it looks as if the fields were actually cut out of a larger area of woodland in a remote corner of the parish. These irregular fields, the result of medieval forest clearances, can be seen over large stretches of England which were formerly wooded. They occur widely, for example, in the Forest of Arden in Warwickshire, in southern Essex, in the Weald, in Wychwood Forest in Oxfordshire, Sherwood in Nottinghamshire, and on the edges of Cannock Chase in Staffordshire.

The recognition of areas of woodland, later cleared by medieval farmers, can be taken even further by employing botanical methods. Recent research by historical ecologists has led to the identification of so-called 'relict woodland hedges'. These often appear to be quite ordinary hedges, but they are usually botanically rich. They contain plants such as dog's mercury, bluebell and wood anemone, all of which are very slow colonizers and, there-

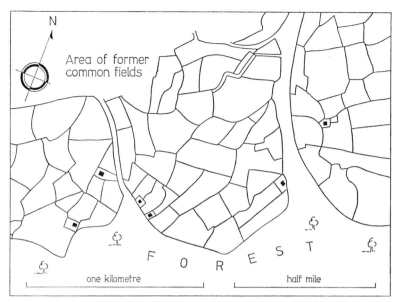

13a Fields formed by forest clearance, thirteenth century and earlier, White-parish, Wiltshire. Botanically rich hedge boundaries.

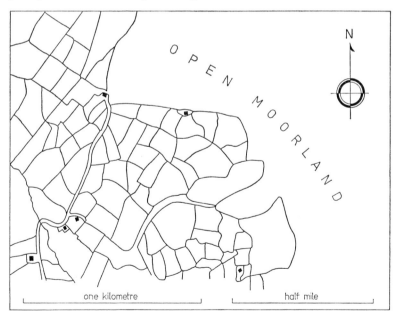

13b Fields formed by moorland reclamation, thirteenth century and earlier, Willsworthy, Devon. Stone wall boundaries.

fore, clear indicators of old woodland. The occurrence of hedges with these species can often point to the existence of ancient woodland cleared in the medieval period when no other evidence is available. For example, the old forest of Sapley, Huntingdonshire, was probably cleared in the thirteenth century, long before any maps were made of the area, and the post-medieval and modern destruction of the enclosed fields there has virtually removed all traces of the process of assarting. The few surviving hedges, however, that follow the existing sinuous lanes, show from their botanical content that the area was formerly part of a forest. Much work remains to be done in refining this method, but the implications for the future study of medieval land reclamation in forested regions are far-reaching.

Another and now well established botanical technique, which is immensely valuable in understanding these medieval enclosed fields as well as others, is that known as hedgerow dating. This involves the counting of the number of different shrub or tree species, excluding herbs or brambles, along thirty-metre lengths of hedge. For reasons not entirely clear even to botanists, the average number of species in a thirty-metre section equals the approximate date of the hedge in hundreds of years. This method has been evolved and checked against dated hedges over much of England and, in most cases, seems to work. The only provisos are that the hedges tested in this way should be reasonably complete and fairly well managed. Badly broken or mutilated hedges cannot be used in this method of dating, nor can totally overgrown ones. The value of this technique is obvious, and, when carefully applied and checked against documentary evidence where it exists, it can appreciably assist in our understanding of fields and their development. We shall return to this technique again in later chapters when dealing with late-medieval and post-medieval hedges. At this point two examples of this kind of work on medieval and later enclosure hedges may be noted.

At Soham in Cambridgeshire there is an area of low-lying pasture land, which was situated along the edges of the medieval common fields. This is now divided into a number of irregular fields which, from the shape of their boundaries, look as if they are successive intakes from the waste. No documents exist to substantiate this process but, by dating the hedges and examining the remains of ridge-and-furrow both near by and actually under one hedge, a sequence of development has been worked out. Thus we can infer that the first field, a small rectangular paddock, was established in the centre of the waste in the twelfth century. Then the rest of the open pasture land was separated physically from the adjacent common fields by a hedge in the thirteenth century or slightly earlier. At the same time, there was at least one other new irregular field enclosed on the waste. Yet another small field was added in the fourteenth century, while a larger one appeared in the late fifteenth century. Thereafter, some time in the seventeenth century, another group of fields was established.

In a very different landscape, at Otford in Kent, using the same technique, it has been possible not only to identify the farm boundaries of the major freeholders of medieval times and to show that they were in existence by the ninth or tenth centuries, but also to locate individual fields dating from before 1100 and their subsequent subdivision in post-medieval times.

The forests and wastes were not the only areas to be reclaimed for new arable land in this period. In the uplands of northern England and along the Welsh borders, as well as on the moors of south-west England, reclamation went on apace. In Yorkshire, many of the great Cistercian abbeys reclaimed vast areas of land and turned them into large arable farms. Elsewhere in the same county, much piecemeal assarting took place and there are many documents which refer to 'old' and 'new' assarts and 'assarts next to the moor'. Not all this assarting was for arable; much was for sheep, for in these upland moors sheep were always important and were to become more so as the medieval period advanced.

All round the edges of Dartmoor, for example, reclamation had started by the tenth century at the latest and continued for at least three hundred years. The isolated farmsteads around the edges of the moors are today still surrounded by small irregularly shaped fields bounded by stone walls which were first made in these centuries (Fig. 13b). The same pattern of irregular stone-walled fields lying around small isolated farms occurs in northern England too. For instance, in the Lake District, many of the tiny farmsteads high up on the fell slopes, each with its associated stone-wall paddocks and with easy access to the extensive high grazings, date from this period. Two such are Parkamoor and Lawson Park, hidden away on the fellside to the east of Coniston Water. The 'park' name is a common Lake District element, meaning an enclosed piece of ground. The ubiquitous sheep in these hills also help to change the landscape completely, and add another form of field boundary. The total absence of trees over much of Lakeland today, when contrasted with names such as Yew Crags, shows how constant grazing totally altered the appearance of the countryside. In addition, many of these upland sheep pastures, some belonging to the great abbeys of the north, were subdivided and bounded by stone walls. In 1284, when the monks of Furnace Abbey were carving out a huge sheep pasture of 600 hectares in Upper Eskdale, they were given 'the liberty of enclosing the pasture . . . with a dyke, wall or paling'. The resulting boundary, in fact a stone wall, can still be traced today across the fells at the west end of Eskdale just below Scafell.

Farther east, on Malham Moors in Yorkshire, miles of extant stone walls mark the division between the great sheep pastures of the abbeys of Fountains, Bolton and Salley, set up in the thirteenth century.

Back in southern England again, the broad open heathlands of southern Hampshire and Dorset felt the impact of the farmers' hands in the centuries before 1300. There are still numerous isolated farms, first recorded in documents dating from the thirteenth and fourteenth centuries, though undoubtedly much older, surrounded by irregularly shaped fields which were cut out of the barren wastes between the tenth and thirteenth centuries (Plate V).

These years also saw the work of fenland and marshland reclamation. In the west, on the Somerset Levels, drainage had certainly started by the twelfth century at the latest. Most of it was piecemeal in the areas not constantly inundated, around the edges of the Levels. Usually the better areas of rough grazing had ditches dug round and across them to assist drainage and so improve and enclose the land for grazing. In some cases drainage was thorough enough to allow cultivation to be undertaken. Low earthen walls were sometimes built to keep out occasional floods, while in a few places larger walls were constructed to prevent even severe flooding. Much of this work involved large-scale effort and organization and, once more, the great ecclesiastical estates led the way. For example, in the early thirteenth century we read of three great 'Hammes', or pastures, that had been created at Bleadon on the River Axe, by the Bishops of Winchester. The surrounding 'sea wall' which protected them was maintained by twenty-three tenants who held their own land from the bishops in return for this work. Many local lords and even peasants also took to reclaiming land on the Levels. Thus Walter de Knowlton was allowed by Glastonbury Abbey in 1281 to retain 30 acres (12 hectares) of meadow which he had illegally made in South Lake Moor. In return, he paid a set rent and agreed to give up the common grazing rights that he held in land on the same moor which the Abbey was then enclosing itself. These old medieval enclosures can still be recognized in the landscape today, usually as small and highly irregular fields, bounded by winding ditches which stand out in marked contrast to the drainage enclosures of later centuries (Fig. 14a).

In eastern England the same pattern is visible along the silt-lands of southern Lincolnshire and north-west Norfolk. There, peasants, lords and monasteries were all engaged in the extension of arable across the level siltland around the Wash. Some of the new land was incorporated into the existing strip fields, but much was enclosed directly into small fields. This process certainly started before the eleventh century and continued throughout the next two hundred years. Again co-operation was needed to carry out the work, often by groups of villages, for the basic requirement in this case was the construction of massive banks

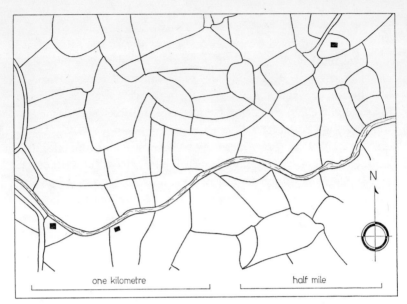

14a Fields formed by medieval fenland reclamation, Kingston Seymour, Somerset. Ditched boundaries.

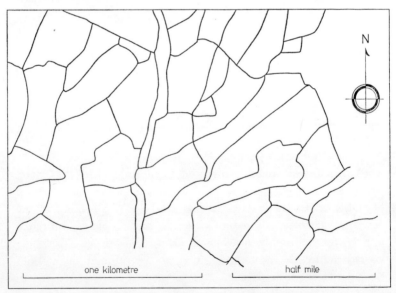

14b Fields formed by medieval estuary marshland reclamation, Wennington, Essex. Ditched boundaries.

running parallel to the sea. Behind these the new land was drained, turned over to rich pastures and even cultivated. Then, as the sea deposited more silt in front of the banks, new banks were erected farther out again and another area reclaimed. As always the mark of this work is still clearly stamped on the present landscape. All along the south Lincolnshire coast, south-east, east and north-east of Boston, the long parallel 'sea banks' can now be seen standing high above the surrounding fields, up to four kilometres from the present sea shore. The fields in this area, too, retain the characteristic irregular form imposed by the medieval drainers' ditches which still surround them.

Farther north, in Holderness, a similar network of irregular drains marks out the new meadows, pastures and occasional arable fields, many of which were reclaimed from the marshes by yet another great monastic house, Meaux Abbey. In southern England too, the great walls of packed clay, originally strengthened with timber and faced with stone, survive marking the boundaries of great 'innings', or sheep pastures, which were reclaimed from Romney Marsh. In the Thames marshes, irregular fields edged by drains bear witness to the medieval reclamation work (Fig. 14b).

In the fenlands of Cambridgeshire, Huntingdonshire and Norfolk we have massive documentation of reclaimed marsh and fen in the centuries up to 1300. Much of this is in the surviving records of the great abbeys, such as Ely, Ramsey and Thorney, but here and elsewhere we have to remember that the work of small peasants and local minor lords, which certainly went on, was probably never written down. Even so, the documentation that survives is impressive. In 1206–7 the records of Ramsey Abbey list twenty-eight tenants working newly reclaimed land in the villages of Outwell and Upwell on the Norfolk–Cambridgeshire border. At the same time, some tenants of Thorney Abbey were drawing up an agreement with their lord regarding shares in new assarts they had made or were about to make. In a survey of 1251 of the Manor of Downham in Cambridgeshire, made for the abbey at Ely, thirteen new tenants are listed as holding 27 hectares of reclaimed land while near by, at Littleport, sixty new tenants were holding nearly 200 hectares of new land. This type of record can be multiplied many times, and shows clearly that there was massive reclamation of the peat and silt fens at this time.

However, it is difficult to see these reclaimed areas in the modern landscape. The characteristic fields over almost all the fenland are highly geometrical ditched enclosures of various sizes. Because of this rigid shape these fields are usually said to be the result of later drainage and the reclamation work of the post-medieval period. This is certainly true in part, but nevertheless it is possible to identify general areas of medieval drainage if they are examined with care. For here it is not the *shape* of the *individual* fields that distinguishes the medieval enclosures from the later ones, but the overall irregular pattern, which is quite different from the rigidly rectangular layout of later times (Fig. 15a). With practice, these medieval fields can be easily established on a map, and the many thousands of hectares of reclaimed pasture and arable land recognized.

Field names once again reveal this process of clearance and reclamation wherever it took place. The common name of Breach or Brake Field, meaning land broken up for cultivation, is one such. The occurrence of this name at, for example, Burwell in Cambridgeshire, associated with 70 hectares of irregular fields, and first recorded as early as 1272, helps us to see both the method involved and the extent of land that was 'reduced' to cultivation. Assart or Sart Field is another name frequently encountered in forested areas, as is Stockley Field or The Stocks, meaning land cleared of tree stumps. Likewise Stubbings has the same origin and at Cottingham in Northamptonshire the name Stubbings occurs as 'Le Newestybbing' in a late fourteenth-century document.

So, throughout the long centuries of the early medieval period, farmers everywhere were extending their land outwards from their villages and making deep inroads into the forests, marshes, heaths, moorlands and fens. It was a slow process, not without its failures and setbacks. Particularly on the coastal marshes and fens,

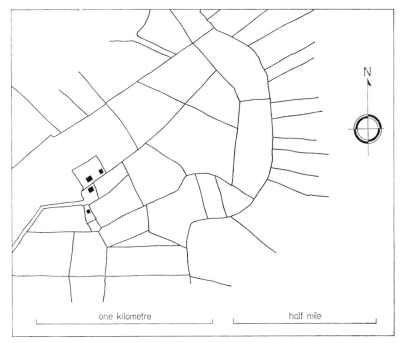

15a Fields formed by fenland reclamation, thirteenth century, Littleport, Cambridgeshire. Ditched boundaries.

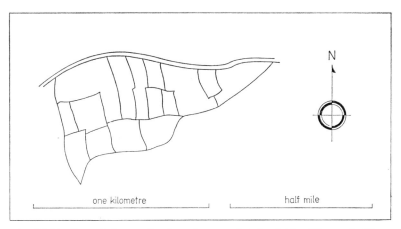

15b Fields formed by medieval enclosure of strip fields, Hinton St Mary, Dorset. Botanically mixed hedge boundaries.

constant flooding was an ever-present threat, which all too often became a reality. Thus in 1251 much of the reclaimed land in Leverington, Cambridgeshire, was 'overflowed and laid waste by the sea'. In the Somerset Levels the same problem existed, and two acres of land held by one Alured at Lympsham were described in 1189 as 'occupied by the sea'. In the far north of England, raids by Scots across the border were a recurring feature, and often caused reclaimed land and even permanent arable to be abandoned.

Even in the forests of the midlands and the south, where no floods or raids occurred, there were problems, especially when the assarting involved the reduction of the invaluable common grazing land. This is illustrated by a case in 1279 at Lydlinch in the Forest of Blackmoor, Dorset, where 'certain malefactors and disturbers of the King's Peace . . . pulled down a certain ditch of Henry Baret . . . with force of arms by night'.

Despite all this the work went on and, by 1300, much of England had been exploited in one way or another by ploughmen or herders. The early fourteenth century marks the peak of agricultural advance. After this time events, whose origins in the main lay outside this country, intervened and helped to change the agricultural landscape of England.

Chapter 6

Late Medieval Fields

Of the various factors which played their part in the changing of English fields during the centuries from 1300 to 1600 the most important was that of population. By 1330 the gradually increasing rise in the number of people in England had ceased and the population may have even been declining. For in spite of all the new land under cultivation, it is probable that the population growth of the previous centuries had outrun the food supply. There was certainly malnutrition and an increasing susceptibility to famine and disease. Onto this weakened population of about 4½ million in 1348–50 came the Black Death, which returned again in 1361–2, 1369 and 1374. Exactly how many people died from the disease is not clear. Estimates have varied between one third and a half of the total population, but in any case it was very diverse in its effect and some parts of the country were hit harder than others. The recurrence of the disease after 1350 kept the population down and by and large it was not before 1450 that real growth started again. Thereafter it rose rapidly, so that by 1600 the population of England was probably back to the 1348 level.

At the basic agricultural level of the amount of land required, these population changes were bound to affect the field systems of England. But they also changed society in various ways, which in turn affected the agricultural systems. First of all, the declining number of people caused a labour shortage which forced up wages. This was accompanied by a surplus of land and therefore a decline in land values. In addition, up until 1500, prices for agricultural products fell or remained stable. The result of these events was an increasing tendency, which had started around or even before 1300, for lords to abandon their land or lease it, coupled with a move to turn from arable to pastoral farming in order to cut costs. The leasing was especially important, for the new tenants were often the peasant farmers who, with higher wages, took the opportunity to invest in land. Many became important farmers in their own right and were able eventually, in a fluid land market, to buy up and consolidate the holdings of other lords and less gifted peasants.

The records of the later fourteenth and early fifteenth centuries show these changes in some detail. There are numerous references to abandoned land in the fens, forests and moors as well as elsewhere, and a reversion of arable to pasture. In the years immediately after 1350 the grain production on the Huntingdonshire manors of Ramsey Abbey fell by half. At the village of Groby, in Leicestershire, the arable land in 1445 was only a third of what it had been just over a century earlier. The evidence for leasing land is also fully recorded; for example, all the manors owned by Durham Cathedral Priory were leased by 1451, and all those of the Honour of Clare in East Anglia, by 1400.

From 1450 onwards yet another change occurred. Pasture land, instead of being kept as a cheap form of agriculture, became profitable through the growth in the demand for wool, not only in this country but abroad. The result was an active reduction in arable land and an increase in pasture where this was possible. There was thus a pressure for the enclosure of former arable land which lasted until the early sixteenth century.

What effect did all these demographic and economic factors have on the landscape and to what extent are they still mirrored in the countryside today? First of all, there was the complete depopulation of villages by the Black Death. This was not as common as used to be thought and certainly relatively few of the thousands of known deserted villages were in fact extinguished by the pestilence itself. Nevertheless, a number were and their common fields disappeared. Only the old ridge-and-furrow, finally grassed over, remained. Much of this ridge-and-furrow exists today around the sites of these lost villages, showing exactly how the last peasant farmers left their fields before they were killed or driven off. Much more common was the massive reduction in the size of villages which, in spite of the pestilence, managed to survive. In these instances the common fields remained, but were sharply reduced in size. Again we can see the result of this in many places. The high downland ridge-and-furrow on the chalklands of southern England and strip lynchets on difficult slopes which have not been ploughed since, are eloquent testimony of the retreat from the marginal lands. On the heathlands of southern England, on Dartmoor, or on the Pennine Hills, summer fires often reveal stone-walled or embanked fields, now normally hidden by bracken or heather, which were abandoned to the waste in the fourteenth century. Even in the more populated regions there are large stretches of ridge-and-furrow which indicate the 'high water mark' of thirteenth-century arable expansion and which were never again brought under the plough.

Some of these areas, however, were not abandoned completely. Many of them with favourable soils reverted to pasture which meant that they could be and were used for grazing. The result was that in many places the abandoned strips of the common fields were consolidated and enclosed to form hedged or walled fields for cattle or sheep. The new boundaries were often put around groups of existing strips or furlongs and their shape was partly conditioned by the earlier arrangement. We still find fields with generally curved sides, of reversed 'S' form, that were produced by this means. Very often these large fields proved to be too big for later farmers and were subsequently subdivided, but their original boundaries can still be recognized (Fig. 15b; Plate VI).

Even where the bulk of the common fields remained, alterations occurred, mainly as a result of leasing or changes in land holding and the development of larger units by the new yeoman farmers. The physical manifestation of this can sometimes be seen in ridge-and-furrow when it is examined in detail. One of the most distinctive features is the result of joining end-on blocks of

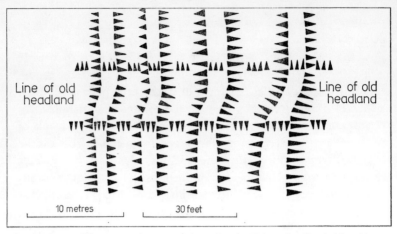

Line of old headland

Line of old headland

10 metres   30 feet

16a   Ridge-and-furrow and associated headlands, Wimpole, Cambridgeshire.

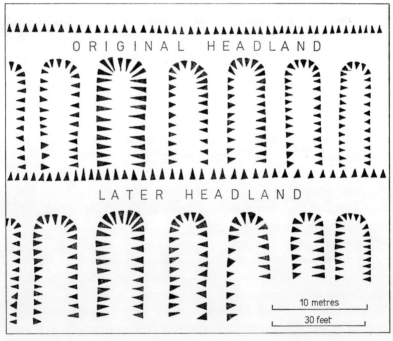

ORIGINAL HEADLAND

LATER HEADLAND

10 metres   30 feet

16b   Ridge-and-furrow overlying older headland, Connington, Cambridgeshire.

strips to make larger ones. These can be recognized on the ground as normal ridge-and-furrow which suddenly rises, twists or kinks slightly before it falls again and runs on. The rise is caused by an older, underlying headland which has been later ploughed over, and the twist by the joining up of two adjacent ridges which were originally not quite in line (Fig. 16b). This occurrence can often be best appreciated from the air after modern destruction has removed the bulk of the ridges, when the older headlands show up more clearly with the traces of ploughed-out ridges crossing them. Even more common are sudden rises in ridge-and-furrow without the twist. This is the result of the same process, but where the ridge-and-furrow was formed anew. Another feature from this form of consolidation is the splitting of one ridge into two. There is a fine example of this at Newport Pagnell in Buckinghamshire, where a number of ridges and furrows suddenly divide into two (Fig. 17a). These, and other features, show exactly how the consolidation of strips took place in the common fields of late medieval England.

Elsewhere consolidation worked in a reverse way. There is evidence in certain places that the old very long reversed 'S' strips were regarded as too awkward for later ploughing, perhaps as a result of substituting the horse for the ox as a mode of traction. Therefore old strips were abandoned and reploughed with straight sides. Such examples have been noted in the West Riding of Yorkshire, and certainly air photographs of parts of eastern Northamptonshire show traces of older curved ridges apparently underlying the later straight ridges which still exist. This process also involved the overploughing of older headlands as the original strips were lengthened.

Another type of alteration of ridge-and-furrow that may belong to this period is the shortening of strips where they run out onto land which had a tendency to flood or was unsuitable for various reasons. In these cases the plough was turned before it reached the old headland and a new one was created inside it, leaving the original ridges projecting from under it. A good example of this is to be found at Wimpole in Cambridgeshire (Fig. 16a) where, at

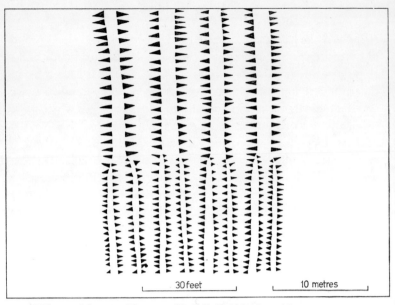

30 feet   10 metres

17a   Ridge-and-furrow, Newport Pagnell, Buckinghamshire.

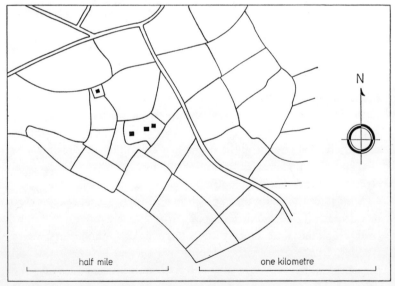

N

half mile   one kilometre

17b   Fields formed for sheep farming, late fifteenth century, Little Rollright, Oxfordshire. Botanically mixed hedge boundaries.

some time before the early seventeenth century, the ends of strips lying in damp ground close to a stream were abandoned.

This kind of alteration indicates yet again how flexible the common fields were, especially in the late medieval period when enterprising farmers were able and willing to carry out such work. Another feature at this time was the appearance of individual enclosed strips of land within the common fields. These almost certainly originated when farmers wanted to cultivate crops different from those growing on the surrounding strips. In the first stages these were sometimes temporarily fenced, but as time went on permanent hedges or walls were erected and a whole new enclosed field, cultivated quite separately from the rest of the arable, emerged. These fields too survive, though it is not always possible to date individual examples as the process was to become even more common later on. In a few places, however, we are able to date these enclosed strips, even if only approximately, by examining their botanical content. Thus at Great Shelford in Cambridgeshire, behind a line of late medieval farmsteads—themselves an encroachment on a former waste—there are a series of long narrow curving strip fields. From their shape they seem likely to have originated as a result of the enclosure of former strips in the common fields. No documentary date is forthcoming, but the botanical content of the hedges suggests that they are some five hundred years old and were perhaps made around 1500.

Although the medieval common fields, albeit often much reduced in size, altered in layout and dotted with small enclosures, survived in many places, notably in the Midlands and the North-East, in other places there was a complete abandonment of the common fields in favour of enclosed ones. This did not happen because of sheep farming, as is often supposed. In fact much of it occurred in the late fourteenth and early fifteenth centuries before the great rise in wool prices. Nor was it done by rapacious landlords, so often the villains of the piece in the early sixteenth century. It was carried out by a multitude of small farmers, by agreement between themselves and their lords, as they strove to break away from the communal agriculture of the past and gain for themselves the opportunities to farm as they wished. This was by no means a universal occurrence; it varied widely from place to place, depending on local personalities, local customs and, most of all, lack of population. In villages which had been much reduced in size and where, therefore, there were few farmers and tenants, it was much easier to come to an arrangement over enclosure than it was where a village was large and many farmers were involved. In the latter villages, problems over common grazing and cropping rotations prevented large-scale enclosure.

If conditions were right, individuals bought and exchanged land to consolidate their holdings and then agreed to enclose them. The result was a curious field pattern which survives in many places. Because the boundaries of the new fields tended to follow the edges of existing furlongs or blocks of strips, they took on a generally curved form which often interlocked with adjacent fields as the old strips had done (Plate VI). Once again it is difficult to date accurately all the surviving examples, for the practice was to continue right through until the eighteenth century. However, certain areas, especially those in the north and west, such as Herefordshire, Shropshire, Lancashire and Cheshire, as well as parts of Staffordshire, Worcestershire and Gloucestershire, certainly seem to have lost the majority of their common fields at this time. We can still see this form of enclosure in many places. For example, in Dorset at Iwerne Courtney, there was in 1548 an agreement between the major landowner and the few remaining small farmers to enclose totally the existing common fields. Today, only one part of their work survives, but it is sufficient to reveal how the new fields were based on the older strip pattern. A similar example in the same county is to be seen at Hinton St Mary. Here the date of enclosure is not known with certainty, though it seems to have taken place some time before the sixteenth century. There too (Fig. 15b) the pattern of surviving fields indicates how they have in fact fossilized the earlier strips.

It is unfortunate that this process of early enclosure by agreement is ill recorded, for the great outcry in the late fifteenth and early sixteenth centuries against relatively small-scale enclosures in other parts of England has tended to take precedence over this earlier large-scale but silent enclosure by agreement. Equally poorly documented is the contemporary enclosure on the uplands of the north, as well as in parts of the dry, infertile chalk and limestone uplands of Wessex and Gloucestershire, where it seems that many thousands of acres of wastelands were enclosed, often for sheep.

From 1450 onwards it was these sheep and the enclosures for them, particularly in the Midlands, that caught the contemporary 'headlines'. There were much controversy, many pamphlets and a number of government inquiries into enclosure and depopulation as a result of the increase in sheep farming in the late fifteenth and early sixteenth centuries (Fig. 17b). In fact probably very little of the total land was enclosed for this purpose. Certainly it has been estimated that it covered less than 3 per cent of the total area of England, and only around 9 per cent in the midland counties, where most protests occurred. The protests were voiced largely because the enclosure involved the eviction of farmers by lords who wanted to increase their profits by turning the land over to sheep. The earlier enclosures by agreement had rarely involved eviction and thus no protests. When in 1498 William Cope evicted sixty people from the village of Wormleighton in Warwickshire and enclosed 100 hectares of arable with new hedges and ditches, his action led to a series of petitions and legal proceedings that went on until the 1520s.

These new sheep pastures were often very large and almost no new hedges were made. Sometimes it seems that each of the original common fields was hedged and became the new pasture. Thus in 1547 the 400 hectares of pasture at Pultney, in Leicestershire, were divided into only two fields, while at nearby Knabtoft one pasture covered 240 hectares. It was soon realized that such fields were too big and many were broken down into smaller, but still considerable, fields of 4-8 hectares. Again, with careful examination on the ground, it is sometimes possible to identify

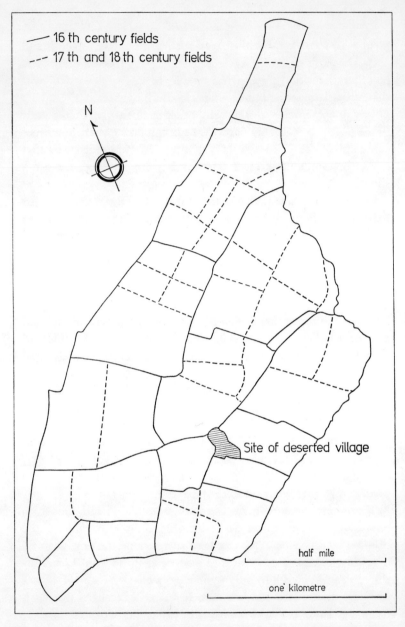

16 th century fields

17 th and 18 th century fields

N

Site of deserted village

half mile

one kilometre

18 Field pattern, Papley, Northamptonshire. Botanically mixed hedge boundaries.

these original large pastures and their later subdivisions. For example, at Papley, Northamptonshire, the village, always a small one, was partly depopulated in 1499 when the then owner, the daughter of a rich wool merchant, destroyed seven houses and enclosed 80 hectares of land. In 1539 her son was brought before a court charged with enclosing more land. By studying closely the existing ridge-and-furrow, the present field shapes and the botanical content of the hedges, together with a number of early maps, it is possible to see the original large sheep pasture fields as well as the subsequent hedges put in to subdivide them after 1632 (Fig. 18).

While all this retrenchment, retreat and change was going on in certain parts of England, in others, where population remained stable or even grew, or where special conditions for products prevailed, the steady reclamation work of earlier centuries was maintained. In many of the forested areas of the country the assarts of the woodland continued as they had always done and the same irregular fields appeared. In the Weald of south-east England, in the Forest of Arden in Warwickshire and elsewhere, encroachments occurred. Thus, at Pulham in Dorset, we read in a document of 1412 that in 1376 Cirencester Abbey had assarted a large area of woodland which the Abbey 'hold and occupy . . . in severalty still'. At the nearby village of Stoke Wake in 1390, 'Edmund Sycock appropriated and enclosed a piece of the King's land 10 perches long and 7 feet wide and worth one penny yearly'. On the coastal marshes and in the fenlands, too, reclamation continued, though undoubtedly the importance of sheep here played its part. For example in Kent, the Prior of Canterbury (1449–68) spent £1,200 on reclaiming Appledore Marsh, and later Priors continued the work here, and also at Monkton in the Isle of Thanet. In the south-west, on the Somerset Levels, the old drainage and reclamation work went on. In all these areas it is still possible to find places where the actual fields and intakes of this period are visible. But they are only patches, for the succeeding centuries were to see changes on an even larger scale than ever before.

Chapter 7

Seventeenth- and Early Eighteenth-century Fields

The seventeenth century saw many changes in the agricultural landscape of England. These were the result of social and economic movements as well as of technical advances of such an order that some historians have seen this period as the time of real 'Agricultural Revolution'. The basis of these events lay, of course, beyond mere agriculture, for the whole of society was in a state of flux. New ideas were pouring forth in books and pamphlets, new experiments were being tried and innovations developed. Political instability, social movement, increasing overseas trade and an expanding known world all played a part. At the same time the population rose from about 4½ million in 1600 to around 6 million by 1700, and this inevitably produced a demand for more agricultural land and/or increased yields.

However, it is important to see this agricultural 'revolution' in its true perspective. It was not a revolution in the usually accepted sense of a complete sweeping away of the past; that was to come in the next century. It was in fact more a preparation for the later revolution, whereby ideas for new crops, cropping techniques, agricultural machinery and enclosure were developed, put to the test and accepted or rejected, so that all was ready for the massive agricultural changes of the late eighteenth and early nineteenth centuries.

Nor must the changes in the fabric of the landscape be overemphasized. Much of the country was untouched physically by the new ideas of the seventeenth century. The areas where the common-strip fields still existed in 1600, especially the Midlands and south central England, and east Yorkshire, by and large retained their overall structure in 1750, even though in detail they had been altered. Outside these areas the common fields had already largely disappeared in the two centuries after 1300. Elsewhere in the forests, moors and marshes, the old-established enclosed fields continued in existence. The basic framework of English fields remained stable, though important minor changes took place within this, and in certain areas considerable local alterations occurred.

The main innovations of this period were threefold. First there was the introduction of what is variously called convertible, or alternate, field-grass, or up-and-down husbandry. This is the system whereby arable land was put down to grass for a number of years to rest and pasture land ploughed up for arable. In fact this method of agriculture had been advocated in the early sixteenth century and was indeed widely practised before 1600. Secondly, many new crops were introduced at this period. The most important of these were roots, such as carrots and turnips, and grasses, together with clover. These crops produced several benefits. They enabled more stock, especially sheep, to be kept, and the resulting increase of manure allowed more flexible rotations and higher yields. In turn the clover and grasses added nitrogen to the soil and so increased fertility. Other crops grown in specific areas, and generally on a much smaller scale, often depending on local demand, were cabbages, flax, hemp, woad, saffron, rape and even potatoes.

The third advance was the introduction of new implements, though this was on a very limited scale and they were not widely used. Various experiments with drilling machines took place in the late seventeenth century, but it was not until 1701 that Jethro Tull invented a satisfactory model and even then it was not used extensively until after 1750. Likewise, attempts to drain the heavier claylands and so improve their value both as arable and pasture were started as early as the middle of the seventeenth century. But again these methods were employed in only a few areas.

What of the fields themselves? In the localities where the common-strip fields still existed considerable alterations were made to cope with convertible husbandry and the new crops. As has been stressed earlier, the common-field system, far from being rigid, was extremely flexible and the seventeenth century saw the incorporation of many new ideas within it. In particular, individual strips were removed from a common rotation to be put down to grass for ten years or more, and often enclosed permanently. There had to be agreement among the farmers for this to be done, and a number of these survive in documents. On the ground, too, one can see how these individual grass strips or leys existed and how they appeared. For example, at Wimpole, in Cambridgeshire, a map of 1638 which shows all the common-field strips also marks strips of grassland within them, there termed either 'leys' or 'baulks'. As they were emparked soon afterwards, the ridge-and-furrow of these fields still exists on the ground, and these leys can be identified. In fact they are normal groups of ridges identical to the adjacent ones, and it is clear that they were temporarily out of cultivation at the time the map was made.

In some areas these leys were permanently taken out of cultivation and fenced or walled by individual farmers, again with the agreement of all. For example, in Raunds, Northamptonshire, an agreement was made in 1664 to enclose a large area of the former common fields. This land, known as Stanwick Pastures, can be identified and the new hedges surrounding the various enclosures still exist (Fig. 19a). There the fields have long curving sides that follow exactly the ridge-and-furrow of the earlier open furlongs which is still visible inside them. Botanically, too, the hedges confirm the date since they contain an average of three species per thirty metres and so are around three hundred years old.

Elsewhere, too, the surviving open fields were gradually nibbled away by this form of piecemeal enclosure. In the far north, in Cumberland, detailed work has shown how this took place. At Hayton, land belonging to the Church, which was described in 1603 as being in strips, was in 1710 recorded as

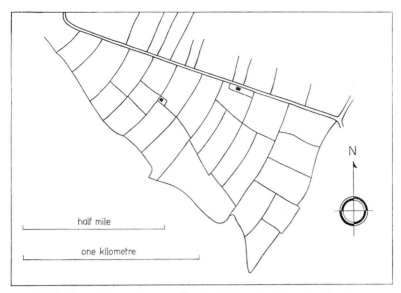

19a Fields formed by enclosure of strip fields, 1664, Raunds, Northampton-shire. Botanically mixed hedge boundaries.

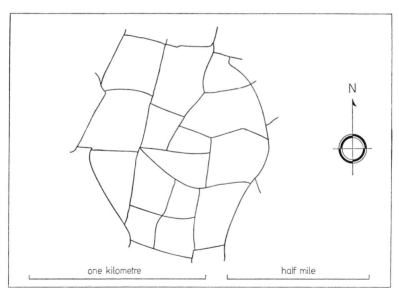

19b Fields formed by clearance of forest, 1625–30, Motcombe, Dorset. Botanically mixed hedge boundaries.

'anciently enclosed', and there are innumerable other examples. Sometimes the resulting enclosure followed the old strips or fur-longs, as it did in Raunds, but elsewhere more rectangular fields appeared which disregarded the old system. These, however, still tend to have a rather irregular pattern overall, quite unlike the later eighteenth- and nineteenth-century enclosures with their rigid geometrical appearance.

A fine example—which though undated by documents is prob-ably seventeenth-century—may be seen at Shenstone in Stafford-shire, where both strip-like fields and rectangular closes occur. Another may be seen at Grassington in Yorkshire, where in 1605 several strips were sold and the new owners began the process of exchanging, buying and selling with a view to consolidation and enclosure. By 1720 one of the main open fields had been trans-formed into a series of long walled parallel enclosures, still with the reversed shape imposed on them by earlier strips (Fig. 20a). This enclosure by agreement often led to difficulties between the farmers, some of whom wanted enclosure while others did not. One curious result of this may be seen at Charminster in Dorset, where in 1577 the lord and some of the tenants wanted enclosures and others objected. The outcome was an agreed redistribution of land so that a part of the common fields was enclosed and the rest re-allotted to those tenants who wished to keep the old system.

This piecemeal enclosure often led to the complete obliteration of some common fields by the late seventeenth or early eighteenth century. But the agreements which made it possible could also result in the immediate enclosure of the common fields, if this was so desired by the farmers involved. In many places, especially where the landowners were powerful and enterprising and the tenants few, the advantages of enclosure for the new convertible husbandry practised, and for the new crops, provided the reasons for total enclosure. Unfortunately the detailed records of this kind of enclosure have rarely survived in a form that accurately dates them. In fact it is probable that this practice was far more common than has hitherto been realized. For instance in west

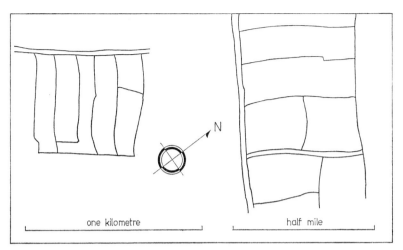

20a Fields formed by enclosure of strips by agreement, seventeenth century. Stone wall boundaries.

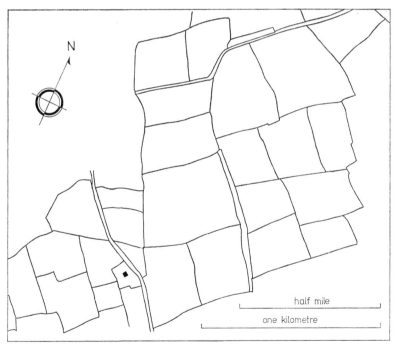

20b Fields formed by enclosure of strips by one landowner, seventeenth century, Croydon, Cambridgeshire. Botanically mixed hedge boundaries.

Dorset there are a number of parishes which certainly had common fields at one time but these had disappeared by the eighteenth century when the earliest maps were made. No record of enclosure exists, but, curiously enough, it has been discovered that in a number of seventeenth-century churchwardens' accounts for parishes in the area, notes were made to indicate that the bounds of the parishes no longer needed to be perambulated as they were now fixed by the new field boundaries.

Elsewhere the information is more definite. In one small area of Cambridgeshire there is evidence that a whole series of villages lost their entire common fields at this time, probably as a result of their being owned by large and far-sighted landlords. For example, at Wimpole the Chicherley family enclosed all the common fields there between 1638 and 1686. At the same time, at nearby Wendy, Arrington and Croydon, the common fields disappeared between 1546 and 1700, probably because the Chicherleys owned these parishes as well. Immediately to the west, the parishes of Tadlow, East Hatley and Hatley St George also lost their common fields, which were all largely owned by the St George family. Most of these parishes still retain the characteristic field shapes of this form of enclosure, despite modern destruction (Fig. 20b). The fields are relatively large, between two and four hectares, generally rectangular but with slightly sinuous sides.

In other areas of England the same massive enclosure took place. Most of the Vale of Pickering in east Yorkshire was enclosed between 1560 and 1760 and divided into a multitude of small fields. In south-west Oxfordshire, too, enclosure was rapid, over half the area being divided into enclosed fields by 1650.

The seventeenth century also saw the beginnings of formal enclosure by Act of Parliament which was to become common after 1750. As early as 1602, an Act was passed whereby the fields of Radipole in Dorset were finally swept away. However, this kind of parliamentary enclosure was very rare and it was enclosure of the common fields by agreement that was the main feature of this period. But if agreement to enclose could be carried out successfully, equally agreement not to enclose could be achieved. Many people in villages where the common fields remained in existence in the seventeenth century, and more especially the smaller farmers, feared enclosure. They rightly saw that it meant the loss of the valuable common grazing rights over the arable fields and wastes. Without these, many small farms could not continue to be economically viable. So there was in many areas an active movement against enclosure which in the early seventeenth century led to disputes, inquiries and even riots where it was attempted. Nevertheless, the new crops and methods of farming were seen as too important to ignore—witness the development of ley strips mentioned earlier. So many villages took active and communal steps to improve their position during this period, while still keeping the common-field strip system in being. Various changes were carried out along these lines. In south-east Worcestershire the seventeenth century saw the development of more flexible multiple-field complexes, either to make more crop rotations possible, or to allow a separate open field to be used for specialized crops. Elsewhere villages which had only two or three open fields reorganized the arrangements to make three, four or more fields. For example, at Barrington in Cambridgeshire, a terrier of 1613 states that at Christmas 1610 a 'Middle Field' was formed out of parts of the old east and west fields.

How far this reorganization of holdings affected the physical arrangement of the fields is unknown; perhaps by not a great deal, but there are examples on the ground which show actual relay of strips. At Turnworth in Dorset, there is a series of normal strip lynchets lying parallel to the contours on a steep hillside which has cut through and thus destroyed the lower ends of another set of strip lynchets set askew to the slope. These are unfortunately undated, but they may reflect the rationalization of older fields to cope with the improved methods of tillage.

Even in the areas already long enclosed there were changes between 1600 and 1750. These often took the form of the rationalization of the larger sheep pastures of the fifteenth and sixteenth centuries and the tiny medieval assarts of even earlier periods in

order to make fields of a generally more convenient size for the
improved methods of tillage and stock raising. In the forest areas
particularly, the small 0.25-hectare assarts were often enlarged
by the removal of intervening hedges (Fig 13a). Where large
sheep pastures existed, these were split up into roughly rectangular fields. This has already been noted as occurring in Northamptonshire (see p. 117 above and Fig. 18) but it also occurred elsewhere.

At the village of Clopton in Cambridgeshire, which had been
finally depopulated and the land enclosed for sheep farming in
1489, the large sheep pastures of 20–25 hectares were divided
into rectangular fields of 8–10 hectares some time in the seventeenth century. In this particular parish, there is further evidence
on the ground, for ridge-and-furrow appears in each of these new
fields. Though superficially it is identical to ridge-and-furrow of the
common fields, more careful examination reveals distinct differences. The ridge-and-furrow is quite straight and fits the new
seventeenth-century fields exactly. More important, at each end
there is a seven-metre-wide headland lying inside the boundary
hedge onto which the ridge-and-furrow runs. That is, the ridge-
and-furrow was formed after the establishment of the hedges,
not before, as the headland had been built up by the plough turning inside the field. Thus we have ridge-and-furrow clearly dated
to the post-medieval period, and having nothing whatsoever to
do with the common-strip fields. This occurrence of late ridge-
and-furrow in seventeenth- and eighteenth-century contexts
within enclosed fields has been noted elsewhere. It takes careful
examination to recognize it and to distinguish it from the older
varieties, but it is important that this should be done, otherwise
a misleading impression of medieval agriculture will be gained
with a consequent loss in knowledge of later agricultural practices.

The steady reclamation of the remaining wastelands went on
during this time in any areas where open land survived. Again
in Cambridgeshire, in Little Gransden parish, until the late
seventeenth century there was a small wood of about 17 hectares

which had been left when the surrounding land was cleared from the woodland before the eleventh century. In 1670 this wood was felled and the land enclosed—or as a survey of that year tells us 'Memoranda that little Hound Wood new stubbed is lett. . . .' The site of the wood is still visible as an irregular heart-shaped area bounded by a thick hedge and divided into three roughly rectangular fields. In the same survey there is another note: 'Item 60 acres of pasture being divided into 3 sev'all closes . . . adioying upon Great Wood'. These three fields now exist as roughly rectangular blocks. In other places the enclosures from the woods and wastes were much more extensive. One such was a complete farm of 120 hectares enclosed from the waste at Berkhamsted, Hertfordshire.

In many places large areas of surviving woodlands had remained intact until the seventeenth century, due to continued royal interest in them. In the late sixteenth and early seventeenth centuries many of these forests were officially disafforested and turned over to farmers for the first time. Again the amount of enclosure varied from place to place. In Whittlewood Forest, Northamptonshire, 330 hectares were granted by the King in 1629 to Sir Simon Barret with permission to convert the woods to arable. Soon afterwards the oak trees were felled and the land divided up into a series of roughly rectangular fields. In the West Country at the beginning of the seventeenth century, there were still vast areas of forest in north Dorset and west Wiltshire, around Gillingham, Melksham and Chippenham. By 1650 most of the woods had been cleared and what was left was estimated to cover only about one twelfth of the land it had previously. To look at one specific example, Gillingham Forest, which was disafforested in 1624. Within twenty years, about 1,000 hectares of land were cleared and divided up into large fields (Fig. 19b), most of which exist today, and provide a landscape very different from that of the smaller irregular fields around them that date from the medieval period. Elsewhere in the same county piecemeal enclosure of forest, wastes and commons went on. Thus in the Vale of Blackmoor a small area of woodland known as Beaulieu Common, lying across the boundary between Pulham and Buckland Newton parishes, was enclosed by agreement between the landowners of both parishes in 1700 and 1724. Farther to the north-west, in south Wiltshire, another Royal Forest, that of Melchet, was disafforested in 1610. Within this area, in the parish of Whiteparish, the trees were felled and the land divided into fields. These fields still exist today (Fig. 21a).

Much more common in the forests and on the heaths were encroachments by small landless labourers. As a result of rising population, as well as of enclosure and the subsequent loss of common rights elsewhere, many poor families moved away from the old villages and settled on whatever land remained unused. Cottages appeared on roadside verges, in clearings and along minor streams, on heaths, forests and moorland edges. Sometimes the development of local industry produced this migration. The result was a scatter of smallholdings, based on the highly irregular field pattern made by these small farmers as they strove to develop a new life.

While such encroachments are typical of moorlands and heaths in particular there were also large-scale clearances in these types of landscape. Again in Dorset, 160 hectares of land were enclosed on the heaths in the east of the county by Sir John Banks of Kingston Lacey, and all the resulting fields can even now be identified as large sub-rectangular blocks of from two to four hectares. On the hills and moors of the north, the same process took place. In Northowram, near Halifax in Yorkshire, a document of 1604 tells us that sixty-four people had made enclosures from the waste; while at Langfield in the same county, in 1615, there were complaints that over half the 360 hectares of upland wastes had been enclosed. Many of these fields can still be seen just below the 1,100-foot contour. They are all walled with stone, generally rectangular in shape, and between 1 and 2 hectares in extent.

The best known of the new reclamations of the seventeenth and early eighteenth centuries were those in the marshes and fens. The first half of the seventeenth century was characterized by wide

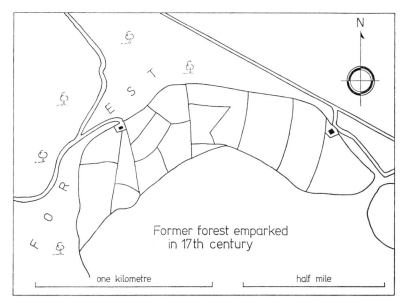

21a Fields formed by reclamation of forest, early seventeenth century, White-parish, Wiltshire. Botanically mixed hedge boundaries.

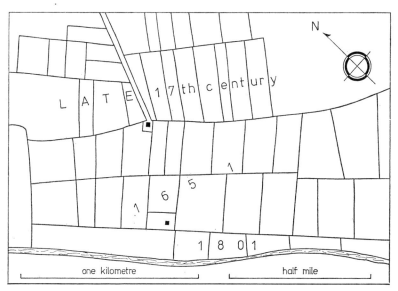

21b Mid seventeenth-century and later fenland reclamation, Swaffham, Cambridgeshire. Ditched boundaries.

interest in draining land as part of the general agricultural improvement. Many schemes for drainage and enclosure were mooted and ideas put forward for lifting water from marsh and fen. New landowners, aware of these developments, and with the determination and financial resources to improve their holdings, appeared. In all the areas of fen and marsh, drainage work commenced. In the eastern part of the West Riding of Yorkshire, the lower courses of the Rivers Don and Thorn were drained and enclosed, while the great Dutch engineer Vermuyden was brought to England in 1626 to drain Hatfield Chase. In Lincolnshire, the Isle of Axholme marshes were also reclaimed at this time. In all these places the modern landscape remains dissected by innumerable straight drains cutting the land up into rectangular fields.

In the Somerset Levels also there was major reclamation work. Some of this involved the seaward extension of the marshes and their subsequent improvement for pasture. Barriers of brushwood woven between stakes and even low stone walls were constructed on the tidal mudbanks, to speed up deposition from the silt-laden waters of the high spring tides. Vegetation then gained a foothold and helped further deposition to transform the mudbanks into fine pasture within ten years. In time more land farther out was taken in by this method. Such work was extensively undertaken in the tidal estuaries of the Axe and Parrett Rivers between 1597 and 1640. In the Axe estuary there are records of 120 hectares being reclaimed. These newly drained areas can be identified, though it requires careful examination to visualize the stages involved. This is because, as the land was extended, the older banks were abandoned and allowed to decay. Nevertheless, in some places it is still possible to see, on the ground, slight traces of these early banks only a few inches high and others show clearly on air photographs.

Much more important were the attempts to drain the peat fens of the Levels, especially on land belonging to the Crown which had the authority and resources to carry it out. In 1618, James I decided to drain King's Sedgemoor and he made an agreement with local landlords to execute the work. Nothing came of this at that time, however, and further efforts during the reign of Charles I also failed. Elsewhere the attempts met with more success; Alder Moor in the Brue Valley was successfully drained and broken up into rectangular ditched fields before 1640, and other smaller areas were reclaimed at the same time or later.

However, the largest drainage works were carried out in the fenlands of Huntingdonshire, Cambridgeshire, Norfolk and south Lincolnshire from the mid-seventeenth century onwards. Many schemes were planned in the early seventeenth century, but partly from lack of capital and partly because of major objections prompted by fear of the loss of grazing, fishing, wildfowling and peat-cutting rights, little was achieved. Some local lords did undertake work at this time. At Littleport in Cambridgeshire, Sir John Peyton bought an estate in 1602 and within a few years he had embanked and drained 600 hectares of fen and divided it into twelve plots of meadow, while another 120 hectares were enclosed (but not embanked) and a further 80 hectares were in the process of being enclosed.

Then in 1630 plans were made for massive drainage work in the southern fens. In that year one of the largest landowners, Francis, fourth Earl of Bedford, agreed to undertake the drainage of all the fens in Cambridgeshire, Huntingdonshire, north-west Norfolk and part of south-west Lincolnshire. In return the Earl was to have 38,000 hectares of land, of which 16,000 hectares were to be used to maintain the drainage and 4,800 hectares were to go to the Crown. In 1631, thirteen other wealthy businessmen joined the Earl and, calling themselves 'Adventurers' because they adventured their capital, formed the Bedford Level Corporation. The Corporation obtained the services of Cornelius Vermuyden to supervise the work. Vermuyden's main job was the construction of major water courses to carry the waters of the upland rivers of the Nene and Ouse across the fens, to reduce floods and also to drain large internal regions of the fens. This work commenced in 1631 and continued until 1637, when the fens were declared 'drained'. Actual enclosure of land was not involved in this instance, merely the construction of channels to eliminate flooding, and in any case there was an outcry when the work was finished that most of the fens were still constantly inundated.

Then the Civil War intervened and work stopped. Vermuyden returned at the end of the war and improved the drainage by carrying out the construction of a number of other massive water courses. By 1652 this was finished and the fens again declared drained. Then, and only then, were the 38,000 hectares which were to be allotted to the Adventurers laid out. These were blocks of land of varying size, scattered all over the fens. Most of these blocks can be seen today, and some are still called Adventurers' Lands. With a little practice one can learn to recognize both the outer boundaries and the internal division drains of both these and the unnamed ones by their shape and layout when compared with the later enclosures around them (Fig. 21b). More rarely one can find on the maps similar blocks of land, called Undertakers' Lands, which were those allotted to the men who actually *undertook* the drainage works, *i.e.* the engineers.

Immediately the advantages of these new enclosures were seen, other landlords started similar work. Whole areas of fenland were quickly drained, enclosed by ditches and subdivided into rigidly rectangular fields by further ditches. Only very detailed documentary work can date these fields accurately, but once this has been done the actual stages of reclamation can be identified on the ground by the changes in the overall pattern of field shapes which still survive (Figs. 21b and 27b). Farther north in Lincolnshire, though a little reclamation work was carried out it was on a limited scale and mainly by local lords. In 1660, for example, some marshes were enclosed by a group of landowners in south Lincolnshire around Whaplode and Holbeach.

At first much of this work was successful. Not only were there greatly improved pastures but cultivation was introduced on land which had never before been ploughed. At Willingham near Ely, onions, peas and hemp were seen growing on the fens by 1657, and farther north near Southey, flax, hemp, oats, wheat, coleseed and woad were visible. Soon, however, problems emerged. One was the silting up of the great estuaries of the Nene and Ouse on the south side of the Wash. This tended to hold up floodwater farther back in the fens and thus cause inundation. Of far more consequence was the shrinkage of the peat. As the water was removed from the southern fens, the peat compacted and shrank, so that the surface level of the newly drained land fell below the level of the drainage channels which carried away the water. The rivers, too, had to be embanked, as they flowed above the surrounding land, and in flood times their banks often burst and submerged the fields. The result was that by the early eighteenth century much of the newly enclosed and drained land was constantly under water and disaster threatened. Both these difficulties, however, were solved in the eighteenth century. The estuary problem was eased slowly by the construction of new channels, while the peat shrinkage was tackled by the introduction of wind-driven pumps or windmills which scooped the water from the low-lying fields into high-level drains. By 1750, under the impact of these machines and drainage schemes organized co-operatively, the fenlands improved again and further reclamation began.

Finally, in looking at the fields of this period we must turn to other regions to see another aspect of this age of agricultural change and improvement. This was largely connected with the growth of sheep farming, mainly on the chalklands of southern England but in other areas as well. In the late seventeenth century particularly, the sheep kept in England probably far outnumbered those of medieval times. All contemporary observers mention the large numbers of sheep to be seen, especially in southern England. This great increase was achieved in a number of ways. First, improved crop varieties, especially clover, produced better feeding. Secondly, there was a great deal of enclosure of former open downland, partly in order to control the grazing more efficiently and so enlarge the flocks, but mainly for use as arable on which the sheep were folded in order to improve the crops themselves. This latter movement led to large areas of the former rolling downs of Wessex being divided up into roughly rectangular fields of considerable size. There are many documentary references to this break-up of the downlands during the seventeenth century.

At Collingbourne Ducis in Wiltshire, the major landowner 'did yerely newly breake upp and eare a parcell of the downe'. In 1614, at Bulbridge near Salisbury in the same county, there were 30 hectares of 'newe broke arable ground belonging to the Sheep-sleight'. On the ground, the evidence of this type of enclosure is still clearly visible. Thus at Piddletrenthide in Dorset, high on the downs, there is an extensive tract of land covering some 160 hectares and divided into a number of subrectangular fields up to 10 hectares in extent with two much larger fields of 20 to 30 hectares each. In the centre is Doles Ash Farm, a building which dates from the seventeenth century. The whole area was probably broken up and enclosed at this time (Fig. 22a). Back in south Wiltshire, at Whiteparish, almost all the open downland there was divided up into large fields at various times in the seventeenth and early eighteenth centuries, primarily for sheep.

However, the great increase in sheep during this period led to serious difficulties. The major one was a lack of late winter and early spring feeding. At most other times of the year fodder of various kinds was available in reasonable quantities, but there was always a shortage in the early part of the year. This meant that the numbers of sheep kept were severely restricted. The problem was solved by the development of various types of water meadows. The idea was to run water across valley bottoms or gentle hillsides early in the year and so produce a growth of the pasture. The first attempts to do this took place in the sixteenth century and by the seventeenth century it was widespread in certain parts of south and south-western England.

In its simplest form, artificial channels or leats were dug along the contours of a shallow valley and water led into them from a dammed stream. Then the water was released through a series of hatches or sluices to run down the valley side back to the main stream. This was put into operation throughout the late winter and then the sheep were turned onto the land when the grass was in short supply in the early spring. It was a method widely used in the West Country, and has also been recognized in Hereford-shire, Oxfordshire and Cambridgeshire from the late sixteenth

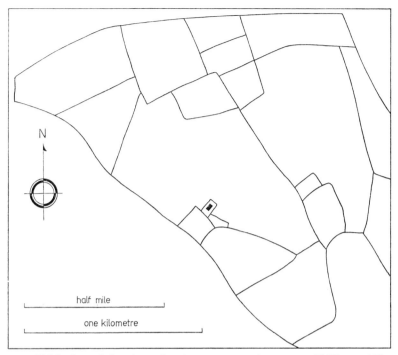

N

half mile

one kilometre

22a Fields formed for sheep farming, seventeenth century, Piddletrenthide, Dorset. Botanically mixed hedge boundaries.

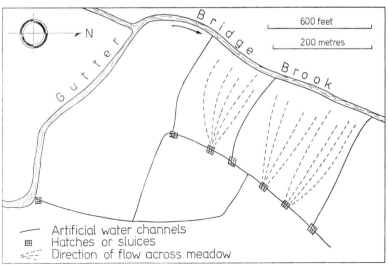

N

Bridge

Brook

Gutter

600 feet

200 metres

—— Artificial water channels
🔲 Hatches or sluices
⤙⤙⤙ Direction of flow across meadow

22b Watermeadows, seventeenth or eighteenth century, Swaffham Bulbeck, Cambridgeshire.

century onwards. Traces of these meadows with their leats and hatches can still be seen in many of the low-lying valleys (Fig. 22b).

A further development of this technique, called 'drowning' or 'floating upwards', was carried out in wide flat valleys. Here the main stream was dammed and the pent-up water forced back over the whole meadow. This was also used in Wessex, and occasionally in the Midlands. This system, however, imposed its own restrictions, for it could be employed only in level valleys and the grass it produced tended to be rough and of poor quality.

The best and most widely used form of water meadows was that known as 'floating downwards'. It was, perhaps, developed in Herefordshire in the late sixteenth century, but by the end of the seventeenth century it was widespread in the chalklands of southern England where it was best suited to the physical and agricultural conditions. The process involved the building of a highly sophisticated network of carefully graded artificial channels which were designed to distribute river water over the alluvial pasture and drain it off again. The river or main stream was dammed, and a 'head main' constructed to carry the water to a complicated series of 'water carriers', or long ridges, which had drains or channels along their spines. These ridges were either arranged in rectangular blocks or fitted into narrow curving areas, depending on the land available. Apart from the drains, these ridges appear very similar to ridge-and-furrow (Fig. 23a, Plate VII). During the 'floating' of these water meadows, the aim was to have a continuous movement of water along the brim-full channels in the ridges which spilt over, ran down the ridge sides into the furrows, and so back to the river.

The development and use of these water meadows during the seventeenth and eighteenth centuries played an essential part in the agricultural economy, because they allowed far more sheep to be kept than would otherwise have been possible. The result of this work still figures as a characteristic feature of many of the valleys in the chalklands of England. Tens of thousands of

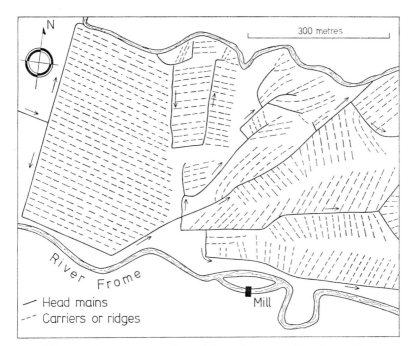

Within image 1: N, 300 metres, River Frome, Mill, Head mains, Carriers or ridges

23a Watermeadows, seventeenth or eighteenth century, Dorchester, Dorset.

Within image 2: N, half mile, one kilometre

23b Fields formed by parliamentary enclosure of common arable, Slawston, Leicestershire. Thorn hedge boundaries.

hectares of land retain the ridges, drains, head mains, dams and sluices, now mostly long abandoned. In other types of country too, such as the Midland claylands, one can still find remains of small areas of water meadows laid out in the seventeenth and eighteenth centuries.

Chapter 8

The Age of Parliamentary Enclosure, 1750–1850

The second half of the eighteenth century saw the development of the agricultural revolution in its stricter terms. The ideas and techniques evolved over the previous two hundred years were now accepted by the majority of farmers, and the industrial revolution began to provide the capital and equipment which had been lacking before. There was a great increase in the amount of clover and grasses sown, and turnips, swedes, potatoes and other root crops became common. Many new and improved implements were introduced such as new types of ploughs, drills, threshing machines, reapers and harrows, though in the main they did not come into common use until later in the nineteenth century. Livestock was also improved by selective breeding but, although this had started long before 1750, it was not until the late eighteenth century that it became widespread.

In the landscape itself other developments took place, most of which are still to be seen. These involved the complete alteration of the appearance of many parts of England as well as minor changes elsewhere. The most important of these was the virtual extinction of the old common-field systems, usually by means of formal Acts of Parliament. This process had already begun on a small scale before 1750, but during the late eighteenth and early nineteenth centuries almost all the remaining common fields disappeared as a result of these Acts. Much of the country was unaffected by this, for the common fields had long since disappeared or had never existed. But in the Midland counties, as well as parts of north-east England and to a lesser extent in East Anglia and southern England, the countryside took on an entirely new appearance.

The open, bare, unhedged landscape was transformed into a series of rigidly geometrical fields, each bounded by hawthorn hedges (Fig. 23b, Plate VIII). The physical process of this enclosure was complex, even after the legal work of organizing and guiding the necessary Acts through Parliament had been achieved. All the existing strips in the common fields had to be surveyed and their ownership and value fixed. Then the land had to be redistributed, new roads and lanes set out, drainage organized, disputes settled and, finally, the new fields established. Yet all this was done in a remarkably short time for thousands of villages. It was normally achieved within two or three years of the passing of the Act of Parliament, though it sometimes took a little longer.

It is this enclosure landscape which is so familiar to travellers in the Midlands today. The straight hedgelines, the numerous trees in the hedgerows, the small copses or woods in corners often planted later as fox or game coverts are typical of this region. Yet for all its apparent antiquity, it is relatively modern in the long development of English fields. Botanically, too, its recent appearance is obvious; the hedges rarely have more than two species of shrubs and the majority are often entirely of hawthorn. An observant traveller will see traces here of the old ridge-and-furrow, showing how the old common fields were arranged with the later hedges cutting across them (Plate III).

The sizes of the new fields varied greatly, partly depending on the number of farmers involved and the amount of common-field land they had held. Where there were many people holding small farms in the old common fields, the new fields were usually 2 to 4 hectares in size. Larger farms had fields of 20 to 25 hectares. However, the latter soon proved to be too big, especially for grazing purposes, and there was a later process of dividing them up into neat four-hectare parcels soon after the formal enclosure.

Incidentally, elsewhere at this time there was also much enlargement of the older piecemeal enclosures in forests and fen as, with the new stock farming and arable methods, the original sizes proved to be too small. The result was a general evening up of the size of fields all over the country. This uniformity must not, however, be overstressed, for there remained considerable variation in size.

Many of the Acts of Enclosure passed in this period did not involve the removal of entire common-field systems. Many were simply to finalize the process of enclosure which had been going on piecemeal. This was particularly true of areas where there was a long history of this kind of enclosure. Thus in Dorset only sixty parishes had Acts of Enclosure passed to end their common fields, and half of these actually dealt with the tiny remnants of old strips, the rest having disappeared long before. In addition, there were also some remaining common fields which were enclosed by agreement between landowners and for this reason no Act of Parliament was ever passed.

Though the parliamentary enclosure of the common arable fields in the late eighteenth and early nineteenth centuries is the most commonly known aspect of agricultural change in this period, in fact it was overshadowed in most parts of England by another event. This was the continued enclosure of the wastes, either by Act of Parliament or by agreement. For example, in northern England the complete alteration of the landscape followed from the enclosure in one form or another of the upland moors. From 1750 onwards the moorlands were divided up by mile after mile of dry-stone walls or earthen banks. In 1777, at Malham in the West Riding of Yorkshire, a writer described the upland pastures as 'of great extent . . . [having] . . . been lately divided by stone walls' (Fig. 24). In the North Riding of York-shire, some 20,000 hectares of upland moors were enclosed between 1815 and 1850, in County Durham over 8,000 hectares and in Northumberland 6,000 hectares. These new enclosures did not always result in a change of land use. Most of it remained pasture, although much was improved by burning or ploughing and reseeding with grass. In many places the new walls ran up and

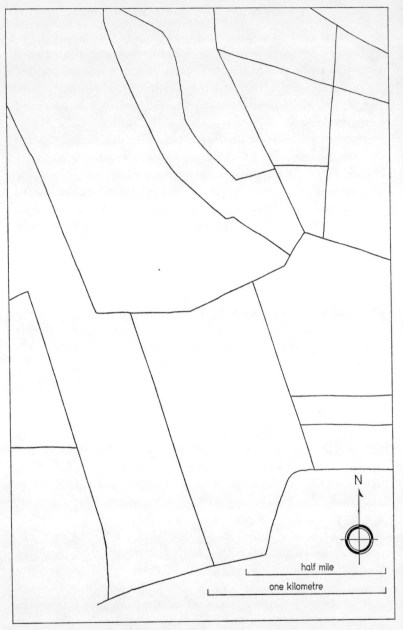

N

half mile

one kilometre

24 Fields formed by enclosure of moorland, late eighteenth century, Malham, Yorkshire. Stone wall boundaries.

over the remains of ridge-and-furrow or strip lynchets, showing that the land had once been ploughed, though abandoned to the waste centuries before (Plate X).

Some of the better parts of these uplands were indeed cultivated, especially during the Napoleonic Wars when demands for home-grown crops increased dramatically. After a few years such marginal land was abandoned and reverted to pasture, but today there remain traces of this period of cultivation in the form of a type of ridge-and-furrow known as 'narrow rig'. It has the same general pattern as the traditional ridge-and-furrow, but is always under 5 metres across, furrow to furrow, usually running in exactly straight lines, and always low, being only a few centimetres high. Where it can be dated, it always seems to be of the late eighteenth or early nineteenth century. Narrow rig is relatively common on the uplands of northern England, but also occurs in Shropshire and Staffordshire where it lies within the new rectangular fields which were cut from the waste in the early nineteenth century. It is also found, as we shall see, on the downlands of southern England.

In addition to the large areas of enclosed uplands, there was a continuation of the small encroachments on the wastes (Plate II). As the extractive industries in particular developed in the Pennine valleys of Derbyshire, Cumberland, Lancashire, Northumberland and Yorkshire, miners and others reclaimed small patches of ground, enclosed them by walls and struggled to implement their meagre incomes by agriculture. These enclosures have endured, as have similar ones in the older mining areas of west Cornwall, where again tiny irregular stone-walled fields can be seen running out onto the hostile moors.

The forests and heathlands, too, continued to be enclosed, either legally or illegally. Some of this work was on a truly massive scale. For example, in Cheshire in the early nineteenth century, there existed a large area of heath covering about 4,000 hectares, technically still the Royal Forest of Delamere. Fifty years before, it had been much larger, but the surrounding villages had all enclosed their common grazing land into the characteristic rectangular fields by means of various Acts of Parliament. The surviving forest was formally enclosed by Act of Parliament in 1812. Most of the land remained Crown property and was planted to timber, but over one third was granted to people with various local rights to be enclosed in the by now familiar way into large hedged fields.

Heathland elsewhere was often broken up, too, following Acts of Parliament. The great heaths of Dorset saw much enclosure at this time, as major landowners strove to divide them up into large rectangular fields, edged by earthen banks. Others did not require formal legislation and reclaimed the heaths without it. In most cases the legacy of their efforts can still clearly be seen (Fig. 26a), but where the work was done at times of high prices and unusual demand, the land has reverted to heath again. Here the banks around the former fields can only be discerned after fires. On Brownsea Island in Poole Harbour, the owner in the late eighteenth century reclaimed some 300 hectares, but it was soon abandoned and the land reverted to bracken and heather. However, a recent disastrous fire there revealed all the old hedge banks as well as traces of the contemporary narrow-rig ploughing.

Again on these heaths there was much piecemeal enclosure by landless labourers and small farmers. In the New Forest of Hampshire, study of the distribution of gorse has revealed that it is usually coincident with small closes or paddocks bounded by low banks. Some of these also have traces of narrow-rig ploughing within them. Documentary evidence has indicated that most date from the late eighteenth or early nineteenth century when it was only just economical to farm such places. Elsewhere in the New Forest, there are of course countless existing small fields, especially around the villages. These fields are bounded by the characteristic gorse- and bracken-covered sandy banks that also date from this period, and have remained in use up to the present day.

Old woodland, too, continued to be cleared. The typical geometrical field layout associated with exactly straight roads and lanes, the product of the enclosure surveyor, can easily be

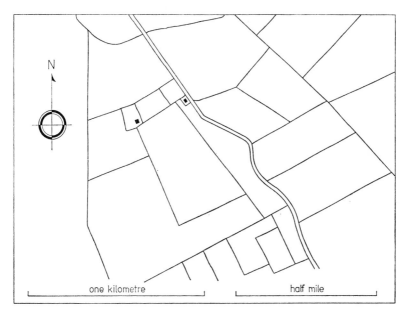

25a   Fields formed by forest clearance, 1857–8, Wychwood, Oxfordshire. Stone wall boundaries.

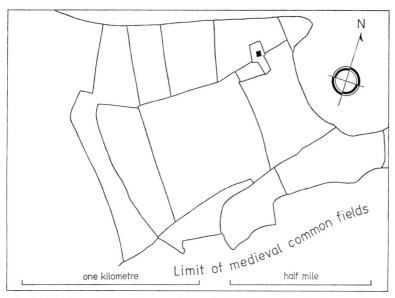

25b   Fields formed by enclosure of downland, eighteenth and nineteenth centuries, Whiteparish, Wiltshire. Thorn hedge boundaries.

recognized on the ground today. A great part of the former Needwood Forest in Staffordshire has such a landscape, as does Charnwood Forest in Leicestershire, the latter dating from 1829. In Oxfordshire also much of the remaining woodland of Wychwood Forest was cleared and replaced by long straight stone walls bounding the new fields (Fig. 25a). Most of this was achieved through Acts of Parliament, and in other areas too the enclosure was legally enforced. Thus in Dorset nearly twenty separate Acts were passed to clear and enclose woodland in the Vale of Blackmoor alone. In 1797, almost a third of the parish of Holwell was divided up into neat oblong fields following an Act of Parliament.

At the same time private agreement between landlords, or action by individual enterprising landowners, cleared woodland without recourse to any legal body. Again in Dorset, at Glanvilles Wooton, there are 80 hectares of land still divided into long rectangular fields which had been open woodland in 1839 but were enclosed by 1847. Likewise in Northamptonshire, at Southwick in the former Rockingham Forest, a small group of large rectangular fields appears to have been cut out of the forest a few years after 1830 (Fig. 26b).

On the limestone and chalk uplands the same process of enclosure went on. By 1848 a contemporary visitor saw the north Lincolnshire Wolds as 'an unbroken succession of large farms'. On the level plateau south of Lincoln itself, the land was described as 'clean and bright, all the hedges kept low and neatly clipped'. Yet, fifty years before, both regions were largely open pasture and downland. The chalklands of Wiltshire, Dorset, Hampshire and Sussex were also largely broken up in these years, much of the work again achieved by Acts of Parliament though much private activity went on as well (Fig. 25b). At Compton Abbas in Dorset, it was an Act of Parliament of 1853 that resulted in the enclosure of the downland there, but at Durweston Common, not far away, the local landowner reclaimed all the rough downland on his own behalf and then cultivated most of it. In addition there are many areas of these downlands which still

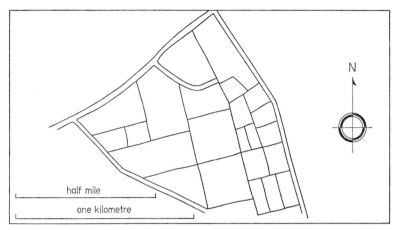

26a   Fields formed by enclosure of heathland, 1858, Alderholt, Dorset. Thorn hedge boundaries.

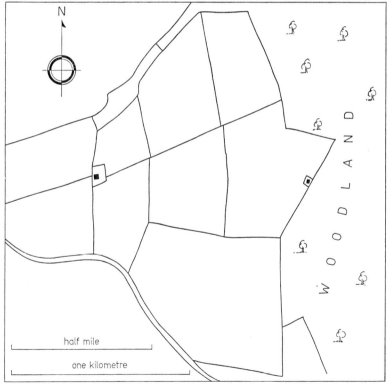

26b   Fields formed by forest clearance, mid nineteenth century, Southwick, Northamptonshire. Thorn hedge boundaries.

have narrow rig on them, showing the short-lived ploughing of the early nineteenth century.

The marshes and fenlands of whatever size were also largely reclaimed. Chat Moss in south Lancashire was finally drained and enclosed by 1833. Many small areas of marshland in Shropshire disappeared at the same time and similar work went on elsewhere. On the expanses of the Somerset Levels large-scale reclamation was accompanied by the laying out of rigidly rectangular fields bounded by the ubiquitous straight drains. In many places the modern landscape displays a pattern of groups of geometrical fields arranged in large blocks which fit into one another. These blocks represent individual stages of reclamation by various land-owners who together finally reduced the open marshes to a regular and monotonous scene (Fig. 27a).

The same picture can be seen in the fenlands of eastern England. Here, too, both parliamentary Acts and private agreements led to the virtual elimination of undrained fen and its replacement by countless rectangular fields edged by drains (Fig. 27b). In all these areas, the development of steam pumps in the early nineteenth century greatly aided the work, for it enabled water to be moved efficiently and relatively cheaply. It was particularly important in the peat fenlands of Somerset and Cambridgeshire where the continued shrinkage of the peat, as the water was removed, led to the constant lowering of the land surface.

Outside these fens and marshes and the light limestone and chalk areas, much of the enclosure of the late eighteenth and nineteenth centuries was on heavy soils. This was especially true in the former common-field regions of the Midlands and in the old forested areas elsewhere. In such districts mere enclosure was not enough; some improvement of drainage had to be achieved in order to allow full use of the land whether as arable or pasture. This was effected by the development of underdrainage. The work involved the cutting of either parallel or herring-bone patterns of ditches across the new fields, which were then packed with brushwood or stones and filled up with soil. This method was in fact developed in the seventeenth century and practised in a few

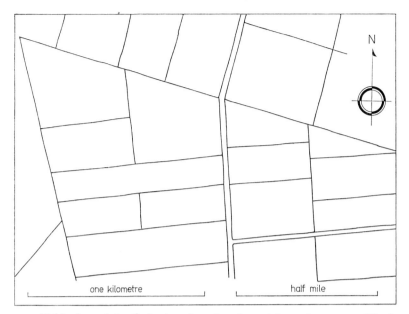

27a Fields formed by fenland reclamation, late eighteenth century, King's Sedge Moor, Somerset. Ditched boundaries.

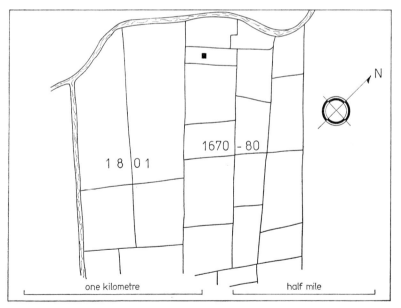

27b Fields formed by fenland reclamation, late seventeenth century and 1801, Swaffham, Cambridgeshire. Ditched boundaries.

places in the early eighteenth century, but was little used generally until the nineteenth century. Another method, that of 'mole drains', was also invented in the eighteenth century. This involved the dragging of a metal plug or 'mole' below the surface of the ground by means of either horses or a windlass and cable. This produced small circular drains across the fields. Again, however, it was not widely used until the next century. The development of an industry which could produce cheap drainage tiles or pipe drains helped as well, and by 1850 large areas of heavy land were being underdrained in various ways. This work both improved pasture and allowed cultivation of land hitherto unusable for arable crops.

The consequences of this type of drainage and its later continuation can still be seen today, particularly from the air. On many fields which are permanent pasture, the slightly sunken drainage channels running in parallel lines or in a herring-bone pattern may be recognized, and the same channels appear in arable land as crop marks on air photographs (Fig. 28a). Sometimes a certain amount of care has to be exercised when looking at these for, again on air photographs, drainage channels look remarkably like ridge-and-furrow. The position is made worse in some regions, where the drains were cut below the furrows of existing ridge-and-furrow. It takes a certain amount of practice to differentiate between all these features.

Once more the results of this great agricultural expansion may be seen in the field names, often still in use today. Many of the new fields produced by this great period of enclosure were given rather mundane names usually based on their size. So the Twenty Acres, the Fourteen Acres, etc., become extremely common. Some, however, tell us of the new crops now widely in use. Trefoil Close at Hinckley in Leicestershire is named after clover. Carrot Ground, Turnip Close and Potato Ground also reflect advances in agriculture. Some of the new fields which were remote from all habitation were often named after far-away places recently discovered. Thus we find New South Wales Field at Barnet in Hertfordshire, New Zealand at Croxton in Cambridgeshire, and

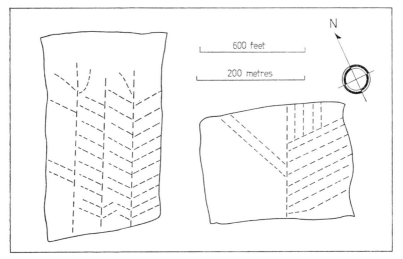

28a Pattern of land drains, Hackleton, Northamptonshire, visible as ditches.

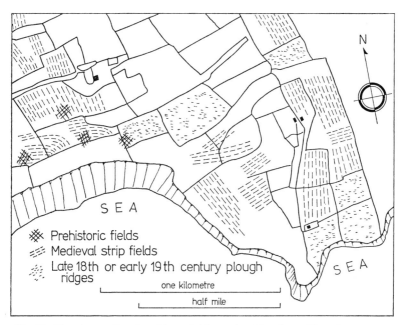

28b Prehistoric, medieval and later field remains, Tyneham, Dorset.

Botany Bay at Monks Kirby in Warwickshire. Elsewhere important events and people of the period were commemorated at this
time—hence we have Waterloo Close at Cobham in Berkshire,
Nelson Close at Elwick in Derbyshire, and Inkerman at Selston
in Nottinghamshire.

Chapter 9

Modern Fields

The last hundred years have seen no slackening in the alterations to fields and field systems in England. Indeed, as with much else, the rate of change has increased. The general agricultural depression which affected the country from 1870 to 1914 virtually brought the expansion of agricultural land to an end and much was actually abandoned. In a few places where the common fields still remained they were finally enclosed into the usual rectangular shapes. Thus the common fields of Ailsworth and Castor in the Soke of Peterborough were not enclosed until 1898, those at Totternhoe in Bedfordshire in 1892, while those at Grimston in Dorset were enclosed in 1907. Elsewhere changing conditions and specialized developments saw new and unusual field forms appearing. In certain areas, especially close to the larger towns or where good railway communications existed, there was a development of small holdings based on market gardening, and the result was a break up of existing fields into a patchwork of small plots of less than 0.5 hectare.

In other places curious fields appeared. Around Newmarket in Suffolk the enlargement of the long-existing racehorse breeding industry based there led to the growth of an almost unique form of fields in the late nineteenth century. The area was already one of large geometrical fields, resulting from parliamentary enclosure of the late eighteenth and early nineteenth centuries. Now these were lined with thick shelter belts of trees and subdivided into small paddocks, also edged by wide tree belts or plantations. In areas such as the Wessex downlands, where farmers on lighter soils survived the depression more successfully, old hedges were removed in order to cut costs and huge prairie-like fields appeared.

This removal of hedges was a process which was to go on increasingly all over England as the twentieth century advanced and, indeed, it is still continuing on a huge scale today. The mechanization of agriculture in the last sixty years has led to the constant enlargement of fields and the destruction of thousands of miles of hedges and walls. Over broad stretches of England the general appearance of the countryside is reverting to a pre-enclosure one. The trim and well-wooded hedged landscape, for one hundred to two hundred years a feature of parts of lowland England, is being rapidly changed. Where boundaries are needed they are now often of wire. Modern technology has been able to produce many varieties of cheap fencing material, notably barbed wire, which was first introduced in the 1870s and became relatively common by the end of the century. It is of some interest to speculate what England would have looked like if barbed wire had been available by, say, 1750 or even earlier.

The impact of the two world wars also changed the agricultural landscape. The pressures and incentives to take more land into cultivation led to the virtual end of the grass-covered downlands of southern England, while elsewhere the sandy heaths came under renewed attack. The results, in the form of huge fields up to 40 hectares in extent, bounded by wire fences, still remain and are in fact being modified to become even larger. The wreckage of the wars also produced strange field shapes. Abandoned airfields have often been reclaimed, at first the concrete runways being left untouched. When these were later removed the lines remained as boundaries, leading to an unusual pattern of fields (Plate IX). A similar picture emerges from the sites of disused army camps.

Modern events and technology are also recorded in field names. The existence in Dorset of Pylon Field and Bomb Crater Field shows this well. A paddock in Sussex, called Beatle Close after the well-known pop group of the 1960s, is perhaps the ultimate in the long history of field names.

At this time, in the second half of the twentieth century, the fields of England are being changed more than ever. On the whole, modern demands on agriculture are resulting in the removal of our heritage of fields built up over 10,000 years. Even so, as has been indicated in the previous chapters, much yet remains for us to see, at least for a few more years, of the agricultural past of England. Indeed in a few places the history of English agriculture is more than usually well preserved, for those with eyes to see, in the form of superimposed systems of farming. One such is near Malham in Yorkshire. There, on the hillsides above Gordale Beck, are large areas of prehistoric fields, cut into and partly destroyed by strip lynchets of the medieval period which in turn are overlain by dry-stone-walled fields of the nineteenth-century sheep pastures (Plate X). In a very different locality, at Tyneham in Dorset, where the existence of the army firing range has protected the land from twentieth-century developments, the same pattern is visible. One can see fragments of prehistoric fields projecting from the sides of medieval strip lynchets that have in turn been broken up by stone-walled fields of the seventeenth century, inside which are traces of late eighteenth-century narrow-rig ploughing (Fig. 28b). Lastly, at Harrington in Northamptonshire, there is a large tract of finely preserved ridge-and-furrow of the common fields, which has been dissected by channels of seventeenth-century drainage works, and surrounded by hedged fields of the eighteenth century.

Yet there is even more to see if special care is taken in looking closely at existing fields. For fields can also tell us about other aspects of English history. This is because when a piece of land, formerly used for non-agricultural purposes, was abandoned, the area was often hedged or walled to be incorporated then, or later, within the surrounding field system. Thus it is sometimes possible to recognize former occupation sites or even lost villages from the pattern produced by the existing field boundaries. At Caldecott in Rutland, the site of the former village of Snelston, finally abandoned in the fifteenth century, has for long been unknown. Yet on a modern map its site is obvious as a series of small irregular paddocks set in the centre of a large area of geometrically arranged fields. When the village was abandoned its site was divided up into small irregular fields and put down to grass, while its former common fields continued to be cultivated by the farmers of the nearby village. These fields were finally enclosed in the late eighteenth century, and the new enclosed fields were laid out in the usual form around the older paddocks.

Similarly, at Raunds in Northamptonshire, there are two abandoned sites, Mallows Cotton and West Cotton. Mallows Cotton has long been known, but the location of West Cotton was lost. A glance at a map (Fig. 29a) indicates, however, an area of small irregular fields, again adjacent to the rectangular fields of a later period. Examination of these small fields reveals that they enclose the site of the hamlet of West Cotton, the house sites of which still exist as earthworks in the permanent grassland.

Other types of land use unconnected with agriculture can also produce field systems which tell us of their origins. Again in Northamptonshire, in the Lyveden Valley west of Oundle, the greater part of the landscape is divided into huge fields which date from the late fifteenth-century sheep farming there. More recently they have been enlarged to cope with the massive arable farming programme of the 1960s and 1970s. However, in the middle of this area lies a small, near-square field, surrounded by a narrow belt of trees. This covers the remains of a late sixteenth-century garden, which was started but never completed.

Away in north-west Norfolk, near King's Lynn, the marshes along the Ouse estuary are covered by rectangular ditched fields, mainly dating from the eighteenth century when drainage work was being carried out in this region. But at one point a ditch has a very curious form, where it suddenly swings round in a series of short straight runs with sharp acute angles. The recognition of this suspicious feature led to the discovery of a rare seventeenth-century Civil War gun battery, around which the later drainage ditch had been cut, following the line of one of its sharply angled bastions.

Much more common are the long curving lines of hedges or walls which can often be traced over wide areas and found to

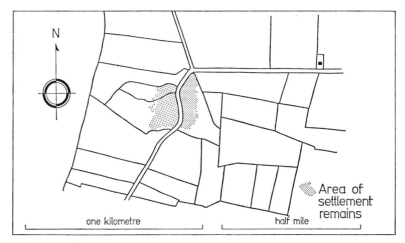

29a   Site of lost hamlet of West Cotton, Raunds, Northamptonshire. Botanically mixed hedge boundaries.

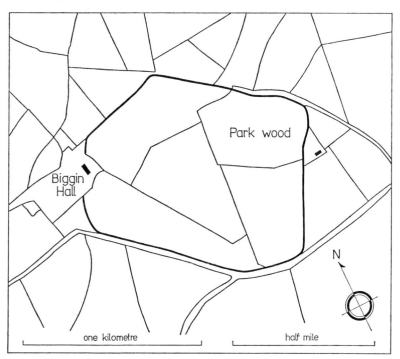

29b   Site of medieval deer park, Oundle, Northamptonshire. Mixed, botanically rich hedges on earthen bank.

enclose tens of hectares. When such hedges are examined they are frequently seen to be situated on large earthen banks, with internal ditches. The existence of names such as Park Wood, Park Farm and Park Fields associated with these curving embanked hedges can lead to the identification of medieval deer parks (Fig. 29b). These deer parks were constructed in their hundreds all over this country in the medieval period in order to contain deer. They then provided a constant supply of fresh meat for their owners, as well as a favourite recreation when the deer were turned out and hunted across the adjacent countryside.

In other places extremely unusual field shapes can tell of land use of a special kind in the past. For example, at Easton on the Hill in Northamptonshire, near Stamford, there is a long narrow field only 50 metres wide but over 1 kilometre long. This is part of the racecourse which belonged to the town of Stamford and was first laid out in the eighteenth century. The actual field which survives is the Mile Course added to the original layout in the early nineteenth century (Fig. 30a).

In a few places there even survive the mutilated remains of medieval-type common fields which have never been enclosed for one reason or another. One such is at Laxton in Nottinghamshire, while others exist on the Isle of Portland in Dorset, at Braunton in Devon and at Soham in Cambridgeshire (Fig. 30b, Plate XI). While these are now worked in ways the medieval farmers would not recognize, the patterns of unhedged strips covering large stretches of countryside are the last remnants of an archaic way of agriculture.

We have already briefly mentioned the value of field boundaries in historical-botanical terms, but it is worth looking at their purely botanical importance in more detail. There can be no doubt that hedges have a considerable natural history interest. They not only provide in themselves the environment for many species of birds and insects but they also contain a wide variety of shrubs, trees and other plants. More important, they act as linear connections or corridors along which both animals and plants can move from place to place and so enrich our landscape. The elimination of

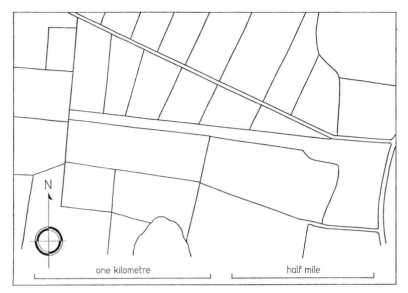

30a   Site of early nineteenth-century racecourse, Stamford, Lincolnshire. Thorn hedge boundaries.

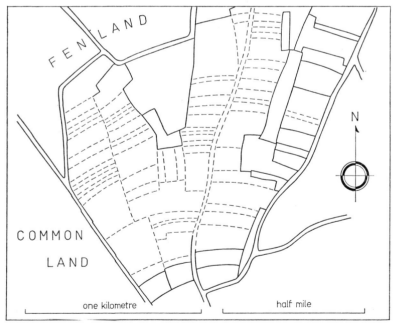

30b   Remains of medieval common fields, Soham, Cambridgeshire. No physical boundaries.

hedges as a result of modern agricultural methods is destroying the habitats that the hedges themselves provide as well as removing these links between woods and copses. As a whole, therefore, our natural history heritage has been slowly impoverished, and indeed in some places utterly destroyed by the increasing removal of hedges.

Perhaps for the great majority of the population of England today, fields, in the terms that this book has dealt with them, are only seen on holidays or on weekend trips. The urban dweller of the twentieth century may be forgiven if he thinks that fields have no relevance to the pattern of towns. But in fact nothing could be further from the truth. The traces of fields lie all around and in most cases have largely determined the shape and layout of our nineteenth- and twentieth-century urban expansion. It is obvious that any urban development has to have boundaries and that these boundaries are largely conditioned by pre-existing land ownership which the builder, developer or the local authority has acquired. Thus the form of most building estates, whether large or small, is fixed by the earlier boundaries of fields of various dates (Plate XII). The actual effect on the existing urban pattern of the old fields varies considerably. In modern large-scale suburban development it may be very little, though it still plays a part. In small-scale development of both the nineteenth and twentieth centuries the layout of the older fields often had or has an immense influence upon the appearance of the estates, on the arrangement of streets and even on the size and shape of the subsequent gardens.

Almost any town in England demonstrates this. For example, in Cambridge the whole pattern of streets and blocks of houses, developed from 1820 onwards around the town, is directly related to the geometrical field pattern laid out by the surveyors and enclosure commissioners who planned it, for purely agricultural purposes, a few years earlier. At Peterborough, the arrangement of housing estates and their roads, developed in the nineteenth century as the town expanded rapidly, was controlled by the existing pattern of roughly rectangular fields which had been formed as a result of seventeenth- and early eighteenth-century enclosures. In Nottingham, because the common fields of the town still existed in the early nineteenth century, expansion was prevented and the town was forced to build houses on every available garden, orchard or yard. Then when Parliamentary Enclosure finally took place in 1845 a large number of small new fields became immediately available for urban development. The result was a number of building schemes on individual fields quite independent of each other which often produced a curious and hopelessly inconvenient street pattern. At Leicester 'from 1885 to 1914 piecemeal growth continued to change an agricultural landscape into one of pavement and brick. Fields and farms . . . retained a vestige of identity in the process'. Likewise Liverpool retains in its modern layout evidence of its older fields. Leeds is another town which shows well the effect of the older field systems on its growth. Especially in the suburbs of Hunslet and Armley each block of nineteenth-century terraces, as well as the pattern of twentieth-century estates, is rigidly controlled by the pre-existing fields and their ownership. Every change in the alignment or direction of terraces is caused by an earlier boundary. Particularly interesting are corner houses, built askew to the main building line to fit in with an earlier irregular field hedge. This same pattern can be seen even in London, where most of the suburbs built after 1800 reflect the pre-existing field shapes of the old countryside.

The Future

So the traces of the history of agriculture are etched on the English landscape. Today much of this is being removed for ever. But what of the future? Are we to continue to see the removal of all field boundaries and other relics of our agricultural past? At present it seems so. Fields are quite unprotected, unlike ancient monuments, buildings of architectural importance, sites of special natural history significance and even individual trees, all of which have some form of protection, however inadequate. Anyone can, and frequently does, remove field boundaries without any form of control.

Of course it is impossible on this overcrowded island of ours, with the consequent pressures for more food, increased farming efficiency, more houses, more roads and so on, to keep fields exactly as they are. And indeed, as we have seen in the previous chapters, fields have been continuously altered throughout man's history to take account of new methods of agriculture and economic and social pressures. In addition, historically speaking, many of our fields are relative latecomers to the landscape. In many places the great hedgeless open spaces of the countryside are now a reversion to their medieval appearance. Nevertheless, while the complete preservation of fields is not possible, necessary or even desirable, it may be that some thought should be given to fields in the future for a number of reasons.

First, the very fact that they tell us something of our past, of the aims, achievements and failures of our ancestors, may be regarded as a useful social amenity. In present-day society with its increasing mobility and rootlessness, more and more people are striving to find an identity with the places in which they live, work and play. The existence of fields with a traceable history is part of the total historical environment that can be explained and understood and may lead to care for the environment as a whole. In addition the existence of fields, either hedged or walled, gives this country an aesthetic value which other countries sometimes lack. The well-wooded hedged landscape of the English Midlands, for example, for all its lack of magnificent scenery, is something one cannot see in the endless prairies of the central United States, or even on the rolling lands of western Europe. The variety of field shapes and field boundaries in every part of England gives it a character and beauty that few other places can rival. Furthermore, without fields our rich natural history environment would inevitably be that much poorer with less of interest to see and enjoy.

The continued wholesale destruction of fields on the present-day scale will certainly lead to the increasing poverty of our environment in historical, ecological, social and visual terms. It is something that should not be allowed to happen. What is needed is a detailed survey by archaeologists, historians, natural historians and planners in which they could examine certain key areas and organize their future conservation.

We cannot totally stop the destruction of fields over most of the country; the techniques of modern farming, and more especially the demands we collectively as people put on farmers for increased food production, preclude it. However, it may be that some small areas of high historical, visual or botanical interest could be preserved. Though we cannot expect individual farmers to bear the undoubted cross of such work, certain corporate bodies, such as the National Trust, could, with some financial assistance, carry out work of this kind.

But even this may not be enough. We should also be thinking of the new fields of the future. These will perhaps be quite unlike anything that has existed up till now and used for entirely different purposes. For example, some field boundaries in the future may have to be thought of as screens. This is, of course, already being done on a considerable scale to cover up unsightly industrial buildings. But it can hardly be said that this type of monotonous screening was started in order really to improve the visual quality of both the rural and the suburban landscape. Massive tree belts of considerable width, planted not with flowering cherry, conifer or poplars as is so often seen but with a variety of more natural hardwoods, would help to hide much of the necessary wreckage of the present and future landscape. And this planting should not be carried out in regular lines with identical trees, all carefully spaced—a method so beloved by many landscape planners. It ought to be arranged in flowing lines with a variety of species in random order. In addition, these same screens could well be used in our urban areas to break up the endless concrete, tarmac and neatly mown grass verge vistas. Occasionally this has occurred almost by accident. On a modern housing estate in Bournemouth, the existence of long belts of trees, which have been preserved almost intact during building development, has produced a splendidly varied appearance on the estate, which gains much from these tree-lined boundaries.

163

In the rural areas, though it is impossible to re-create field boundaries as we know them, much could be done by the careful planting of small copses at certain places to break up the general bareness of some of the present countryside. Well-planted and sited, such woods would improve the landscape and need not be either large or valueless in agricultural terms. With the present increase in the demand for timber of all kinds, woodlands could be made economically viable. Perhaps in these or other ways a new generation of English fields might be added to the long history of the country's landscape.

Select Bibliography

Agricultural History Review, The Journal of the British Agricultural History Society, published twice yearly.

Baker, A. R. H., and Butlin, R. A. (eds.), *Studies of Field Systems in the British Isles*. Cambridge University Press, 1973.

Bowen, H. C., *Ancient Fields*. S. R. Publishers, Wakefield, 1961.

Chambers, J. D., and Mingay, G. E., *The Agricultural Revolution, 1750–1880*. Batsford, 1966.

Crawford, O. G. S., *Archaeology in the Field*. Phoenix House, 1953.

Darby, H. C., *The Draining of the Fens*. Cambridge University Press, 1968.
    (ed.), *A New Historical Geography of England*. Cambridge University Press, 1973.

Fairbrother, N., *New Lives, New Landscapes*. Architectural Press, 1970.

Field, J., *English Field-Names*. David & Charles, 1972.

Finberg, H. P. R. (ed.), *The Agrarian History of England and Wales*, Vol. 1, pt 2. Cambridge University Press, 1972. Vol. 4 (1967). *See also* Thirsk, J.

Hoskins, W. G., *The Midland Peasant*. Macmillan, 1965.
    Fieldwork in Local History. Faber, 1967.

Kerridge, E., *The Agricultural Revolution*. Allen & Unwin, 1967.

Tate, W. E., *The English Village Community and the Enclosure Movement*. Gollancz, 1967.

Thirsk, J., *English Peasant Farming*. Routledge, 1957.
    (ed.), *The Agrarian History of England and Wales*, Vol. 4. Cambridge University Press, 1967.

Williams, M., *The Draining of the Somerset Levels*. Cambridge University Press, 1970.

Index

Index

Forest clearance, Neolithic, 21–2;
medieval, 94–9; late-medieval,
117; 17th-cent., 127–9; 18th-
and 19th-cent., 143–8
Fountains Abbey, sheep pastures
of, 100
Fox coverts, 140
Frampton, Dorset, prehistoric and
medieval fields at, 84; Roman
hamlets and fields at, 62
Fritham, Hants, Roman plough
marks at, 26
Furlongs, 58, 79–80, 85, 109
Furnace Abbey, reclamation of land
by, 100
Fyfield Down, Wilts., prehistoric
fields at, 29, 31, 41; ridge and
furrow at, 83

Game coverts, 140
Gardens, abandoned, 156
Gillingham Forest, Dorset, 17th-
cent. clearance of, 127
Glanvilles Wooton, Dorset, 19th-
cent. enclosure at, 146
Glastonbury Abbey, medieval
reclamation by, 101
Goats, Saxon, 70
Gordale, Yorks., fields at, Plate X
Granaries, Iron Age, 39
Grantchester, Cambs., village plan
of, 89, 93
Grassington, Yorks., 17th-cent.
enclosure at, 122
Great Shelford, Cambs., late-
medieval enclosure at, 113
Great Wymondley, Herts., alleged
Roman fields at, 58
Grimston, Dorset, enclosure of
common fields at, 153
Groby, Leics., abandonment of
land at, 108
Gun-battery, 17th-cent., 156
Gwithian, Cornwall, prehistoric
plough marks at, 26; Bronze Age
fields at, 29, 31; Saxon ploughing
at, 69, 80

Hambledon Hill, Dorset, Neolithic
camp at, 23
Harrington, Northants., fields at,
155
Hatfield Chase, 17th-cent. drainage
of, 130
Hatley, Cambs., 17th-cent. enclos-
ure at, 124
Hawthorn, 15, 140
Hayton, Cumberland, 17th-cent.
enclosure at, 120
Headlands, 82, 84–6, 93, 110–11
Heathland, reclamation of, medieval,
128, Plates II and V; 17th-,
18th- and 19th-cent., 144
Hedgerow dating, 98–9, 113, 120
Hedges, 15, 67–8, 72, 95–6, 113,
115, 120, 140, 144, 146, 153–4,
156, 160, 162, Plate VIII
Hemp, 119, 132
Hen Domen, Mont., ridge and
furrow at, 80
Herb paris, 96
Hermitage, Dorset, medieval forest
clearance at, 95
Higham Ferrers, Northants., 80–1
Hill forts, 44
Hilton, Dorset, medieval forest
clearance at, 95
Hinckley, Leics., field name at, 150
Hinton St Mary, Dorset, late-
medieval fields at, 105, 114
Hoes, 21, 48
Holbeach, Lincs., 17th-cent. relama-
tion at, 132
Holderness, medieval reclamation
at, 103
Horridge, Devon, prehistoric
fields at, 31
Horton, Wilts., strip lynchets at, 91
Housesteads, Roman fort and
medieval fields at, 91
Hunting, prehistoric, 19
Hut circles, prehistoric, 36, 39

Ice Age, 19
Infield-outfield, 62, 68–9, 74–5

170

Trailblazing the Way from Victim to Victor

THROUGH THE ASPERGER WINDOW

LYNN JONES

ISBN: 0995678626
ISBN-13: 978-0995678620

DEDICATION

To my dear friend, Joan Cossins.

Thank you for all you have done for me and
others rejected by the world.
For befriending me in 1994 when I was at a very low ebb.
For being there through the turbulent years and for giving
your time and professional skills as proof reader.
Our friendship is richer for the experience.

ACKNOWLEDGEMENTS

First of all, the more I understand myself, the more I understand and love my mum. Thank you for everything, most especially for holding the family together.

To my husband Geoff, my sons Justin and Matthew, and my grandchildren Hollie, Lewis, Archie, Harry and Rosie, I love you more than you could ever know.

To my father, sister and her family – love and suffering have run together. Thank you for all that was good and the learning that came from all that was difficult.

Relationships with my step-mother, brother-in-law and the people who fired his bullets have been pure suffering. From that suffering I gained understanding and personal growth that enabled me to find my place, life purpose and voice in this world. Thank you for the lessons that have enabled me to rise up and make a difference in the world.

My friends are far too many to list. They will know who they are. Thank you for love and friendship. I remember Janet Palmer who was a friend, neighbour and child-minder who also sang Ave Maria beautifully at my wedding to Geoff.

To the friends I let down because of my changes, please accept my heart-felt apology. I especially mention Joan Hyde as a dear friend who became disengaged when I felt a misfit and moved away from married friends at the time of my divorce.

Sincere thanks to all who have worked to complete this book: Nicky Marshall who has worked as my mentor and publisher; Julie Merrett who has been my life coach; Joan Cossins who has supported me through the years and proof read the book; Yvonne Bishop for photography and most recently Laura Barnett as artist for the logo and book cover.

CONTENTS

FOREWORD

Rachel E. Gingell B.A.(HONS)Psych

Lynn and I first met during a lunch break at a mental health seminar being held at a local University. As we later discovered, Lynn attended in her capacity as a survivor of poor mental health services and trainer of health care professionals and me as a representative for the Bristol Disability Equality Forum. We both went outside for a breath of fresh air and we exchanged our first hello. My initial and abiding impression of Lynn was that of a woman full of indignation as she told me she had been diagnosed as schizophrenic. The indignation in her voice was palpable. My immediate response was to tell her unequivocally that the diagnosis was incorrect and I gave her my phone number, inviting her to contact me if she wanted to talk at some point in the future. A lasting connection had been made. A few days later Lynn called me and we arranged to meet for a chat over coffee.

I should explain that I am an independent psychologist and my unequivocal response to her 'diagnosis' came from my heart and was based on years of trying to support people who had fallen through the cracks of the psychiatric 'care' system. These people had become victims of a system and practice that perpetuates mental illness, offering no concept of 'recovery'. Her profound love for her family is central to Lynn's life and she has fought hard to keep her family together and to heal her wounds and theirs after her traumatic experiences at the hands of mental health professionals. Lynn described herself as a victim of the very people who were supposed to be there to help those of us who have experienced mental distress. Being the indignant and persistent woman that she is, she began to take on the system failures as a woman in recovery with a story to tell and a mission to fulfil.

We met on a regular basis for quite a while – sharing life stories and experiences, tears and smiles as we negotiated the early steps on Lynn's path of recovery. We didn't always agree on everything we discussed – but we respected our differences and moved on. At some point, after months of discussion and sharing, I recognised what I considered perhaps to be a missing piece vital to the jigsaw of Lynn's life. Before I offered this potentially vital piece to Lynn, I gave the matter very serious consideration – I wanted to be relatively certain that I was correct. During one discussion I offered my opinion that Lynn may have been dealing with undiagnosed Asperger's Syndrome, which would have made difficult issues in family even more challenging for her to make sense of. Being Lynn – now well along her road of recovery – she threw herself into researching everything she could find on this form of autism. The information she found resonated with both aspects of herself and her family life she had always struggled with; this knowledge she used to advance still further from being a victim of her past to becoming the victor she is today.

On her journey to heal herself and her family, Lynn also acts as a life coach to those in need of her insight and expertise in empowerment, has been actively involved with universities and health services in training professionals on the vital concept of recovery and campaigns on behalf of people not as far along the path of recovery as she now is. The indignation I first noted during the first conversation we shared served to sustain her as she fought to make sense of her experiences. Over the years this righteous indignation has transformed into unshakeable strength and conviction and the confidence to write her story – no more will Lynn be a victim and she will do what she can to help others move from victim to victor.

Today, many years later, we are sisters in spirit, and lifelong friends. I love and respect this bravely honest woman – her book is an inspiration for everyone with an interest in mental health, recovery and liberation from inappropriate paradigms in 'treating' people who are, or have been, in the care of mental health professionals. We all live in a society where much is still to be learned about mental health and wellness – Lynn's voice most definitely must be heard.

GLOSSARY OF TERMS

Adrenaline: A hormone secreted by the adrenal glands that prepares muscles to run away or fight in response to fear.

Affirmation: A statement that helps positive thinking.

Archetypes: Jung, who followed after Freudian psychiatry, put forward a theory that there is a primitive mental image inherited from the earliest human ancestors, and it is supposed to be present in the collective unconscious.

Asperger's: Asperger Syndrome is a lifelong developmental disability that affects how people perceive the world and interact with others. (The National Autistic Society).

Authoritarianism: Authoritarianism is a form of management characterized by strong central power. Authoritarianism is for the purpose of control and oppressors have low or no accountability.

Depot: Regular injections of anti-psychotic drugs.

Dharma: Encompasses ideas such as duty, rights, character, vocation, religion and customs considered appropriate, correct or morally upright.

Dysfunction: A disturbance in the usual pattern of activity or behaviour – dysfunctional families or societies.

Dyspraxia: Poor coordination displayed by some

children.

Frequency:	A wavelength on which a radio or television signal is broadcast and to which a receiving set can be tuned.
Genius:	The prevailing character or spirit of something. Exceptional intellectual or creative power or other natural ability.
Gravity:	Keeps everything on planet Earth from spinning off into space.
Ideology:	Belief.
Inflation:	Price rises.
Jung:	Early psychiatrist who followed on from Freud.
LSD:	An hallucinogenic drug made from lysergic acid that was used experimentally as a medicine and is taken as an illegal drug.
Meditation:	The action or practice of meditating.
Oppression:	Inequality, where one seeks to have power over another person or group.
Parable:	A simple story used to illustrate a moral or spiritual lesson.
Projection:	A theory in psychology in which humans defend themselves against their own unconscious impulses or qualities (both positive and negative) by denying their existence in themselves while attributing them to others.
Psychiatry:	The study and treatment of mental illness, emotional disturbance, and abnormal behaviour.
Stigma:	Shame.

Trauma: Extreme shock and suffering.

INTRODUCTION

This book is the story of my life as I see it and my interpretation of events. The need for soul-searching came about because of a shocking experience with the medical profession that knocked my world off its axis so that nothing made sense. Survival depended on getting answers and I lost the Summer of my life, but I have reached understanding.

Like most people, I considered that my childhood was normal. As an adult I re-examined early memories and was shocked to find dysfunction and emotional abuse. Life can be compared to a building in that both are built on foundations. Some buildings can be torn down and built again, while others are underpinned to give added strength. Underpinning my life has given it added strength and enabled me not only to uphold and develop, but to transform myself into a better person.

Before the trauma I looked back on my life with happy memories of childhood and had a balanced view of my family and saw them as good people. The book has been a transformational journey that plumbed the depths of emotional pain and old wounds were opened for healing. I studied the nature of abuse as it applied to me. What we focus on we attract more of. For me it was more abuse.

As a child I was religious, but lost faith in the church as I looked to them for healing through the spirit of the Gospel teachings. My belief system totally broke down. I lost faith in the authorities and formed a new unconventional belief system that challenges convention born out of the man-made ideal of how life should be. It would be easy to dismiss the church in total, but I know there is goodness in some ministers and church members. Reverend Alister Palmer is the one priest I consider outstanding and he is my priest. I had a few years where I attended his church in a neighbouring district and thankfully he and his lovely wife Sally have moved into my district and now attend the same church.

In order to understand my life, I have read books for over 40 years on personal development, the meaning of life and the transformational power of spirit. Starting as a non-thinking person who accepted what was said, with full trust in the authorities, I have released dependency on the church and medical professions. I have tried to give both the church and the medical profession the benefit of my findings, but came to the sad conclusion that I am unconventional. This means that what I give is rejected by conventional groups that uphold the balance of power and the way things are.

I have put out theories with some acknowledgement from experts in their field, but the fact remains that change does not come from the top, but from the ground up. I have purged my soul over and over and laid my soul bare to put out an honest account of my true life story. The need to find and put out what is true to me leaves me feeling vulnerable to attack not only from the professions who represent various schools of thought, but also from people who are bullies. In my experience, it is easier for victims to forgive oppressors than it is for oppressors to forgive victims that challenge and expose them. The greatest sin is to think independently or contradict the official or unofficial authority of the powers that be.

Throughout my life, I have constantly faced and

overcome fears. The fear of annihilation is a real one. My story shows that if the offenders can't ignore the person who challenges them they trash the theory. If they can't do that then they go on to trash the person.

My story and findings will not be a perfect fit for any person or school of thought. I am not aiming to destroy anyone's view to supplant it with my own. I appreciate receiving different viewpoints myself, as they can add a new dimension to my own view of the world. I describe this as a kaleidoscope that changes the picture. I find it incredible that although we all come from one source, all life journeys are different.

Some readers will be familiar with the psychology and spirituality lines of thought within the book and for others they will be new ideas. From my own experience of reading new ideas I have found it difficult that when I get to the back of the book there is a glossary of terms that would have helped me if they had appeared at the beginning of the book. For that purpose, I have put a glossary of terms at the start of the book, for beginners. Recommended reading is shown at the back, for those who would like to follow up some of the themes or understand schools of thought that have influenced my thinking.

When I have shared my findings in the past, people work with them in different ways. After all my time and effort working through to understand, some people are lucky enough to accept the punch line and go off to make simple changes in their lives. Others like to take an in-depth view and take time to think about the concepts.

My hope in putting out my work is that as my story has inspired nurses in the mental health field and student doctors, it will also resonate with the contribution of other groups of victims and disadvantaged people as they travel towards healing. We meet in the oneness of our humanity, but each and every one of us is totally unique in our choice of path to understanding and peace.

The realisation that I had Asperger's came late in life. I had slipped the net of the medical profession, which made my life like the ship that started out one degree off course to end up hundreds of miles in the wrong direction. With the right point of reference, I was able to re-evaluate myself yet again to get my difficulties into perspective and to understand them. Finally, I felt confident enough to share my alternative view of the world. Although my findings might clash with those of others, my story is written from my heart.   My deepest wish is that my heart felt experience will resonate with others and touch them in the depths of their suffering so that they too can find peace.

Chapter 1

EARLY DAYS

As a post-war baby, I was born into the world the day after the National Health came into being, at 7.00 am on Tuesday 6th July 1948. In many ways my life has been privileged, as I haven't known war and have always had access to health care. This was a time when there were no expectations for women. My life script was to grow up, get married, have children, and that was it.

I cannot remember the first 18 months of my life when I lived with my family in rooms in Lawrence Hill, Bristol. My earliest memory was living in a spacious three bedroomed house in Lawrence Weston, Bristol, with a large garden, on a new housing estate. Although money was tight, the Second World War was over and life had exciting possibilities. People felt as though they had received a new start.

I was a happy child with a zest for life. I had a huge capacity for love, forgiveness, generosity and appreciation, which are spiritual qualities. Most likely these qualities gave an impression of buoyancy and the ability to bounce back. This disguised the fact that underneath it all I was a distressed child. With any understanding this could have been picked up by the medical profession, due to the fact that I was accident prone, had nose bleeds and wet the bed. These are all signs of a disturbed child. With hindsight, I have lived my life as mildly autistic with High Functioning Asperger's. I am wired differently from the average person. I also suffer from dyspraxia, which means I need extra time and support for practical tasks. If doctors had understood the condition, my needs might have been met.

My mother constantly said, "Be good, be good" or,

"Have you been good?" I asked, "What do I need to do?'"
She laughed, saying, "Children are innocent. They don't
know right from wrong." I was looking for a definition of
the word 'good'. I went to Sunday School and loved it. We
constantly sang, "I'm H-A-P-P-Y" and I am sure this was a
positive affirmation for me, and I continued to sing it at
home. At Sunday school I was finding my definition of the
word 'good' in the teachings of Jesus and I watched nuns to
learn how girls should behave. My family script was to
grow up, get married and have children. My own secret
script was to be a nun.

Moral and social values were better in years gone by,
because good behaviour was encouraged with regular
reminders of 'Do a good turn every day', 'Keep Britain tidy'
and stories of 'The Good Samaritan'. As a literal child, I
took the teachings to heart.

Trauma has been a consistent part of my existence,
present before birth, into conception, early years and
throughout much of my adulthood. The account of my
traumatic early life was given to me by my older sister
Patsy. This has helped me to understand and overcome
the family dysfunction.

My sister was three and a half years older than me
and born in the war, living in rooms in a house in
Lawrence Hill with Mum and Dad. We shared this with my
maternal grandmother. Life sounded traumatic when Dad
came home on leave or returned after the war, as he did
not get on with Granny Ford. My sister's descriptions of
the scene sounded like a Brian Rix farce. People were
running in and out of rooms in the house. Mum was the
youngest of eight children. She was a sickly child who was
doted on by her mother. I can imagine Dad's irritation as
Granny Ford answered for my mother, but it was still
difficult to come to the realisation that he threw Granny
Ford down the stairs.

Dad was back from the war as I was preparing to
enter the world and I was born a week early, at 39 weeks.

Mum said, "When Patsy was born she was pretty, but you were ugly because you had yellow jaundice and had to be put in the sun". When a woman gives birth, her body floods with a hormone to love her baby and even if the baby looks like a monkey she sees the baby as beautiful. From studying psychology, I understand that when a woman is emotionally unwell, the love hormone does not flood in for the baby, which is possibly why my mother had a weak bond with me.

The move to our own home came when I was 18 months old and my grandmother went into the workhouse. She died of a stroke when I was four years old and I have no memory of her.

My father was the second child and the eldest male in his family. His parents were young compared with my maternal grandparents. Dad was born Mitchell, which was my maiden name. He was a little boy who doted on his father, but he was to hear the news that his father had died because he had been crushed at the docks where he worked. My grandmother spent several years as a lone parent, before remarrying and becoming Florrie Mogg, giving birth to more children in her second marriage.

Dad had lived a very hard life as a child, being a runner for his mother, making trips to the soup kitchen. Poverty meant that he went to school wearing odd shoes and Granfer would call him out of school to run errands. Granfer Mogg did not know good health, eventually losing his legs to gangrene. While he was employed, he worked at the local baths, where his family had the chance to swim. The family became strong swimmers and Danielle, the granddaughter of Dad's brother Bill, swam for Wales.

Dad's survival had depended on his mother, which set up a game whereby she was master and he was slave. The game continued with whoever took the place of the eldest female. This was to my detriment as the younger sister. A touch of cruelty seemed to add to their enjoyment of the game.

I loved my grandmother, but my sister hated her. Nan Mogg had been difficult with my mother, giving food to my father, but not to my mother. My sister was aware of this and carried resentment on behalf of my mother. I was Nan's second favourite grandchild and Granfer's favourite.

Mum was a hard worker. Every day she went through the house from top to bottom: dusting, polishing the furniture and linoleum floors. Each day was set – Monday for laundry, Tuesday and Thursday for walking a long distance to the shops. Mum's aim was to provide a protected environment for us to grow up feeling safe and secure. In those days working class women did not go out to work and I can remember her repeating to herself, "What a life, I wish I was dead".

Mum was a very shy lady, but she did make two very good life-long friends named Joyce and Doll, who were as close as family. Doll lived across the main road and Joyce lived next door. My mother was particularly squeamish and could not cope with blood, so we were regular visitors to Joyce as my mother called out, "She's bleeding again". Mostly Mum and her friends visited each other for morning tea and in the afternoon, they got together for knitting sessions, as all wool garments were handmade. My Mum was extremely gifted at knitting, but could never give herself any credit. When neighbours were stuck with their knitting Mum would sort it out for them. Sometimes the pattern was wrong and Mum would identify the mistake and alter the pattern. Many years later when knitting was done by machine and computerised, it became apparent that knitting was complicated and mathematical.

Dad worked in the aircraft industry. He was a copper smith by trade, but he spent his working life as a shop steward and convenor. I loved my Dad, especially in childhood and I am sure that when I was a child he loved me. He carried me everywhere on his shoulders and as Patsy was bonded with Mum, I was Dad's constant companion.

I can see now that Dad had been affected by life's inequalities. He was extremely short and had been teased about his height in the RAF. People remarked how much Dad was like Norman Wisdom. One day, as a child, I went into town and saw Norman Wisdom laying a penny chain for charity. I couldn't believe that I was looking at my Dad's double!

Another thing that affected Dad was that he worked as a blue-collar worker, which meant he worked with tools. Young people who had started in the office would enter Dad's workspace and refer to him as 'Mitchell', while he was supposed to respond with 'Mr.' to the youngster.

Effectively, Dad was suffering from oppression and wanted equality. The thing he did not realise was that his claim to status depended on being the eldest son. In this way the pecking order in our home resulted in my sister being right and successful, while failure was my lot and I was blamed for it. In spite of the unfair treatment in the family, I would later in life take up his fight for fairness and equality.

My favourite times were Christmas and holidays, when the family were together and I was given time. Generally, tensions in the home were difficult. Mum was frightened of anything going wrong, because Dad would explode. My sister coped by trying to be invisible and unheard. She was frightened. The problem was that I was a different type of character and my sister shrieked at me when I made a noise, such as rustling paper on a crisp packet, eating noisily, or making a sound. I would go up in the air with shock and shriek back at the attack, which resulted in one of the parents stepping in, and then the trouble my sister had been trying to avoid actually occurred. Often it would result in Mum walking away and staying out for hours. It has been difficult to feel safe in life after the experience of explosions coming from nowhere and for no reason.

Mum would say to Patsy and me, "Don't tell your

father or there will be trouble". I tended to repeat everything, so I wasn't told anything, but it seemed my sister became a confidante for Mum. The result of this is that my sister lived in a closed way and hated me for being open. She continued in this way into her marriage until her death, doing things in the home without consulting her husband. She justified it saying, "If I don't tell him there will be only one row, whereas there would be two if I told him".

My sister read Enid Blyton, *The Secret Seven,* while I preferred *The Famous Five*. She saw herself as the hard done by sister and I was the horrid little sister within the stories.

I enjoyed school and Mum said that on my first day I didn't look back to wave because I was so keen to go in. I remember my first teacher as a very attractive brunette called Miss Lester and finding my peg to hang my coat. I was in the top five for reading in the infants' class. For some reason reading came easily. The fascination with words has continued throughout my life. Writing with my left hand was difficult and when I joined my mother in writing letters to an uncle, he asked, "Who taught your Linda to write – a Chinese man?"

With hindsight, I skimmed the surface of subjects and if it stuck that was good, but as was often the case, subjects didn't come easily to me, especially maths and geography. As a child with a lot of energy, games and sport were my favourite subjects, leaving me with happy memories and feelings of nostalgia.

It was quite a walk to go to the infant school, but Bank Leaze Junior School was at the back of our house and an easy distance. The back garden was steep and the school was literally on an embankment. Singing could be heard in our home, as the school put emphasis on the whole school singing together at assembly.

I loved helping and enjoyed tidying the staff room after the teachers had taken their break. I can remember sweeping the floor, so the cleaners must have loved their reduced workload. With the exception of helping and eating, praise was limited and criticism frequent, so it is little surprise that I became an overweight do-gooder!

Play was mostly outside of the home and much of what we did would not be allowed within modern society. Children would go out at the start of the day and come home at the end of it, calling in for food. I wandered for miles, either doing a circuit through four districts, or taking my fairy bike down a long lane to Severn Beach.

I saw older children playing two-ball against the walls of houses and worked hard to learn the skill. I developed very good hand to eye co-ordination for ball games because of the amount of practice I did. Generally, I had a lot of accidents starting at an early age when I climbed a stack of paving stones and still have the scar on my chin to prove it. I fell out of windows and got my head stuck in gates and jagged buckets that were meant to cover the rhubarb.

Mum believed abuse and danger happened after dark with strangers. If I was late, I would get the cane or be hit with a boiler stick. Mum never explained her fears. The result of this is that I am compulsively early and suffered three types of sexual abuse between the age of three and nine and all by people who were known to us.

For senior school my sister went to Henbury, which was in a neighbouring district. For my year, we were to have a new school in Lawrence Weston. We were to be the first year in and so each year the school population would increase. This was to prove a disadvantage in later life, because without older children I lacked the social development of surviving oppression as well as the normal push and shove of life. I was in a protected and innocent environment due to the newness of the district and the school.

The Headmaster of our modern comprehensive school was a young, dynamic man named Mr. Poster. He described us as 'pioneers'. While that may have been true, we could have been more accurately described as 'guinea pigs'.

I heard the head master say of me, "She hasn't got it", but it was clear that he liked me. I was given the task of being fund raiser for The Pestalozzi Village and I raised a lot of money by selling pins and other items. One teacher really didn't want to buy anything, but ended by saying, "You could get blood from a stone" as she begrudgingly got out her purse. I was also a useful house member when it came to sport and excelled at sprint, table tennis and hockey.

A girl in a wheelchair came to the school and I befriended her, taking her to her classes whenever I could. Suddenly she stopped coming to the school and I thought no more of it. One day all the schoolchildren were sitting in assembly and an announcement was made that the girl had died. I sat and cried, because despite our closeness, no one had forewarned me.

Educationally I continued to skim the surface and wasn't achieving. In the fourth year commercial studies were introduced and this made a big difference, as I was able to engage with the subjects. My sister had not got on well with shorthand, but I took to it like a duck to water and was in the top three in my class. My friend Pam Burgess and I took private lessons on Saturday mornings.

Book keeping came easily and I was fast with fractions and percentages, again in the lead for that subject. My exams were at UEI level and we were told that book keeping was not on the syllabus for UEI, so the subject had to be dropped. We were then put in a class with boys who had been doing mainstream maths, so again I lost it.

Through life I grew up hearing that I was dim and stupid and so much that happened in life reinforced the message. There were a couple of contradictions that confirmed the presence of intelligence, but sadly the good messages got filtered out as I continued to believe I was dim and stupid. One contradiction was that I applied for a job at ICI. Over 100 people applied for the position of shorthand typist and this was the first year they would receive applications from UEI students. At interview they gave an IQ test, which consisted of ticking the right box as well as fractions and percentages. As usual I flew across the page and ended up being offered the job, which would include further training. The other contradiction was when Mrs. Sceens, the teacher for secretarial studies, said, "I wish I had you for another year, as I could really do things for you". I didn't see the compliment.

The 1960s were a wonderful time for young people. I entered my teens in 1961 and left school at the age of 16 in 1964. In my pre-teens I tended to like the same music as my mother, but music was changing. My sister loved Elvis Presley and rock and roll had entered the scene. The first artist I liked for myself was Rick Nelson and on a weekly basis some new wonderful record was being released. With the switch in style, young people were finding an identity of their own. As a young person I had no idea of the sexuality within the lyrics but enjoyed the energy of the music.

Youth clubs were popular and I went to Henbury where they held their club in an old cottage-type house. These were happy days. A few of the boys had motor bikes and I absolutely loved them and had a few short rides, which were exhilarating. I loved speed and had no sense of danger. A new youth club opened in Lawrence Weston, which meant I was able to attend two clubs, where I either danced or played table tennis in high heels to the beat of the music. My greatest regret in life was not having table tennis training, as I played a stylish game and was good as a natural, but didn't have the killer instinct or the few tips that could have made the difference.

Puberty was a difficult time for me. As a child I was resilient and bounced back after slights and difficulties. The emergence of hormones changed resilience to floods of tears as I became very sensitive. I used to do the housework chores for the boy next door while his mother was at work. After doing them one day, he turned to me and said, "You can push off now". I ended up in floods of tears, so when I got back home I turned to Mum for comfort, but she was no help at all in difficult situations, so her advice was simply, "Stay away".

I had always loved Mum's friends and neighbours, as if they were family. This single incident of being used and then told to 'push off' might not sound significant, except that it indicated an attitude towards me that was to lead to further abuse, and the main reason for the collapse of my health and life as I knew it. The positive outcome of this event was that it held the key to my problems, and this was to place me on the path to a continuing journey of discovery.

Chapter 2

YOUNG ADULT

On 4th August 1964, at the age of 16, I entered the world of work. Although I was offered the more local job at ICI, my choice was to work in town as a shorthand typist in a large typing pool at Eagle Star Insurance Company, where the starting wage was 15 shillings higher. My first week of work was a four-day week after the August Bank Holiday. I was exhausted by the difference between school and work. After being top of the class at school, it seemed that everything I typed went into the bin. With hindsight I now realise that I was overwhelmed with the huge pile of files and if my older, wiser self could advise my younger self, she would say, "Remove the sense of pressure by putting the pile aside and focus on one task at a time".

I made some lovely friends who were aged 18 and 19 and they seemed very mature and sophisticated. The world of work brought a significant change in my own development as I adapted to this new way of life. One day, a few months after starting work, I walked past the playground of my old school when the sixth formers were taking a break. They seemed childish compared with my new friends as I had matured in my new work environment.

My mother was most concerned that I should not work in a factory and was pleased that I had found an office job. Like many people in the district, I spoke with a broad Bristolian accent but started adopting the ways of my new friends, which included changing my pronunciation. Mum was unsure about these changes, and once said, "You think you are better than you are".

It was in the workplace that I was introduced to smoking, which was socially acceptable anywhere at the time. Ash trays were on the desks and in ladies' rest rooms. I became a heavy smoker and it was 30 years before I was able to break the habit and give it up.

Towards the end of 1964 I met my first boyfriend called Terry. I was attracted to his boyish charm and his Tiger 110 motorbike. It was the time of mods and rockers. While I was a mod, I enjoyed the best of both worlds. We shared mutual friends at the local youth clubs and went out with my work friends on Saturday nights as a group of eight. We went to the cinema, bowling and out for rides as a couple. Life was good.

Terry had thirteen accidents on his motor bike and I was to join him in the last of these crashes. I suffered two compound fractures, cuts, bruises and a concussion. The accident happened because a car did a U-turn on a busy road and did not notice our motorbike, which hit at the level of the front wheel of the car. Terry slid across the bonnet, tearing a nerve in his leg, while I was catapulted some 30 yards over the front of the motorbike and landed badly on the road. Helmets were optional in those days and it was lucky I had chosen to wear one on the night of the accident, as the helmet had an 'L' shaped rip in it and there is no doubt I would have been killed if it was not for that helmet.

The day of the accident was the day my sister got engaged to Alan, which meant Mum and Dad visited the hospital, then went on to the celebrations. The accident happened on 5th August and I woke up in hospital on 6th August. These dates were to become black days in my calendar as on those days I was to go into hospital for a sinus operation and to be treated for a nervous breakdown. Furthermore, I would be rescued on the M6 after a car I was travelling in broke down in the fast lane of the motor way. It is always a relief to reach mid-August safely!

Up until that time my habit of smoking had been a secret. Dad found out because a friend of his witnessed the accident and told him about the dreadful accident where a young girl was laid out in the road smoking a cigarette. Although Dad had been a heavy smoker himself, he was very disapproving of other smokers who had not gained the victory.

A palmist would say my heart line is long and strong, but my mother's heart line was incredible, as was her ability to care. I have fond memories of the love and support she gave me as she nursed me after the accident. Another of Mum's strengths was her ability to manage money. While I was laid up, Mum took control of my money. When I was better and wanted a coat, she had put aside enough for two coats, and I was probably better off then than at any other time.

I had put my notice in at Eagle Star at the time of the accident, and went back to work six months later with John Harvey Wine Merchants, who kept the job offer open for me. It was incredible to see rush hour traffic stop for me when I needed to cross the road. I was an 18-year-old girl using walking sticks, wearing a mini skirt. The change in job involved two buses across town to work in Whitchurch. The work was interesting and some of the clients were prestigious. Although walking was a challenge, my brain was still quick and I could locate districts from the first two digits of the telephone number or postal code.

It took some time and a few jobs for me to find my niche at work. This happened while I was working as a temp for a secretarial agency. Later on, I took a permanent job at Barnett and Leonard Solicitors. Stanley Trayhurn, who specialised in divorce, was impressed with my work and recommended me to his partner John Foot, who specialised in Conveyancing. I became his secretary. In some jobs I couldn't do anything right, but in this job, it seemed I couldn't do anything wrong. This was my introduction to Dictaphones, which suited me better than shorthand. I have found that the better my senior is at his or her job, the better I am at mine. I became great friends with my colleague Jessie and together we flew through the work. If the secretaries of one of the partners were out, I would step in to help and usually managed to bring their work up to date. Besides John Foot being immaculate at his work, I had no sense of intimidation, which makes a great difference to the quality of my work. With a sense of mischief, I used to enjoy going back to the partners when I had run out of work. Every time, Mr. Trayhurn laughed, Mr. Clough got a little flustered and Mr. Foot gave me a 20-page lease to type.

The over-protected environment of my childhood and school continued at work and in my relationship. Terry and I married five years later in 1969 and we moved to a new house in Whitchurch, which we could afford due to my accident claim. He was an only child. Other than his parents and cousins in Wales, there was little or no exposure to in-laws or the power dynamics within families. I left my lovely job to have a baby.

My life was enriched when Justin was born in September 1974. As a literal person with no experience of babies, I went by the book and now cringe at the fact that I woke him up to give him four-hourly feeds. Luckily, he slept six hours for me through the night.

At 5.30 am I got up with Justin to give him his feed and took the opportunity to use the following three or four hours to get the bulk of the housework done while he slept. In the afternoons we went for walks. Life certainly changed, as everything was geared to baby and his needs.

Every time Justin cried I cried and the health visitor spent time with me. She put my problem down to lack of confidence and wanting to do everything perfectly. Babies lay on their stomachs in those days and each time milk came back and on to the fitted sheet, I changed it.

Life in Whitchurch was good. Terry went out one night a week and I went to the sports centre for keep fit with Janet and Judy, who were neighbours, and into the bar afterwards. We also spent time together sewing, and for a while I was making clothes for Justin and I. My sister was so impressed with one of the dresses, I made one for her. My thoughts went back to my sewing teacher at school, who despaired of me so much that she declared, "You will never pick up a needle again".

I loved my life in Whitchurch. The homes were open plan and we could see the neighbours. We played badminton with our next door neighbours Janet and Neil, over a low fence. Gwen and John lived on the other side and our friendship was like 'the old days'. We used to knock on each other's doors and walk in.

In the early 1970s it was a pleasure to walk to the local shops, where we were served in the old-fashioned way, waiting until the shop assistant finished with the customer in front. Far from being a hardship, it became a social occasion as we chatted to people we knew, instead of standing in a supermarket queue amongst strangers.

I was happy as a young mum in the 1970s as there was still a sense of community and mutual support. I am so pleased that returning to work was not compulsory for young mums. As a result, I avoided divided loyalties and the disruption of my priorities.

Family life was good at that time. Patsy had her two children and I was also a mother. One bus across town enabled us to visit each other. Patsy's daughter Kirstine was born in February 1974 and Justin was born in September of the same year. There are fond memories of the babies playing together, and on one occasion they crawled to the kitchen and showered each other in Ready Brek breakfast cereal. All we could do was laugh and take them into the garden to shake it off.

At Christmas, Patsy invited the whole family to her home from Christmas Eve until Boxing Day. As young people we enjoyed the fun of using sleeping bags in the lounge diner and waking up to the pleasure of all the children being together on Christmas morning. In the ups and downs of life, these were fond and happy memories.

Chapter 3

THE DOWNWARD SPIRAL

My life plan with Terry had been to have three children. The second pregnancy was most welcome for me, coming a little earlier than I had anticipated, as I would have liked to have had a couple of years with Justin before having a second child.   In February 1976 I attended an antenatal session at the health centre. Dr Hughes, my trusted doctor had passed over the clinic to locums and was bringing them into the practice.

After the birth of Justin, I told the midwifery sister that I was anxious about having stitches out. She took me into the operating area and gave me gas and air, but she did not switch it on. This may have been due to a distraction at the time, but my anxiety levels were now heightened as I tried to prepare for a better safeguard should stiches be needed after the second birth. I told Dr Platt, the locum GP who eventually joined the practice, "I have a thing about stitches. Can I please have soluble stitches?" He replied, "No problem" and I went about my pregnancy confident in his word.

1976 was the hottest summer on record at that time and Matthew was born on bonfire night that year. The cord was around Matthew's neck and he was facing the wrong way. Although his birth was over quickly compared to the first, it was traumatic. I had been dosed up with Pethidine and came around when Dr Platt arrived after the birth. I reminded him about the soluble stitches and a sister said, "We don't have any". I passed out and came around to find the doctor had humoured me verbally, but had gone back on his word. He had used ordinary stitches.

I spoke to the senior sister and she promised that I could have a valium injection. When the time came to have the stitches out, she took me to the operating area to give me sedation, put a needle into my arm, and said, "It isn't working". She then put me on gas and air, manhandled me into position and took the stitches out. The mask came away from my mouth as I was distressed with a need to cry, and all that went through my mind was, "I have been conned. I have been conned". I was in shock and feeling badly let down. When it was over I broke down and cried uncontrollably. The staff just left me to it. When I woke up, a new shift had come on duty and staff had given my baby two feeds as I slept due to emotional exhaustion.

In those days mothers stayed in hospital for nine days. For the love of my baby I managed to recover and took him home within the given time. He was a perfect little chap. He slept 12-hour nights when we left hospital and soon went on to sleeping 14 hours. He didn't cry. He waited for his food and after a little grizzle went back to sleep to wake up happy again. To me he was perfect.

After a few days at home I suffered constipation and bled into the toilet. I was beside myself with worry that I had damaged the stitches and could not stop crying, so I was unable to explain what was wrong. Rather than have to explain everything to Dr Hughes, I went to see Dr Platt because he knew about the stiches. As I was leaving the house, Terry said, "Ask for a blood test". I looked at him and said, "Do you think I had an affair?" Terry replied, "No, but I can't see how he can be mine. We didn't make love very often". The remark was so stupid that I did not mention it at that visit, as it took everything I had to keep myself together in order to check if there was a problem with the stitches. They were OK.

Throughout my time with Terry, he said some pretty stupid things and this was no exception. I went for the six-week check-up and did mention to Dr Platt about having a blood test, to shut Terry up. He said, "A blood test would not prove anything and I heard about the denial of paternity from the nurses, as Terry had told them when they had coffee after the birth". I felt so betrayed and this statement put the death blow on my marriage. About 15 years later I mentioned this to Terry and he said, "I did not tell the nurses, but told Dr Hughes some three months before the birth". Dr Platt had lied to me.

The first time I met Dr Platt, after I returned home, he said, "You can come in to talk to me". When I did speak about the stitches he said, "You are becoming neurotic and would have something to worry about if you had cancer". Talk went away from the stiches and on to the marriage, the doctor saying, "Your husband isn't the right man for a woman like you". Dr Platt did not understand and said, "You are confused". I then felt lost and in a state of mental chaos, with a need to understand. When I abandoned my logic, and accepted his, I became completely disturbed and dependent on him to give me all the answers.

Terry did not want to divorce and blamed the doctor for influencing me. I felt again that Terry was not taking responsibility. Just over a year after I gave birth, Terry left the marital home. Forasmuch as I believed I had put everything on the scales to make a balanced decision, I could never have known the emptiness, loneliness and despair I was to feel, or that I was actually a very vulnerable adult about to go out alone in the world.

Life was hard. With no trust in Terry, I chose Social Security as the safer option. The first thing I did was to work out my bills for the year, divide everything by 52 and then set out to put money in a tin to cover our cost of living. Family allowance was put to one side and used for the upkeep of the home and I can remember the sense of pride and achievement as I came home from the post office with my first acquisition, which was a metal tea pot. Any money for the boys went into their Post Office accounts, where it stayed untouched until I gave it to them when they were 18.

Terry left in November. A neighbour came to visit me in early December, because her husband had left and we became good friends and supported each other. Margaret had two boys and we spent many Saturday evenings at the swimming baths, finishing with a chip supper. Although my heart was weighed down with sorrow, and life became heavy going, my boys were the love of my life.

By Christmas I literally had gifts costing £5 for each of my sons. I had formed friendships at Gingerbread, the Association for Lone Parents and my boys were given gifts from the charity. We spent Christmas at my sister's home and she saved the day by buying them lots of toys and clothes to give them a normal Christmas.

Each Christmas we would follow time at Patsy's with a week at Mum and Dad's, returning home in the New Year. We had saved some money and took home a gift of a food parcel. For five years Mum and Dad took us away for a week's holiday either in a cottage at Teignmouth or the Isle of Wight, where the boys enjoyed the beach and had a lovely time.

Mum travelled across town each Tuesday to visit me and each Thursday to visit Patsy. Dad would call after work and Mum and Dad visited on Saturdays, doing odd jobs for me. If anything broke, the children would say, "Nandy will fix it".

Ann was one of my Gingerbread friends. I called one day and Nigel, the curate, was visiting her. He started to visit me and I went back to church. He called at my house almost every day, realising there was a lot of woundedness within me. He had previously worked in psychiatric nursing and was excellent at listening. Women loved him for that ability.

Church life was good in the 1970s and early 80s. Richard the vicar, Nigel, and his wife Jackie were focused on community life. The church hall was a hive of activity with Christmas fairs and other events. Richard and Nigel set the standard and my expectation of clergy for the future. They had set the bar high and after that I was to feel misunderstood by priests and let down by my high expectations.

I had only had one boyfriend and felt my inexperience was to blame for the breakup. Added to that, I had never had a problem of any significance, and felt disadvantaged by my over-protected life. I did have friends and my home was an open house. People called in from early in the morning until later in the day. I did have a few boyfriends to gain some life experience, aware that if I did form a relationship it would have to be marriage, as I was too much of a prude for living together. Although I did not wish to impose my prudish standards on my sons, no-one was allowed to stay the night, unless it was on the sofa. I did not judge others who chose to live together, and sometimes wished I was not so inhibited.

Together with Jackie, who was the curate's wife, and other friends, I attended light education sessions at the Folk House. These sessions were on sociology and psychology. I was fascinated. The leader was Joan Travis, who saw something in me and felt I should focus on working with people. I started reading pop psychology books, and was struck by the fact that many had spiritual themes running through them. Joan introduced me to an O Level Sociology Book. After reading the first page, I had not understood one word, but as time went on I started adopting a sociological language. When my mother visited, she said to me, "I always thought you were dim, but now I don't know what you are talking about".

I started part-time work at a youth club for long term unemployed people in Knowle West, which was a neighbouring district. Employment had for many years been plentiful for the majority, but in response to inflation, mass unemployment was brought about by Margaret Thatcher. Initially there was an outcry from the public and the media at the hard heartedness as people lost their jobs and their homes. Jobs were lost throughout the ranks, but the people at the top were able to take a step down. It was the workers at the bottom who fell off the work ladder, leaving the working class with all their energy and no work.

The employment situation was madness - shoe shops were asking for applicants to have six O' Levels. Wages were an insult. Rather than full time jobs, Sunday became a working day, which made church attendance difficult. The creation of extra jobs reduced the numbers on the unemployment register. This was all a manipulation for the sake of statistics. At the start, people applying for work were told they did not have to work Sundays and could attend church. Within a short while employment was offered only to those who would work Sundays.

Pretty soon the media swung into action and the victims within the system became vilified as scroungers. In the main, the youth club unemployment facilities were used by boys, as they came in to play snooker or table tennis. Girls came in once a week, but the girls were not so much into playing, but needed something constructive to do.

Mike from the employment service used to visit, and I tried to motivate young people to find work. Very little seemed to happen for young unemployed people, and I felt like a babysitter for young adults. Some of the boys got into trouble with the law and I was pleased to set up five-a-side football with the police and the boys. One day, three of the lads were to appear in court. I went with them in the morning, but had to leave at lunch time, before they heard their verdict. That gesture made an incredible difference and formed a bond, as no one else went with them to give support.

I kept in touch with Joan, who informed me that Community Programmes were to be set up, giving long term unemployed the chance of work experience for up to a year. Alongside my work with long-term unemployed, I helped with a church youth club in Whitchurch, and was receiving training in youth work.

In November 1982, Geoff knocked on my door. We had a mutual friend, Rita, who lived in Italy. He called for her address, saying he wanted to write to her. A while later Geoff called again, asking to check the address, as he hadn't heard from her. This was a ploy to meet me, but I was green and accepted him at his word. Geoff said that he was celebrating his birthday and would I make up the numbers for him? I said, "Yes. As I am not interested in relationships, I am happy to be friends". Geoff agreed. Geoff went on to say, "I pass your place of work each morning and could give you a lift". I accepted.

Geoff called quite regularly and bonded with my children. Although I had no plans for a relationship, I found myself falling for this very kind person, and affection was forming between us with a sense of family. This was wonderful after being traumatically betrayed in my first marriage. One day, Geoff took us out and bought Justin a pair of Dunlop trainers and a pair of shoes for Matthew. Justin was over the moon at having shoes with a label and Matthew had to be carried from the car into the house for fear he would damage the shoes!

During the war Geoff was still a child. His parents and extended family stayed at Clevedon. Originally, they used an old bus body, progressing to caravans. They continued to visit at weekends and Bank Holidays, and some still have caravans at Clevedon. The family enjoyed many carnivals, fancy dress parties and celebrations, most of them captured on cine camera.

Geoff had been married before. It was quite an incestuous marriage in that his ex-wife and he were both related to the same cousin on either side of his family. The ex-wife fitted in very well with the family and kept contact after their split. Geoff could not have children, and his ex-wife committed adultery, having one termination and a baby by another man. Geoff was devastated and divorced her because of it. To avoid pity and having his life taken over by his family, he took work in the Middle East.

Early in our courtship, Geoff introduced me to his youngest brother Chris and sister-in-law Ann. Chris was pleased for Geoff and brought gifts of chocolate for Justin and Matthew. Quite possibly, Chris was one of the nicest men I had ever met. He started his career as a ladies' hairdresser and then went on to transporting children with special needs to school.

One day, Geoff and I were at my home and the telephone rang. I answered to hear a man on the other end saying, "I am from the Salvation Army and Geoff isn't a man of this world". This made Geoff sound quite odd. I felt a bit uncertain after the call and it did cast some doubt on Geoff. I looked up the Salvation Army in the phone book and rang them, relaying the conversation. Geoff was quite disturbed to hear me pass on the story to the Salvation Army. They had not phoned me. It was a hoax, and when I gave the man the telephone number of the hoax caller Geoff recognised it as belonging to his other brother, who I will call Damian. Geoff was incensed, and was going to cut him out of his life. I said, "He was probably feeling left out and perhaps I should meet with him".

We went to visit Geoff's brother Damian and sister-in-law, who I will call Carmel. She laughed saying, "It wasn't anything to do with me", treating it as a joke. If it had been a joke, they would have been decent to me, but after that Geoff would walk in followed by the boys, then my sister-in-law totally ignored me. That was typical of our relationship. Exclusion is a female form of bullying, and Damian has used not only exclusion as his form of bullying, but putting nasty remarks behind smiles and laughter. No-one could have known how timid I was in the early days, but they decided that Geoff leaving the caravan group was my doing and I was the leader. As I was told many years later, Damian set out to do everything he could to put me down. He even used extended family to gang up on me. Ganging up on a person in this way actually comes under the dictionary definition of 'mafia'.

I have heard that all families are dysfunctional, but to me Geoff's family has to be the ultimate dysfunctional family. Geoff is the eldest son and, like my father, has suffered 'little man syndrome'. Damian has middle child syndrome, and when he was a child the parents were advised by a child psychiatrist, "Damian feels he can't win. Let him win without knowing you are letting him". Chris was the youngest and painfully thin as a child, and was allowed to eat cake and anything that would increase his weight. Everyone pandered to Damian. Chris was selfless, and I never heard him ask for anything for himself.

Geoff and I married on a beautiful day in July. Our lovely vicar, Richard, took the service and we held the reception at the house, where guests were able to overflow into the garden. Justin and Matthew were page boys and looked wonderful in their outfits. They rose to the occasion and enjoyed the day.

As Chris had been best man at Geoff's first wedding, Damian was best man at ours. As I look back on the photographs, Damian and Carmel looked miserable. I was very happy and pleased with my yellow two-piece outfit that went well with white accessories. A friend told me that my sister-in-law was catty and when my friend told her that Lynn had a choice of two outfits, she replied "Perhaps the other would have looked better".

Geoff and I both went into marriage with emotional baggage that was hard to overcome. Many years later it got back to me that Damian 'advised' Geoff how to treat me within the marriage, but I am very pleased to say that despite experiencing horrendous problems, we have survived.

As I had no experience of travel, Geoff arranged the honeymoon. We went to Spetsis, a Greek Island. Other than delivery vehicles there were no cars on the island and no telephones. Emergency calls went from a loud speaker on a boat out at sea. It was wonderful, but nothing prepared me for the roller coaster ride that was to follow.

Chapter 4

THE DARK NIGHT OF THE SOUL

Life seemed as though it was about to improve for me, but what I didn't realise was that I was entering 'the dark night of the soul', which means death of the old self. This brought about the birth of a new and better person. I was to experience a catalyst for change that I certainly would not have chosen for myself. Eventually I came out on the other side richer, wiser and better for the experience.

Eckhart Tolle is the author of *The Power of Now*, *A New Earth* and *Awakening to Your Life's Purpose*. He describes 'the dark night of the soul' as 'a term to describe what one could call a collapse of a perceived meaning in life ... an eruption into your life of a deep sense of meaninglessness. This inner state in some cases is very close to what is conventionally called 'depression'. Nothing makes sense anymore - there's no purpose to anything'. I can certainly agree with this definition.

I started my new job in June 1983 and got married a month later. The changes were incredible. After living on my own with a lot of time to spare, the only time I had to myself was a ten-minute drive to work. I was in Geoff's house, which was a new environment for me, and I felt homesick for my old home.

As a Supervisor for a government community programme project, it was my job to set up and run a scheme for unemployed people. They would have up to a year's work experience, during which time they would find employment. Their task was to provide a care service for elderly and housebound people in Knowle West, which was an estate close to home.

To start with, all I had was a pad and pen. With that I went out to meet people. My friend Yvonne had been an assistant matron in a home for people with dementia. I went for coffee with her, taking notes about caring for elderly patients and those with dementia. She taught me the difference between the two.

Social workers were particularly helpful, and met with me to discuss the needs of people living in the district. There was provision through health workers, church and home help. My aim was not to duplicate services, but to fill the gaps. One way we did this was by visiting and if a client needed a doctor or an ambulance, we would wait with them. We fetched prescriptions, accompanied patients to hospital and visited while they were there. When they got home we would visit to ensure that they had milk and other essentials.

My team received a commendation from Social Services because we backed social workers when roads were difficult during a severe winter, and reported back to give assurance that their clients were safe and well. At Christmas time some staff members visited clients, taking them a Christmas dinner.

There was little or no support for me within the workplace. The group was made up primarily of male workers for gardening and decorating. The money allocated for female workers was used for gardening and other equipment. I was marginalised because I was in another building and my task was different. I was thirsty for knowledge, and probably came over as intense and strange to the social workers while I drank in all they told me.

Home life was hard as I was working full-time, coming home to cook and clean. The bedroom extension was finished, but Geoff had plans for a lot of building work. He wanted our first Christmas at home and I said that I could not cook for ten people in the very small kitchen. He started work converting the garage into a kitchen. At the same time, he knocked through the old kitchen and dining room. Each day I was coming home to dust throughout the home.

My home in Charnwood Road sold in October of that year and by Christmas the kitchen was finished. The demolished kitchen/dining room looked a dreadful sight, and I asked Geoff if we could get this sorted. He replied, "We have run out of money". I was horrified because when the money for the house went into the joint account I had said, "I haven't had much of a life – keep some money back so that we can go on holidays". He replied "Ok" at the time but now the money was gone.

In order to get money for the dining room, I stopped buying the food shopping and put it towards the cost of the building work. This was the start of going into debt.

Geoff found it difficult for me to do housework in the home. I wondered if his mother only did housework when in a bad mood. It took many years to realise that it was about Geoff being territorial. He showed little or no appreciation for my efforts. My home started to lose its meaning.

The worst part was what happened to my relationship with my boys. Geoff's desire to be a father was so great that I got marginalised as a mother. They were not allowed to be dependent on me. When they asked me for a drink Geoff would say, "Get it yourself". When little Matthew wanted to hold my hand, Geoff would say, "Walk on", although it was ok for Matthew to hold Geoff's hand. Geoff always gave the boys lifts home, well into their adulthood. He would sleep on the sofa until he received a phone call from them. They remained dependent on Geoff into adulthood.

I sank into depression and spent a lot of time in bed, smoked heavily and drank wine to escape my feelings. The consequence of all this was that Geoff looked like a saint, while I looked like the villain of the piece. I appeared to be an awful person, expressing my distress through shouting and swearing.

The life I was living was not the life I had signed up for. I hated TV and when courting, Geoff did not have the TV on. Once married, the TV went on first thing in the morning and off last thing at night. He was a television addict, always needing noise in the background.

Geoff set up a five-year work plan for the house. Other than going out for meals we had no quality time as a family, as Geoff did building work – or nothing. He took his place in the home and I worked round him. One person came into the home, saw my office and said, "Geoff should have this as it is the best room". That was pure sexism, as Geoff took the TV room and I had what was left, which was the room with no TV. I used to withdraw on to the fringes of family life into isolation. The room has since become my sanctuary. I now have my office at one end of it and relaxation space with music at the other.

In the main, Geoff is the easiest going person in the world, and it seemed as though everyone else saw this while I suffered the more cussed side of him. My friend Yvonne called me the downtrodden wife'; while at least one person, a lady who was a gossip, saw me as someone who had been taken off the streets and said that I should be grateful.

The reality is that when I was distressed, Geoff was at his most difficult and the more difficult he got, the more distressed I became. Geoff's family could never know the damage they had caused, not only to me, but also to Geoff and our children.

Geoff's mother was a hefty woman and her sons were not allowed to say no to her. Two of the sons told lies and set up scapegoats rather than be seen as blameworthy in a problem family. On two occasions Geoff's mother pushed me, and if I had not taken running steps I would have fallen over. On one of the occasions I called out to my boys to go careful with the football, as the neighbours got upset when it went over fences. "Go on" she said, with an almighty shove.

A friend of mine asked Geoff, "What was it you liked about Lynn?" He answered, "She always told the truth, whereas I always told lies". I know telling lies was something that bothered Geoff, because he joined me at church and wanted to tackle this as part of his confirmation class.

Some years later I was to learn about displacement. This is key in 'middle child syndrome', where often the displaced child moves away. Alternatively, like Damian, they move to displace others. A child is not able to get angry with a person who provokes their anger, so expresses that anger towards an easy target. This helps me understand my brother-in-law and how he set out to bully and displace me.

Before we met, Geoff spent three months living in Italy after working abroad for four years. He stayed with a cousin named Clare and Rita, our mutual friend. Clare had it worked out that when she came back home, Geoff would be her companion and do all her jobs around the flat. When he married me, I became demonised for scuppering her plans. Each time we met, Clare and her sister Madge called me 'Jayne'. This was the name of Geoff's ex-wife. I discussed this with a health worker and her advice was to play her at her own game and use a name that was just slightly different from her real name. I did and Madge reeled back saying "Aww". She hasn't spoken to me since.

Geoff fitted in well with my family, who were always generous at letting people in. My father treated Geoff like the son he had always wanted. They saw eye to eye in many ways, helped by the fact that they were both short.

For all the negativity in my life, there were strong positives. I had an incredible faith in God, but made the mistake of looking to the church for healing. Tony De Mello says, "We think people have let us down, but the truth is we have misjudged them". My belief system was certainly going to be subjected to a massive collapse and would need rebuilding.

At church one day I went for coffee and met a lovely lady named Jackie Clarke. We chatted and I asked her what she did. She replied, "I was trained in singing and dancing, but life circumstances drew me in another direction". Jackie had a severely disabled son and spent most of her life fighting the system in order to obtain better health and social care for her boy. She went on to say that she was a counsellor, and I asked for an appointment.

Can you imagine groping your way around in the dark, bumping into furniture, and then someone switching on the lights so that you can see? That is how it was after spending time with Jackie. She was a re-evaluation counsellor, having trained in the school of Harvey Jackins. Jackie was an expert in oppression studies and taught me, as I explained my life and what had happened.

Oppression might be 'I am a doctor, you will do what I say'. Internalised oppression is 'I am the patient, I have to do what the doctor says'. What holds the oppressive way of life in place is the fear within the oppressed.

I was an extremely timid person. My voice was light and high pitched, becoming more so when I got distressed. For some reason, other people saw me as powerful and I could never understand how they could see this. The in-laws saw me as the power who took Geoff away rather than Geoff wanting a different way of life.

My way of shopping for clothes was always to look at the price tag and search within my range. My friend Yvonne was a classy dresser and Geoff said, "Don't look at the price tag, but look at what you like". With my new earnings I was able to do this and found that I had good taste. I didn't realise it, but the suits I felt best in added up to power dressing. I felt the same inside, but could forget about myself and get on with the task. I had little self-awareness.

With Jackie's help, I could see oppression in all aspects of my life. She also explained that as children some of our needs do not get met so get carried over into adulthood. They then become frozen so they can never be met because they belong to a time gone past. The solution is to revisit at the emotional age it happened and release the emotion from there.

By the time I met Jackie, I was well read and able to contribute the ideas of parent/adult/child within us. Jackie was able to relate to my learning as an expert in re-evaluation counselling. I made great progress with her and she said of me, "I have never known anyone pick up the ball and run with it as you do".

The job at Knowle Initiative lasted for four years. I was proud of my achievement, having based my own care on values inherited from my mother and religious principles. My group was described as 'as professional as possible for a non-professional group'.

Towards the end of my work as a supervisor, my friend Brenda came to me and said that management were creaming thousands of pounds off the programme. My first reaction was to think she was wrong. She said, "I was a captain in the army and an army friend had been digging and pulling strings for the team". Brenda said, "Your job will be made permanent and the community aid team will get more members of staff". These things did happen and the team that started as twelve members of staff became a team of sixty.

The mysterious friend was never proved to be right and I became obsessional about knowing what was happening. The first manager had lost his job because of dishonesty. After I did fund raising to replace the missing money, it seemed there was more dishonesty. On top of that, my team had suffered a couple of thefts from handbags. I lost sleep and was heading for my first psychotic breakdown.

It was difficult not knowing the truth of the matter. The only other likelihood for my elevation was that one member of staff wrote to the Community programme saying, "You will never have another supervisor like Lynn". It is possible that rather than the information coming from an army friend, gossip could have been coming from head office with feedback to Brenda, who told me, "Management think you have someone in Community Programme pulling these strings for you". On top of all the other problems, I then suffered bullying from management.

Sinus problems raged and I went into hospital as a private patient. On my return the stress at work was as bad, if not worse. I suffered my first psychotic episode, which means I went high, relating life back to the Bible and lost touch with reality. I got through on my own. Stress continued and I left the job to prevent another breakdown.

Geoff could not cope with my distress and our marriage was in crisis. It was difficult at the time of nervous breakdown for me to realise that people who loved me also suffered. After a year home from work, I was to go into breakdown again. When I shared my distress with Geoff, he would reply equally distressed, saying that people only wanted me because of what I did for them. I have come to realise Geoff was describing his experience with family and friends, not my own.

I got back into life quite quickly and played safe by working as a temporary secretary. One of my assignments was with the health service, working for the recruitment and allocations officer. Maureen Dore and her lovely secretary Ann loved working with me. I could fully express myself and when I left they bought me perfume that they felt described my personality, which was *Panache*. My contribution was enthusiastic, but certainly not perfect. I decided that companies rated me not on the standard of my work, but on their level of liking for me.

Work for the health service was so enjoyable that I applied for a job at Barrow Mental Health Hospital as a secretary for the training department. It was while I worked in this department that I identified the sexual abuse I had suffered which was the reason for the collapse of my life. This was a very difficult time and I had to take some time off work to cope.

I loved working in the training department, but hankered for more. This was around 1990 when the role of student nurse was to change. Students were not to have nursing responsibilities, but were to take more of a student role, while health care assistants were being brought in to perform lesser tasks. I applied to be a health care assistant and was accepted.

My time as a worker in the psychiatric field was quite difficult. At interview I said how important training was to me, and I was put on a ward that had little or no interest in staff training, although other wards were keen on training. This was stressful for me, as I needed 150% theory before feeling confident enough to put my toe in the water. Another difficulty was that what was taught in my training did not apply on the ward. It was years later that I learned that what is taught is best practice, but that does not necessarily get carried through.

Health for my sister, father and mother became difficult. I received a phone call saying that my sister was having an emergency operation for a brain tumour and had a 50/50 chance of surviving. It was fortunate she did survive as she had Faron and Kirstine, who were still young children.

Dad had chronic back problems and it looked likely that he would need an operation, with the warning that he could end up paralysed. As it happened, Dad did not go for an operation, but after Mum had been vomiting blood for a considerable time she went for hospital tests.

Mum was a person who buried her head in the sand and did not want to know the result of the test. We all sensed that she had cancer, but for her sake took the unhealthy option of not talking about it. Mum went in for an operation, but after cutting her open she was sewn back up. There was nothing they could do. The distressing thing was that the doctor told Mum about cancer, but left us thinking everything was ok.

As I went to do something for Mum, she did what she had done all her life and said, "No". I said to her, "When are you going to let me in Mum?" Things changed from that point. I gave up my job, money, and hope of a pension to be with her. I got up at ridiculously early times and drove across town to be with Mum at the hospital early. When staff went to wash Mum, she said, "I want Lynn to do it". When we took Mum out in the wheelchair, Dad would ram the bumps in the pavement and Mum would say, "Let Lynn push it". Dad was not happy about my new place in the scheme of things.

In playing the game with Mum, we nursed her at home. I left my family and moved in with Mum for three weeks. My sister Patsy kept her distance and Dad had to call her in to help. Patsy took a week's holiday and after that week on 20th July 1992 Mum, who was reduced to skin and bones, died at 1.00 pm from stomach cancer. The nursing staff congratulated me on the standard of nursing, as Mum had suffered not even one bed sore. For my mother's sake I was glad her suffering was over. For myself, I was devastated, feeling stunned and shocked at the loss.

Chapter 5

BETRAYAL

Following the death of Mum, Patsy and I stayed with Dad for a further week until the funeral. This was possibly the darkest, heaviest time of my life. After holding up to give Dad support, I needed love, comfort and inclusion to get through my grief. Instead, Dad and Patsy were making a new order, as he elevated her as first lady and she gladly stepped up to the plate. Patsy faced Dad, smoothing his jacket and removing bits from his shoulders. It was a similar action that revealed Princess Margaret's affair. Dad and Patsy walked side by side, while I trailed behind, lost and lonely in my grief.

I hear certain sayings, but they don't have full meaning until they apply to me personally e.g. 'Death makes or breaks families'. It was common to hear that families have problems, even fighting at family events. I could never imagine our family having such problems, but it became clear that Mum had held the family together, and it was about to suffer a break that was never to be repaired.

After the death, life felt unreal. The family got together regularly and, unusually for us, we went to the pub quite often for meals and to be together. It was as though my world was in slow motion and I was peeping out to see people laughing and celebrating. It was surreal.

The funeral took place at 9.30 in the morning and Dad chose not to put on a reception afterwards. Dad said, "Hold up, hold up for me". I was later to realise that Dad meant he could not face his own emotion or give emotional support. I did hold up for Dad and Dad's friend said that I seemed high. For the rest of the day I felt so lost, going to see neighbours as I did not know what to do with myself.

Geoff was very upset that I had stayed away under such difficult circumstances. He said, "We all suffered badly with you away. I wish you had come home".

I did not work for almost a year and Matthew asked if his friend Alex could live with us for a while. They were gearing towards their GCSE exams and it was a pleasure to have Alex with us.

My health was suffering due to stomach problems. I was referred to the hospital for tests. I explained to the person doing the exam that I had suffered a breakdown because of medical intervention and we chatted through it. The hospital gave me a date to go back for the result. I was really pleased as I got through it safely – or so I thought.

Within a short time, I was going high, which meant becoming elated, running at high speed and not sleeping. I was heading for my third episode of psychosis. For the first breakdown I was in the dark with no understanding, for the second I identified sexual abuse and after the third I was certain that invasive medical intervention was a significant trigger for a psychotic episode.

True to pattern, as I got more distressed Geoff could not cope, and our marriage was again in crisis and I was in the early stages of breakdown. I went to spend time at Dad's house. As a spiritual person I badly needed healing, but had no faith in the medical profession. As a child I wanted to be a nun and now I could no longer cope in the world. I asked Dad to take me close to my home to visit a nun at the convent. I had met her on a training course and from visits to the district. I took my slippers – I was going home.

If Josie the nun had sat and chatted to me, I believe it would have been OK and I would have gone home. Instead, she went upstairs and left me alone. Unknown to me, she was phoning people for advice and their advice was to call the emergency services. A psychiatrist, GP and social worker arrived to see me.

With my experience of doctors, I chose to speak with the social worker and was so pleased he was there, as after working with this fantastic group of people in the past, it was a huge relief to have him there. They would like to have sectioned me, but fortunately my father agreed that I could stay with him. I warned the group that I could not take anti-psychotic medication due to the side effects. I was prescribed Haloperidol, which is probably the worst drug they could have given me. The only drug that had helped me was Flupenthixol, but the doctor wanted 'the big guns' and ignored my request. In large doses, Flupenthixol is for psychotic disorders, but in smaller doses it can be used for anxiety.

Fortunately, I had regained contact with Helen, my first nurse, and we were due to meet during my difficult period. My agitation was chronic and she went back to work and phoned my wonder doctor James, telling him that I had the worst side effects she had ever seen. After that, James telephoned Dad's surgery. Within a few days I was able to go back to Dad's doctor and say, "Phew, that's better. I can go home now", which would put me in touch with the one doctor who could help me.

Within my situation, stress was the forerunner to psychosis, which meant that I needed help for both stress and sleep. According to doctors, psychosis is a disease and they wanted to come in with 'big gun' medication that was chronically harmful for me.

The surge of adrenalin and energy within psychosis is incredible and I did not feel I could survive another episode. My great fear was that if doctors took it out of my hands again, I would end up abused. It would happen all over again and I could not survive more of the same.

I found employment quite quickly, taking the safer option of part-time work with a secretarial agency. Work was sporadic. Placements required new packages, such as PowerPoint and spreadsheets. While I had some training in these areas and the agency had trained me for specific tasks in the past, young people who had gained experience through schools and colleges were used for the best jobs.

In order to have regular, part-time work I went for two interviews. One was with the police as a clerk putting data on a computer and the other with the health service. I had accepted the job with the police before the health service also offered me a job. I chose to work with the police.

Things did not go well for me. While clerical work is lower paid and less technical than secretarial work, it is an entirely different skill set. Through the passing of time and further understanding, I can see that the culture, my training needs and the work were a total mismatch. I had developed into a thinking person and that certainly wasn't wanted as a clerk and I was a threat to some people.

My best experience was working for an Inspector named Andy Bennett. He was highly respected by his staff and definitely had my loyalty. He looked to my strengths and how best he could use me. Again, in a safe and friendly environment I did well with my work. Unsurprisingly, Andy left the station for promotion. My conclusion with lovely people who act as a buffer between me and a problem is that when they leave, the weight of the problem is felt tenfold. Within a short period of time I left the job feeling depressed and suicidal. By then my lovely James had left his position as GP and a lesser doctor did nothing to help, other than signing me off sick for the duration of my notice, and then put me on a list of the chronically mentally ill.

As usual, Patsy hogged the lion's share of family relationships, but I did call over to Dad's house and he came to visit us. After visits and often during, my mood and energy dropped to a terrible low. When he chatted, he was locked into Geoff and I was sitting outside of it all. One day he walked in the front door and said, "I like your rose tree". I thanked him and he went on to say, "Better than that bloody thing I have in the back garden". That 'bloody thing' in his back garden was my gift to Mum when she was dying, so that she had something pretty to look out on. It was an apple blossom.

Dad used coaches for short stay holidays. He came home from one trip saying that a lady had asked to join his table as she was on her own, and a young couple were hogging all the food on her table. Dad went on to say that he had asked her to join him for coffee. I was really pleased as Dad was far more likely to live longer if he was happy. He had taken Mum's death very badly. He coped well with the practical side of life, but was not doing well emotionally. After telling me, he then told Patsy, who responded, "Well, it is not as though you are getting married". They were married before the second anniversary of Mum's death.

Patsy always knew how to play the game and bought Nora cards that said, "You are like a mother to me". For some reason I could see daggers of hate coming from Nora's eyes towards me. I can think of two possibilities for her hate. One was that she didn't remember having a father as he died when she was 18 months old and Dad would have told her how inseparable we were when I was little. The other thing was that Nora could not cope if everything did not go through her and I usually went straight to Dad.

When the family got together, Nora did not converse, but did a monologue, telling us all how wonderful she had been all her life, the best daughter and the best worker. By this time Justin had a girlfriend called Beccy and when we were around the table together I could see her sinking in her chair, as we couldn't speak to each other while the monologue was on. When there was a break I would ask someone else a question, in an attempt to change the atmosphere.

While Dad and Nora stayed at my home, I could hear her running me down to Dad, but Dad stayed quiet and did not answer. Patsy gave her full support for her own

purposes, but told me what had been said about me. I
called a meeting with Dad, Nora, Patsy, Geoff and myself.
Nora said that I did not want them to get married and I had
said awful things about Dad. By then Dad was registered
blind, but the situation was untenable and I walked away
never to see Dad again. Finally, I also cut off from Patsy, as
she invited everyone to Christmas events, which rubbed
salt into my wounded life of exclusion. Dad died 20+ years
after Mum and survived his second wife, who was older
than he was. I was cut out of the will and Patsy inherited
the entire estate.

On the brighter side, a promotion came through my
post box for training as a Life Coach. I had received life
coaching to help a colleague who was training. I signed up
with The Coaching Academy, not to make money as a
coach, but to have access to coaching, as I love the way it
keeps what is important on track and I have made great
progress from the support I received.

As a non-academic I froze when it was time to answer
ten questions. With support and encouragement, I
completed the questions and passed the diploma with
distinction. After qualifying as a coach, I attended a
support meeting for coaches. Literally within a month of
starting with the group, a man promoted Toast Masters
International. Forasmuch as I loved helping people
progress through coaching, my greatest need was to be
heard. I changed direction and spent two years at Toast
Masters on fast track, where I achieved Competent
Communicator and Evaluator. In addition, I learned a
variety of management skills by experiencing all the roles I
needed in order to run events, from timing talks, to
evaluating the whole evening. It felt good that I had gained
competence and a way forward for speaking out to right
some of the wrongs in an oppressive world.

I went to various agencies and asked them to include
me as a speaker. The Director of Bristol Mind included me
in one of his sessions at the University of the West of
England (UWE). The next year I approached the

university. As the Director did not receive funding to continue his role with MIND and I had received good evaluations from the students, I was taken on to be part of student training.

At UWE I met a man named Tony Fraher, who championed the cause for service user involvement. This was to enable students to learn not only from theory, but also from the experience of people who had suffered illness and from the misuse of power dynamics within the professions. Tony became my buddy and worked for me to have inclusion in almost everything. Throughout nursing, professional conduct dictates that staff and patients do not socialise. The hardest part for Tony was detaching from those teachings and accepting me as a colleague. He eventually became good friends with my family. After that I did workshops at Bristol Royal Infirmary where I started teaching on mental health and later switched to teaching on the subject of Asperger's.

One day I attended a meeting for research at the university. People gathered outside in the sunshine before the meeting. It was there that I met Rae, a pretty petite blonde lady, who was sitting in an electric wheelchair. This meeting was to be the start of huge changes – my belief system was about to be turned upside down.

Rae said, "I am an astrologer and psychologist. I work with people who the services have given up on". As was quite normal for me, I told her about my experience with doctors and Rae invited me to join her at her home. This was to be the start of a lifelong friendship and we are now as 'sisters in spirit'.

In Rae's past she had met a psychologist who became a friend and spent hours helping her at no charge. Rae wanted to give back and left her family and home in Ireland to come to England in order to study. She gave to me, as her friend had given to her, and did not charge for all the wonderful help I received.

From the outset and before doing an astrology chart,

Rae identified me as a typical Cancerian. She said, "Your sun and moon are in Cancer. No one in the universe is more of a Mother than you". As a Jungian psychologist Rae explained, "You have to go careful, because in addition to being the good mother, there is also the devouring mother". With hindsight I can see that as part of having Asperger's my excessive thought processes have been overwhelming, as have my enthusiasms to love through giving, helping and saving the world!

Rae also said that when she did a chart, she would not work with the person if the chart was neat and tidy, as it meant the person was having an easier time than in previous lives, but took on people whose charts were topsy turvy. My chart showed lines shooting all over the place and from this Rae deduced, "You have a large dharma, which means you came into the world to fulfill spiritual duties".

I learned that a lot of my unhappiness was because there was a great difference between the way I believed the world should be and the way it was. I had been brought up in a standard working-class family and attended church. My beliefs about life were in line with what Rae described as 'patriarchal ideology'. This meant that I lived to the male-controlled ideal of how life should be lived.

Rae, on the other hand, went to church at the age of six, noticed that it was all male with no female and did not go back. Rae had a strong spiritual leaning towards the Goddess and all that was natural, including homeopathy. She is a feminist. We build our world on our beliefs and over a period of time my belief system was to be turned upside down. Generally, I was confused and disturbed by the breaking down of old beliefs and felt happier when my thinking became clear.

My family had fallen apart. Although my sons had grown up and had partners, the girls did not want to know me and relationships were fractious. Relationships with doctors were at an all-time low and it seemed I couldn't get on with anyone. I had a compulsion to understand and that compulsion broke through into writing and trying to justify what had happened to my family. Rae's approach to psychology was to know who we are, warts and all and to accept who we are. She helped me to understand other people and where they had gone wrong, but equally to realise where I had gone wrong and what that meant for the other person.

I was introduced to several conspiracy theories and Rae gave me leads to understanding them for myself. It was eye opening and quite incredible to see the evils that would take place to bring about the ultimate male-domination of a one world order. The words 'conspiracy theories' are used to dismiss concerns about what is happening under the cloak of darkness and what might happen in the future. What does strike me is that gross atrocities have happened in the past that can only be described as mass genocide of indigenous people such as witches and Native American Indians. These have all been trivialized.

Another introduction was to Bristol Disability Equality Forum, where I met some incredible people who campaign for the rights of disabled people. Far from being shirkers, work done by the members was amazing. My connection with the group was in line with my beliefs and efforts for equality. Rae was highly respected in the group as a powerful lady who worked hard and achieved great things.

Within my life I had faced some difficult things, such as revealing sexual abuse. I have also done some difficult things, such as giving up smoking. Rae was about to say something that would blow my mind and shatter my world. She said, "I think you have Asperger's Syndrome". After years of working to lift inappropriate mental health labels, this one felt right and all I could think was, "There is something wrong with me after all". I cried.

45

Chapter 6

ASPERGER'S

When the bottom fell out of my world at the age of 28, I set out to make sense of it. Some 30 years on, the new world on which I had built my beliefs was falling apart again. I was like the proverbial ship that began its journey one degree adrift, but ended up hundreds of miles off course. The really good thing about identifying Asperger's was that I now had a point of reference with which to understand and navigate my life.

Rae felt terrible that her discovery had upset me so badly and regretted telling me. She said to me a short while later, "You would rather have a bad truth than a good lie".

The first thing for me to realise was that people are frightened by what they don't understand, so they work to scare away or kill off the perceived danger. After thirty years of independent working to overcome medical abuse, there was another hard slog in front of me and another mountain to climb, still carrying the same emotional baggage.

Rae explained that I had High Functioning Asperger's, which means I am mildly autistic. People with Asperger's look out of a different window on the world and take in information differently. They arrive at divergent conclusions compared with the average person. I could picture the majority of people looking out of the front window where there was a main road with cars and people walking by, while I looked out of the back window by myself seeing a garden, with flowers and birds in a tree. Neither view was wrong, but I had heard so many times over the years that I was in the wrong – perhaps I wasn't after all.

Although autism lies on a spectrum with a lot of variance, people with this diagnosis share some common traits, such as being literal and not understanding nuances or hidden agendas. I progressed from vulnerable child to vulnerable adult because high levels of trust and expectation led either to people thinking I was stupid or to me being bullied.

Within the medical profession, Asperger's is classed as a hidden disability because it is not obvious to the uninformed. Since Asperger's is such a recent realisation, it has been hidden not only from the medical profession and society generally, but also from the people who experience the condition.

To make a comparison – I am left-handed and have learned to adapt to a right-handed world. In addition, there have been some adaptations by the world in recent years, but there are times when I can't adjust and there is nothing to meet my requirements. At university there are chairs with either left or right-handed tables. When there are no left-handed tables I feel a sense of deflation, because there is no provision for me. When I try to use a chair with a right-handed table, my body is twisted and uncomfortable, taking some of my attention away from the task and towards the discomfort.

Left-handedness is realised. Although there is more provision these days, my granddaughter Hollie, who is also left-handed, hates it when she is doing sewing at school and she has to traipse around classrooms looking for left-handed scissors. If a sense of handicap is felt with left-handedness, which is realised and visible, imagine how handicapped a person with Asperger's feels when they are misunderstood, mistreated and distressed because needs cannot be met.

I have felt deflated when telling friends or family that I have Asperger's only to be told, "No, you don't have Asperger's". Some people's response to me is that I am lying, most especially an elderly neighbour who was part of my past. Despite the fact that I have spent years trying to understand, people seem to think their opinion of who I am is more important than my own self-knowledge.

In life, people don't like to ask for what they want, so they play games, often making the other person think the suggestion is theirs. Asperger people can't do this. Because I am direct and ask straight out for what is wanted, it is seen as bossy and demanding and people have set out to prevent me from meeting my need. This adds to my distress, which in turn reinforces the opinion that I am a difficult person. I have heard it said that this is the biggest injustice that people with Asperger's suffer.

I attended a course for health workers, which showed that the average person deals with feelings at gut level, but people with Asperger's can't do this. I am typical of someone who has to take my feelings through the intellect. Since I can't see at an instinctive unconscious level, I have to make sense by intellectualising so I can understand at a conscious level. The result is that I have become articulate on complex matters.

Senses are either hyper or hypo and examples were given of people not feeling the cold and wearing tee shirts when it was snowing. This described me when I was younger. The tutor explained that Aspies, as we are affectionately called, often couldn't tell if the opposite sex were attracted to them. This also applied to me, contributing to my vulnerability as I just thought men were being friendly.

My sense of hearing is hyper, more so when stressed. My hearing was tested and I was classified hyper acoustic, which is in the same category as tinnitus, because noises that should be filtered out are not. Noise that does not affect others can be highly distressing for me. Another chance for the medical profession to identify Asperger's was missed.

My worst experience is at the cinema, where the sound of sweet wrappers, people eating noisily and texting are examples of noises that draw me away from the film and towards the noise. The noises that cause me most distress are the same as I made in childhood, resulting in a screech attack from my sister.

One year I went away for a few days with Rita, a friend of mine. We went to see a show at Torquay Theatre, where my friend took an aisle seat in front of me. I heard talking from somewhere behind me. I looked round, as it seemed safer to locate the noise and the man behind me said, "What are you looking at"? I answered, "Someone is talking". I didn't realise it, but it was his friend who had been talking. He set out to attack me with a tirade, "You miserable cow, he has got a right to talk". He went on and on. I explained I had a hearing problem and his wife tried to calm things by saying, "She has a hearing problem". The attacker then turned on his wife for supporting me. Rita heard the commotion, but didn't realise what had happened and thought he was drunk. I didn't go to the theatre for quite a few years after that due to the shock of the experience.

Lack of mechanical understanding affects me in a variety of ways. Sometimes not seeing is visual, for example boxes get mutilated when I don't see the way to open them and clasps get broken, as I can't see how the mechanics work. Not seeing can also include what is meant and what is wanted. I have a very poor sense of direction and often when I know the way I only have one route. If the road is blocked I am stuck and have, on rare occasions, had to go home because of the difficulty of getting through. Undertaking tasks can be similar in that if my way is blocked, I can get stuck.

Relative to the majority in society, I can see that I have special needs, but in the main I do not feel that I have a learning disability. It is more of a handicap because there is a lack of provision by the majority for the needs of minorities. From my experience 'diversity' is rhetoric, because far from an inclusive society, I, like many others, have felt a social misfit.

In most of my office jobs I received training to undertake the task, particularly when computer work as a PA was concerned. Clerical work is a completely different skill set. Companies deploy people and often fit PAs into clerical tasks rather than look outside for staff. My findings on the matter are that investment for training goes to higher positions, while lower members of staff are 'shown' what to do by operators.

A learning style test indicated that my style of learning is theoretical. I had an equal score as a pragmatist. As a reflector I was a few points down. Activist is way down the list and that explains why I need 150% theory before dipping my toe in the water for the practical side of the task. I had problems with one person who trained me. She showed me what to do using a comparison with changing gears – put this here and put that there. My need to understand what I was doing was totally ignored. I tried to explain that this wasn't meeting my need, but she felt blamed. In response, the team set out to put every bit of blame they could on me, resulting in a witch hunt during which I was constantly set up for reprimand.

Understanding of the brain has shown that when we are learning we use a certain part of the brain. When we have gained competence, another part of the brain is engaged. I found it interesting to understand that when we get frightened, however competent we are, the activity reverts back to the learner brain. David Beckham was given as an example in that he is a very gifted football player, but if he is nervous when taking a penalty, he can be way off in his attempt to score a goal. In my own situation, it feels as if my brain freezes when I am frightened.

Did doctors pick up on Asperger's? No. My experience with doctors was very much like going down in water because of their mistreatment, and then they iced the water over, as at no time did they hear me or take responsibility. Instead they heaped more mental health labels on, to keep me down and in my place. Luckily, I did find the equivalent of ice holes where I could come up and be heard as part of my recovery.

My friend Rae moved to Ireland, which was an incredible loss for me, especially as her home was in such a remote place. The bus service only ran on a Saturday and that got cancelled. Communication depended on the postal service, as signals were poor due to living at the end of a peninsula.

As a lifelong learner, I attended some Saturday courses organised by Jackie Hawken, who is a Buddhist. One of her exercises helped with feelings and I made an appointment to see her 1:1 on a private basis. To my delight Jackie was not only a clinical psychologist but she also had a good knowledge of female Asperger's. In addition to Rae's work with me, Jackie was able to explain the behaviour of others towards me and how or why I suffered difficulties in relationships. Both psychologists agreed that I had Asperger's.

I had become a compulsive writer. My feelings were so difficult that everything went through my brain at terrific speed. Writing was a safety valve, whereby feelings could spill out on paper and I could make sense of my world.

Before the Asperger's diagnosis I asked my trusted GP, Dr Rogers, if I could see a psychologist as I needed to understand my thoughts and overcome my writing compulsion. The word 'doctor' was equivalent to abuse because of the trauma from my experiences; it would be unhelpful to see a doctor as I had lost faith in the profession. Unfortunately, the psychologist that Dr Rogers approached passed the referral to a one stop mental health team. After looking for protection, I was seen by Dr Everett who was a psychiatrist and not a psychologist, which put my trauma into overdrive.

My whole reason for the appointment was to discuss the compulsion, but when I received my medical records there was no mention of my concern in the letter to the GP. No reference was made to the reason I attended. I asked why the psychiatrist thought I was bullied. He gave me no answer but put in his letter, "She probably came over as an oddball at work". All the signs of Asperger's were there, but again the correct diagnosis got missed. Unhelpful remarks were also added to my records. Despite my medical records being totally off course and effectively rubbish, medical opinion carries a lot of weight and can do a lot of damage, if and when records are needed outside the health profession, for such things as insurance claims or hospital tests. Further problems can come about as future decisions will then be based on this erroneous diagnosis.

Dr Rogers had kindly agreed to receive my writing, which was my way of making sense of my world, but these workings were to be held as if they were in support of a criminal conviction. This enabled the medical profession to deny any responsibility for the problem, keeping me down and in my place as 'mentally ill'. My relationship with doctors was dire.

Einstein was also up against the system and it is believed he had Asperger's. He is my ultimate example of someone whose abilities were low in some areas and at genius level in others. It was believed that Einstein could not do simple maths and would not be able to manage his money, yet he went on to give humanity 'The Theory of Relativity'. The reason Einstein and others achieve great things is because autistic people apply single minded focus to the task.

I also am obsessional and will spend the rest of my life working to change the medical profession. A lot of harm has been done to patients despite the Hippocratic Oath to 'do no harm'. My inspiration for challenging the system is Patch Adams, whose part was played in a film by Robin Williams.

The things I most dislike and yet like about myself stem from Asperger's. The difficult part is when buttons are pressed triggering my weakness. It has been like touching a nerve and I have shouted a lot. My voice used to be a couple of pitches higher, which I realised and hated when I heard myself on an answerphone. I worked to bring my voice down a couple of levels and Rae pointed out that when I get upset my voice becomes higher in pitch. This shows that I have become disempowered. I have been harshly judged because I lose control when upset, but it always felt strange to me that no one seemed to see what had upset me, or the distress I was suffering. The shouting returned me to my default position of scapegoat. My reaction made me the villain of the piece, once more.

The thing I like about myself is my level of integrity, which I continue to work on. Dr David Hawkins wrote a book called *Power vs. Force*. The gist of the book is that each of us has a calibration relative to our levels of integrity. Integrity leads to courage, with the highest level of integrity being love. Christ and Buddha would be two examples of the highest levels attainable. When I look at the people who have bullied me and worked to have me excluded, a common factor is that their integrity levels have been low. An aid to my own happiness is to know and live to my core values, which are truth, integrity and love.

If someone said to me that they could wave a magic wand and make me 'normal' if I wanted it, my answer would be no. Integrity plays a major part in my relationship with myself. It is my yardstick to measure as I search for truth. If I suddenly had the means to be devious, it would mean I would need to work to overcome it to get back my desired levels of integrity.

One thing that carried through from vulnerable child to vulnerable adult was that it is easy to see the ideal. My blindness has been relative to the harm in people and I have been hit time and time again by the harsh realities in the world. I have read that spiritual mastery is starting life with the innocence of a child, negotiating the realities of human nature and then emerging with the innocence, wonder and attributes that were within us as children. I am reaching a point where I see and accept some of the harsh realities in human nature and the underlying forces throughout society.

Chapter 7

PSYCHOSIS

The psychotic episode was awesome to the full extent of the word. Imagine you suddenly found yourself outside the earth's atmosphere and in outer space. That is how I describe my experience of psychosis. On the one hand there was a vastness beyond imagination. It was terrifying. On the other hand, there was a sense of richness that I could only describe as the genius that is said to be in madness.

Typical of a female with Asperger's, everything has to go through the intellect over and over again, to make sense of the world. It is exhausting. Psychosis hit me like big bang theory and my mind was thrown into chaos. Once out of the psychosis I kept going back to draw meaning from the experience. It was very confusing to be one with the vastness of time and space. By repeatedly analysing the experience after the episode, I could see that there is an inner universe where we are one with time, space and each other.

We have scientific proof of rockets going outside the earth's atmosphere and into space. We can all see and believe the evidence of a universe beyond anything humanity could understand or control. I had broken through the boundaries of mind and entered the far reaches of my inner universe, unable to prove my experience.

We know when we have been dreaming, because we wake up and go about our day. I describe my psychosis as living in a dream state, but it wasn't a case of waking up, but of trying to go about my normal life in that state. Sometimes my new dreamy way of being was drifty and funny, while at other times I was living a nightmare.

I call these dream and nightmare states 'heaven and hell'. Within the heavenly state I experienced a oneness with all time and space and everything within it. Hell was to be alone within the totality of time and space. I felt doomed, thinking, "It is right and I am lost".

There are stages to sleep. Within the sleep pattern there is REM (Rapid Eye Movement) that happens within the last four hours of sleep. This is when we make sense of our world. Loss of sleep can lead to severe sleep deprivation and that can then become full blown psychosis. I found that lack of sleep brought the dream state into my waking life.

There are two types of psychosis: 1) Schizophrenia, which is said to be ongoing, and 2) Manic Depression, more recently renamed Bipolar, which can come in episodes. I had three episodes and would call them manic depression. Even when feeling on a high, what lay underneath them was a very deep depression.

With high and low as my points of reference for going out of my mind, I saw two ways this worked for me.

The first was to describe the entry into psychosis as a rocket going into space through increasing pressure, until it takes off. In my life I had traumatic events from early life that had not been resolved. Fear within my work situation was so great that due to lack of sleep, I was frightened out of my wits and into the far reaches of insanity. I needed an escape and the only place I could go was out of my mind. A rocket needs fuel and what powered my breakdown was adrenaline, which is the fuel for fight or flight, as we are part of the animal kingdom.

The second way is by entering space beyond the world of the mind through guided meditation, which I now teach students. We live in the world and are on firm ground, safe in a room in our home, on a street, in a town, etc. The ground starts to rumble and breaks apart and we drop through the world we know into the void.

We build our worlds on our beliefs as to who we are in the world and our place and relationships in it. Mind is a build-up of beliefs. The word that would describe the crack in my world is 'heartbroken'. There is a relevant line in the film *The General's Daughter*: "The one thing that is worse than death is betrayal". Another significant line is from the film *What Dreams May Come*: "Good people go to hell because they can't forgive themselves". Within my guilt complex, the deepest guilt was not holding up as a mother. Because I was not able to function, my boys would feel abandoned and betrayed by me. I can remember thinking, "If I can't be there for them, I will put the world right for them".

In my life I had hit some lows and lived an ongoing drama, but after entering the world of psychosis I knew life could never be the same again. As part of psychosis, there is a heightened awareness that holds a touch of genius. It may come in snatches and then disappear, but these snatches were as rough diamonds to me and I had to go back over and over again, sifting to gain clarity concerning the gems of insight. In life I was poorly educated, but in psychosis I loved being the mad professor, seeing a scientific element in the experience and trying to cure all the ills of the world. I can quite see why mathematicians and scientists leave off medication in order to access their heightened state, as it contains a touch of genius triggering progress in given fields of study or work.

My experience was terrifying and for a great many years I had a huge fear that I could go back into it. Now that I have distanced myself with time and understanding, I value the experience and the richness of breaking down beliefs inherited from family and social conditioning, thus forming more appropriate beliefs for myself.

In the build-up to breakdown, or breakthrough as some call it, I tried to get closer and closer to the Bible for a sense of safety. All of a sudden it seemed as though the Bible was in me and I was in the Bible. Jung, the psychiatrist who followed Freud, showed that within each of us there are archetypes. Some of these are more prominent than others. I see this as part of the whole array of genes within us. I believe that what I saw was archetypes within me, and that the Bible contains the whole story. A greater mystery than any of us could imagine. I believe that Christ is the ultimate archetype within each of us. I believe that the birthing of the Christ consciousness within is the immaculate conception and as Jung said, "There is no birth of consciousness without pain".

I had a very strong sense of 'Joseph syndrome'. As the younger female in the family, it felt as if I had been oppressed to the point of being buried by the family. With strong faith in God I knew that I would come through. At the time of writing I have progressed to teaching student nurses and doctors. I also work on committees with health professionals.

Joseph is known for his coat of many colours. By coincidence I had a colour assessment for my clothing, which turned out to be the brightest in the box. I also felt in touch with Moses as I crossed the wilderness of mind, as a seeker of truth. By coincidence, it is almost 40 years since I started the journey back to make sense of my world.

On the edge of breakdown, I could hear the most heavenly music. It was soft and beyond beautiful. It was as though I leaned in to hear and tipped over the edge and into another state that the world knows as insanity. I wrote about this some years later on an internet site and about four others had had the same experience. One was a musician and he could not replicate the beautiful sound. Since then my friend Emma shared with me that science has found that the universe gives off a vibrational rate that is musical. These discoveries can be found on the internet.

We are human and being. Like the world, humanity knows gravity. The being side of us is like space, where there is no gravity. Experiments have been done with LSD to try to experience the psychotic state. I can't think why scientists didn't ask the psychotic person, because the dream state and a good trip are similar, while the nightmare and a bad trip are also connected. The reason people on LSD think they can fly and then die jumping out of windows and off cliffs is because they are in touch with the sense of non-gravity within themselves. They do not realise that inner being is within the body, which is like a cage.

As I read newspapers or watched the TV it was as though they were talking about me. This is very common for people experiencing breakdown. The reason this happens is that we become aware of our oneness, but still can't understand the universe that is in fact beyond division. All goodness and evil are within us. At first, I felt responsible for wonderful cures in the world, after that for all that was wrong in the world. There is a story that says there is a good wolf on one shoulder and a bad wolf on the other – which is stronger? The answer is, the one you feed.

I have come to believe that as we have the duality of humanity and divinity within us, the opposite poles of consciousness work like the radio in that these states are like channels on the radio. Further to that, there are frequencies on these channels, which explains why when something is said it can be interpreted in different ways by the people who receive the message. My best example would be the biblical parables, which can be understood on several levels.

After leaving the psychotic state, I found it an interesting study. At an early stage in my experience everything said during appointments with Dr Platt came back to me, word for word. It was quite incredible.

In fact, everything we have said, done or thought is stored within us. In life we can only live with ourselves and the awful things we have done by denying blame and justifying the selfish, spiteful things we do. Within my breakdown the self-deception was taken away. I saw all the things I had done right or wrong as well as all my selfish motivation in otherwise kindly deeds for others, and worse than any wrong doing, was when I did nothing. The day of judgement is within us and that is when we will go beyond delusion, facing ourselves and the truth that is within our hearts. I found the day of judgement truly horrifying.

In psychiatry, therapy should not be performed on people who are experiencing psychosis, because patients sense something, but cannot understand what is happening. My conclusion is that the psychiatrist Dr Ralph gave me therapy and I became highly confused as a result. It was as if I was trying to communicate with him on the surface but he was listening to something else, as though there was a conversation going on under the table. We see comedy sketches where radio stations are changed, making complete nonsense of the conversation. My world became totally confused as though channels were being changed during a conversation.

Just after the second episode, I wrote the following poem that captured my experience.

REALITY

Is it real?
Is it there?
Does anyone know?
Does anyone care?

To spend yet another sleepless night
With the mind working fight or flight.
To work through the mind's deceptions,
Sifting through the varying perceptions.

With no thought for personal cost,
Is the search for reality lost.
To lose the here and now for the there and then,
Not to know how, or even when.

To be high in all its gladness,

Searching for the genius in madness.
To be low in all its despair,
Knowing that somewhere it's there.

Is it a mind that is breaking?
Or a mind in the making?
There is no turning back, no denial,
Once the mind has been put to trial.
                              Lynn Jones (1988)

Why has psychiatry got it so wrong? Psychiatry is known to be an interpretive science but is sadly lacking in understanding. Conclusions are way off mark. As a woman in a man's world, I know what it is to be considered an inferior species. I can understand why psychiatry was shunned as non-scientific by the medical profession. The message in both situations is that if you want to be equal, you have to be the same.

Psychiatry is a philosophical subject. Science is about what can be weighed and measured. This might apply to the brain, but mind cannot be weighed or measured. Psychiatry contains the uncontainable. It attempts to put boundaries on the boundless with medical models. A diagnosis is then followed by medication, in line with the side of the profession that treats diseases of the physical body.

Another reason I see psychiatry missing the mark is that, again in line with medical model, a consultant takes a top down approach, resulting in actions being instigated at the highest level. He assesses the patient, decides what the problem is and the treatment that will be given. People who have suffered mental health problems are the real experts, as we have experience.

As a better way of working, service users suggest a Recovery Approach. This is a client centred way of working where professionals are seen to listen and to take the lead from the service user. This way of working keeps responsibility with the service user, either for managing their illness or recovering completely. The main aim is for service users to terminate their use of medication and use of the health services.

The consultant writes to the GP surgery, where the family doctor is given direction. Many older service users will be on drugs for the rest of their lives. Until recently, service users were not allowed to see medical records, but now they are. My own file has the potential to do much damage to my credibility if I were to make any form of insurance claim or complaint.

It is known that doctors and nursing staff cannot help people who are using alcohol or street drugs and that the problem can only be tackled once these behaviours have stopped. From my own experience I feel there is little or no difference with medically prescribed drugs.

We know from history that people suffering mental health problems were put in strait jackets for the purpose of control. This form of control has changed to 'chemical coshes' or 'chemical strait jackets'. Patients moved about like zombies, unable to control their saliva as it drooled from their mouths.

My experience of psychosis happened when I was 40 years old and I had a strong sense of personal responsibility. A lady doctor was speaking to my father when he accompanied me to the health centre and I turned to her and said, "Look, I know it is difficult for me to understand, but would you mind talking to me, because I am the one who has to take responsibility for this".

There is an expression 'feel it to heal it'. While I feel there is a place for medication in the short term to help with crises, I know that when mood altering substances are taken we lose the ability to find ways of coping. That is a great pity because suffering leads to understanding, and overcoming problems leads to personal growth.

If psychosis can be likened to dream states, it seems

reasonable to think that it could be better understood with techniques used for dream analysis. My psychologist friends find it incredible that I can gain so much from my dreams. Rae said, "You have the ability of a psychologist for making sense of your dreams". Jackie is very impressed with the symbolism within my dreams and what I make of them.

My understanding of dream interpretation came from a book *Gestalt Verbatim* by Fritz Perles who promoted gestalt, which means 'wholeness'. Dream interpretation made sense to me, as I read a dream about a person riding a camel in the desert. Firstly, the lady was the rider of the camel who spoke as the rider, then she spoke as though she was the camel. When the lady spoke as though she was the sand, she said, "I am fed up of getting shit on". It was a eureka moment for me – I GOT IT. From that point I got a lot of feedback from my dreams. Initially the interpretation might have been shallow, but eventually greater depth came through, with richer meaning.

The word 'patient' means 'passive'. The psychiatry profession needs to move from a control style of management to enabling the service user to take the lead as a responsible person in the healing relationship.

If psychiatry knew a better way, richness could be gained from the psychotic experience by helping us to reap meaning out of the confusion. Instead of something worthy being drawn from the service user, further suffering comes about in the form of stigma. To be explained in another chapter is the fact that society has a ruling elite with an underclass. When people fall out of grace and are stigmatised, they drop beneath underclass to become outcast and are no longer valid in society.

There is a saying 'People who break down show the symptoms of a dysfunctional family'. Whilst I can see the truth of this, relative to my own family, I believe the greater part of the dysfunction is in the social structure. The word 'stigma' comes from the Bible and relates to people being marked. By not holding up and thus showing the symptoms of distress, it is as though we have let the side down.

When Dr Platt did not understand he called me 'confused'. Another way doctors keep the power position even when they don't understand is to put the patient down with labels such as 'grandiose and bizarre'. My question is, when doctors call people 'grandiose', is it a diagnosis or putting what they are themselves on to others – known as projection?

Psychosis was an incredible experience, but one I would not wish to revisit. Treating people who have suffered psychosis as discards is as tragic as throwing away diamonds because they are not recognised in their original rough states. My greatest wish for the mental health service would be to stop the controlling style of management and facilitate healing by gathering from the experience its incredible richness.

Chapter 8

SPIRITUALITY

Writing on the subject of spirituality should be easy, as it is so close to my heart. Words ought to just flow. Finding an entry into the subject has been quite difficult. I am reminded of a child asking, "How will I know when I am in love?" and the answer is, "When it happens you will know it".

Spirituality, like love, is an experience. Love and spirituality feel the same to me. The world becomes a nicer place and I am transformed into my better self.

Spiritual gurus explain that trying to clarify the experience to those who have no personal knowledge is like trying to describe the colour green to a blind person. For some reason academic descriptions of spirituality are so complex that meaning gets lost in the interpretation. I would define spirituality as 'an altered state of consciousness that is one with all, but exists on a different plane'.

Within the world we know of division between male and female, black and white. We are all aware of wars between both religions and nationalities. Schools of thought have been formed and division comes as a result of the language of the schools. I want to use an inclusive language, but know that when words such as 'God, Goddess, Allah', etc. are spoken, unity gets lost, because when words of one school are used, people with a different language or belief system may well switch off. It is hoped the words 'source of our being' will be acceptable and fully inclusive. Spirituality is beyond division, it is the oneness that is common to all of us within time and space. This makes us brothers and sisters in spirit.

Can I please ask that when words and beliefs differ from yours, that you stay with it rather than switch off?

Throughout much of my life I have been religious, with my roots in Christianity. When I needed healing and looked to the church I was let down. Although there are wonderful priests and others in the church, I have also met misogynists, narcissists and lots of egotists within the priesthood. They call for conformity rather than unconditional love and acceptance within the church. I felt marginalised to the point that I left the church several times to become a seeker of truth. I found that there is no such thing as an absolute truth. I have felt the transformative power of spirit within me as I find a better level of 'true' within, by seeing and then releasing what is not true. Transformation has taken me from insecurity, doubt and fear to inner strength and faith in the process.

In the chapter on psychosis I said that there was richness in the experience. The breakthrough from mind to another place was entry into the spiritual realm, with all the vastness of oneness within time and space. To the human side of us, this is terrifying as it is realised that life as 'Lynn' is temporary and we see with horror the stark reality of our own mortality. From the formless, 'being' side of our nature, death is natural and in it we re-experience bliss in oneness.

I compare the evolution of humanity to the growth of a tree in that however tall it grows, it needs feeding at the root if it is to survive. As people, we need feeding in body, mind and spirit. Spirit has been so marginalised and negated in our world that many of us do not realise it is missing, and we compensate by taking in more food for the body and mind. The result is obesity in the western world, plus an increase in mental health problems as well as burnout.

Within the church I received a spiritual feed from the word within the readings and the sermon. I drew from the message how to live in love with the source of our being, the self and one another. On many occasions I have sat in an empty church, felt the tensions ease from my body and then taken in positive energies from the atmosphere. This was a wonderful means of restoration for me, but I was not understood by others and the distress from church relationships became greater than the benefits received.

Females with Asperger's need to make sense of their world and I spent many years reading, studying and putting learning together with my experiences. I came up with theories on spirituality and put them out as mail shots. Professor Brian Thorne gave a positive response to my theories, as did Professor Walter Wink. Both happened to be Christians. Professor Thorne formed a bridge between Christianity and client-centred counselling; writing books entitled *The Mystical Power of Person-Centred Therapy* and *Person Centred Counselling and Christian Spirituality*. Professor Wink wrote *The Powers That Be*, in which he showed that each person and group has an angelic and a demonic spirit. I was interested to read that 'when people get together, one person or group sets out to have power over another. If the other does not acquiesce, there are problems'.

In my life I notice the angelic spirit when people go out to enhance the lives of others, as compared with the demonic spirit which sets out to displace and cause people suffering, by cutting them off from loving relationships and personal growth.

My first model showed that each of us has a false self that is fashioned in the world and a true self that we were born with. Religion talks of dying to the old and being reborn in the spirit, which I believe fits my model. On this day of writing, the saying on my Zen calendar is 'We must be willing to get rid of the life we've planned, so as to have the life that is waiting for us. The old skin has to be shed before the new one can come'.

My second theory was that we have poles to the mind and that the subconscious is merely a pole that needs to be in balance with the superconscious. The animal and spiritual aspects of our humanity are played out in consciousness. We are as earth to these electrical energies. As human beings, the survival instinct runs together with the spirit of love which enhances and enriches life.

To me, humanity is like the prodigal son who has wandered out and needs to find his way back. So where did it go wrong and how did we lose touch with spirituality?

The roots of humanity and source of spirituality were indigenous, which means native and original. Two examples of indigenous people are Native Americans and women who tended the earth. They were in touch with rhythms and cycles.

Indigenous groups were hunted and slaughtered. It seems strange to me that the genocide of gentle people can be swept under the carpet so successfully and all in order to dominate. Fortunately, there is a return to Eastern philosophy and natural healing, but certainly not in mainstream living.

I found the truth of spirituality in nature when I visited Jackie, my latest counsellor, who is a Buddhist. Before visiting her for my appointments I spent an hour in an estate where there are lawns, trees and a path leading into woods with a stream. In that environment all my senses were touched. I heard the songs of birds and running water, saw trees with the sun shining through the branches, smelled the woods, felt the gravel under foot and got simple pleasure from seeing dogs with their owners and children with their parents. My counsellor explained that this was mindfulness and I certainly felt good being restored by taking some time in nature.

Harm for me has been twofold. It wasn't just that what was natural was taken away, but that something unnatural was put in its place. In academic circles, it is called 'patriarchal ideology'. That means a male-controlled system of social belief. It means that an elite and privileged group of men set out to determine the social norms, or the way we should all live.

Far from being civilised, it was the law of the jungle under which privileged people at the top formed a social order. This left men like my father feeling inadequate in the scheme of things. Men were then given power over women. Until recent years the law allowed men to hit women with a stick, up to a certain size and weight. Police did not get involved in home disputes because it was considered 'domestic'. Women's lives and bodies were solely for the use of men. I read that women could suffer female mutilation up until 1936 for pleasuring themselves.

Patriarchal ideology saw a surge in male ego, where knowledge was bestowed on authorities for power and control of the masses in social issues such as health, education and religion. The acronym for ego is Edge God Out. The natural order was moving towards the unnatural and that has become the norm. Possibly my most alternative view of the world is to see natural ways as The Tree of Life and the unnatural way as The Tree of Knowledge. In the Bible we are told we should not eat from the Tree of Knowledge, but within my logic, this is just what humanity has done.

In addition to chronic exploitation of the masses to keep the elite with power, possession and privilege, humanity has been subject to corruption.

I listened to a four-part series on YouTube called *One Century of Self*. True to Rae's prediction, the recordings have been withdrawn. The talk was about Freud delving into the subconscious. He found something so awful that it had to be controlled. However, he did share his findings with his nephew Bernays, who changed the face of advertising by bypassing conscious reasoning and appealing to the unconscious drives. Selling cars and cigarettes became sexualised. Bit by bit moral boundaries became eroded, as unacceptable behaviour came about and after initially being frowned upon, became the norm.

From there I looked at what are dismissed as 'conspiracy theories'. The ideas shown in the conspiracy theories seem too mad to be true. Having studied the nature of abuse, the bottom line is politics with its hidden agenda. I believe mankind is corrupt and evil enough to cause mass extermination to follow the instruction on the Georgia Stones, to reduce the world's population to 500,000,000 to achieve a one world order and domination. While there might be some red herrings in the conspiracy theories, I would ask you to take a look for yourself, as there is a lot of evidence out there.

Due to my interest in power, I was given a book by a sociologist named Freidson entitled *Professionalism Reborn*. This showed that in English speaking countries there is a ruling elite that has a hidden agenda and an underclass. One example I see of a hidden agenda is that there are loving people who want to ease suffering through assisted dying to save loved ones from horrendous deaths. The hidden danger that I see is that people who work to reduce the population would support the cause until it is law, and then manipulate it to reduce the population. Holland has walked the path of assisted dying and warns of the slippery path, as pressure is put on people to end life for financial reasons.

One charge nurse working in a hospital said, "Politicians have to be psychopaths to make some of their decisions". I can certainly agree with his statement. As I looked up 'elitism' on the internet, YouTube showed *Wounded Leaders* by Nick Duffell, who explains 'British Elitism and Entitlement'. Nick Duffell attended boarding school and is therefore able to explain how our leaders are wounded because he attended school with them.

Children are sent away from their mothers at the age of seven or eight and spend time crying because of the separation. School detaches them from emotion and replaces it with 'rational thinking'. These people are damaged, but given compensation through a sense of entitlement over and above others. Emotion is deemed to be irrational and, as women are emotional, this has been medically classified as 'neurotic'.

Within the church, one of the vicars had been to boarding school. At the end of his time in the community, a large meeting was called to reveal bullying. Amongst the information on wounded leaders is 'narcissism', which is defined as 'seeks grandiose validation while negating others'. While it is easy to feel a victim to wounded leaders, recovery is in realising the victimhood of what it feels like to be the offending party. Somehow, recovery from our experiences is not only to move beyond resentment to acceptance, but also to find compassion for the damaged child who grows into a wounded leader.

The makeup of the male is said to be testosterone fuelled. He competes for rank, while the way of the female is to co-operate. Within my alternative view of the world, I see the problems of the world as being a direct result of killing off Mother Earth and Motherly Love, which are the nurturing and life sustaining qualities in life.

Spirituality is life itself, yet focus has moved from life-sustaining attitudes towards materialism. The body houses the spirit and there should be reverence for the body as the temple of the spirit. When a mother feeds her baby, she doesn't just give milk for the body, but emotional wellbeing through holding and caressing it. Wellbeing is sustained through emotional touches. Children need to be cherished, but due to the exploitation of women, many lone parents are forced out into the workplace. Abandonment of the child experienced at the top of the social scale has now reached all social classes.

Women have been considered inferior, and if we want to be equal we have to be the same as men, doing twice as much to be considered half as good. If it is true that it takes five men to do the work of one woman, perhaps the ratio of women in management needs to be one in five!

Professor Brian Thorne says, "All children need to be cherished". Further to that, I can see that everyone needs to be recognised. For emotional wellbeing all people need to have a sense of worth in the world, and I believe much of the problem is that the love of the world is conditional, since there is a belief that love is in short supply. People are compensating for lack of love with materialism and status symbols. These do nothing for emotional wellbeing, but rather feed the ego and widen the divide between people.

Some years ago, I set my mission statement as 'To make the world a better place. Where love and abuse run together, stop abuse by exposing the domination system, and bring love by promoting the need for spirituality'. I am on the verge of achieving my life purpose. As a seeker of truth, I would like to bring truth to expose the lie that has corrupted life through the ages.

If our divided world is to heal, it will be by going beyond division to the oneness of our humanity, towards the life source itself. The answer to male domination of humanity is not to put the male out and the female in, but to appreciate whole life as the integration of male and female throughout creation. I believe that humanity is part of the evolutionary process and that we are progressing from our animal to our spiritual state.

Philosophy has shown that thought is known to be unreal, yet we have built and in fact worship schools of thought. According to my view of the world, these schools are as the Tower of Babel, each one speaking in its own language. They are like empires that uphold the injustice of the social system.

The church operates as a hierarchy with an organisational chart. From outside the church looking in, I like the present church leaders Pope Francis, Justin Welby and the Bishop of Bristol. Good people in the church suffer depression as they pray fervently for Earth to be as heaven, sometimes questioning if there is a God at all.

There is a parable that refers to 'the old flask cannot hold new wine'. To me the spirit of the word is the new wine, and the old flask is the patriarchal way of life. Unless and until this false premise is exposed, the spirit of the word cannot be fully alive to answer the prayer of St Francis, which reads:

> *Lord, make me an instrument of your peace,*
> *Where there is hatred, let me sow love;*
> *Where there is injury, pardon;*
> *Where there is doubt, faith;*
> *Where there is despair, hope;*
> *Where there is darkness, light;*
> *Where there is sadness, joy;*

> *O Divine Master, grant that I may not so much seek to be consoled as to console;*
> *To be understood as to understand;*
> *To be loved as to love with all my soul.*

> *For it is in giving that we receive;*
> *It is in pardoning that we are pardoned;*
> *And it is in dying that we are born to eternal life.*

To me, patriarchal ideology is in direct opposition to spiritual laws to live and love in peace. These laws are the answer to the Lord's Prayer that we might know a holy way of life on Earth as in heaven.

> *Our Father, which art in heaven,*
> *Hallowed be thy Name.*
> *Thy Kingdom come.*
> *Thy will be done in Earth,*
> *As it is in heaven.*
> *Give us this day our daily bread.*
> *And forgive us our trespasses,*
> *As we forgive those that trespass against us.*
> *And lead us not into temptation,*
> *But deliver us from evil.*
> *For thine is the kingdom,*
> *The power, and the glory,*
> *For ever and ever.*
> *Amen.*

At the crucifixion, Christ prayed, "Forgive them, for they don't know what they are doing". I believe that in turning away from the light we have wandered into darkness. Having gone through the Dark Night of the Soul in the depths of my depression, it is my hope and prayer that my alternative view of the world will to some degree help bring us back to the light of spiritual glory.

Chapter 9

UP AGAINST THE SYSTEM

The turmoil of my mind led to the need to understand and bring order out of chaos and facilitate change. The biggest difference has been in relationships, which have put me up against the system. Although some relationships with professionals are still difficult, it is as though I had moved from being blind to being able to see. My sense of facing something huge and impossible has shifted, and I now have a better sense of owning my own power.

The significant factor in my new relationship with the world is the way I rebuild my trust with myself and God. Historically, my life fell apart because my belief system collapsed. By rebuilding trust in myself and also in God I am more aware of the power of faith. My current view is that the system within the world is made up of individual authorities with collective power. This upholds the domination rights of the class system.

In my early life I was pro-authority. In line with Sunday school teaching, I honoured not only my mother and father, but also doctors, police, church plus Uncle Tom Cobley and all. So, what catastrophes could have happened to destroy my faith and demolish my childlike, idealistic view of the world?

While I was going into breakdown at the age of 40, something happened in my brain. I had a word for word replay of the early surgery visits and Dr Platt's counselling, which overrode my opinion in favour of his. By the age of 40 I had gained experience working with people and was horrified at what had been said to me. When the doctor did not understand he called me 'confused' and I certainly did become deranged when my way of thinking was ignored. In addition, he said, "Your husband is immature, insensitive and manipulating. He isn't the right man for you". At the time I did not realise that the doctor was wrong to behave in this way. Thinking this was some new breed of doctor putting psychology into the practice, I adopted his judgemental way of reasoning to analyse everything in order to make sense of my world.

I first met Dr Platt in February 1976 at antenatal clinic. When my medical records were received from the health centre many years later, Dr Platt had referred me for a psychiatric appointment saying he knew me at the time of my divorce and that I did not know the meaning of the words I used. He ended his letter with, "I refer an interesting girl".

The collapse stemmed from Dr Platt exposing me to a phobia at the time of giving birth, yet all evidence that should have been on record to support me and get my circumstances back on track had been removed from my file. The letter had the power to cast doubt on me knowing what I was talking about. It also insulted my maturity. This was the beginning of the end for me, as psychiatry became misdirected, resulting in drastic distortion of the facts, misdiagnosis and mistreatment...

My introduction to psychiatry was an outpatient appointment at a health centre. This was the first of four outpatient appointments. With an incorrect referral, Dr Ralph, the consultant psychiatrist, put my problem down to either my marriage or to a chemical reaction. Far from there being no reason, within my emotional baggage were such things as sexual abuse in childhood, trauma suffered from the phobia, a miscarriage, a divorce where I had not grieved and bullying at work. The final straw happened at work when I was told that management was creaming thousands of pounds off the programme. The breakdown happened after I had a sinus operation and I was unable to hold up under the weight of the problems. I was confused, because it felt as though I was being annihilated, but I didn't know what was wrong with me that I should be treated this way.

Through the four outpatient appointments Dr Ralph giggled into his tie. I found this really difficult as I wasn't aiming to be funny and the message received was, "Your concerns are not only ridiculous, they are laughable". It seemed he was not listening to me and I wondered what he was hearing. This is when the messages from the world turned into a series of languages that became like interchanging radio stations. I suffered mass confusion as I tried to make sense of my world.

At the fourth session I asked what was wrong with me, to be told, "Nothing. What you need is marriage guidance". I was greatly relieved as I could sort that out, but what Dr Ralph didn't say was that he had marked my file 'psychosis or schizophrenia'. I was told to wait ten days before going to the doctor for a prescription. On taking the medication, I had an orgasm and kept getting in the bath because I felt dirty. This was before I discovered that I had been sexually abused.

By my reasoning I had suffered 'psychiatric violation'. This was because Dr Ralph had been a sexual therapist for almost twenty years and operated with Transactional Analysis, which was devised by Eric Berne. Part of Berne's work was shown in a book *Games People Play* and one of those games was 'Rappo'. The tragic thing was that when I spoke about the violation some years later, professional people put it down to my mental health problem. Some think that the drugs 'messed with my head'. My opinion is that doctors either know what they are doing and the practice is unethical, or they don't know what they are doing and are incompetent.

I was discharged from outpatients. Being on medication was like holding a table tennis ball under water, so when I left them off, I went high. I was in a difficult state: wanting to go to bed day and night, but every time I lay down, I needed to get up. Eventually I went to bed one night and woke up around midnight feeling suicidal. I crashed out in the local psychiatric hospital in the early hours of the morning.

If doctors wondered why I presented like someone from a concentration camp, it was because extreme fear had become terror due to the psychiatric experience. It was a weekend when I landed in the hospital. I was frightened when I met psychiatric patients, wondering what I had done and what I had got into. The group of patients on the ward could be described as 'colourful' and some did appear a bit weird, but there was a sense of realness about them as if the masks that get shown to the world were off.

On the day Dr Ralph came on duty, I went for a walk. Staff then asked me to stay around. My stomach was in a terrible state. It felt as though my gut wanted to explode, so I kept going to the loo, but only managed to pass wind. Someone on the ward was filthy and had splattered all the loos around the villa. I was horrified to realise that it was me who had been making such a dreadful mess and at a physical level this showed the terror I was feeling inside. Within days I was sent for a hospital appointment to check my stomach. Instead of sympathy from the nursing staff, I was refused medication for the stomach the first time I asked, as the member of staff had taken a dislike to me. Taking anti-psychotic medication was terrible and experienced staff said I had the worst side effects they had ever seen. This was not helping my relationship with the medical profession.

It was decided by the staff that I needed time out, and other than regular observation, staff kept their distance. Staff nurses were frightened of my intensity, so didn't engage with me. Helen did sit down with me to have a chat. Just thinking about this brought tears to my eyes 27 years later, as it meant so much that she had crossed the line breaking my sense of isolation as she connected with me. Helen went back to her colleagues and said, "She is off the wall, but she is talking sociology". Where I had been reading and taking courses to make sense of my world, I had adopted a language of sociology.

I was an in-patient for five weeks, spending some

further time as a day patient. I used the villa as a life line as I went in daily to visit others. Helen became my key nurse and offered me a chance to chat. After listening to me with all my issues going around and around, she broke the concerns into four problems, and from there set out to find solutions. Typical for a female with Asperger's, I imitated Helen's way and took up a solution focused approach for myself.

Taken as a whole, the psychiatrist in charge of my care was a good person who was highly respected by his team. His way of working was a saving grace for me, as he worked to keep responsibility with the patient. He trained his staff to work with patients as adult to adult rather than being as a parent to a child. Another thing to appreciate was that he did not force medications, electric therapy or incarceration on his patients. I can forgive people who make a mistake. Although I was terrorised by the interventions, I do believe it was a mistake because he was wrong footed by Dr Platt's referral. In addition, the original diagnosis was wrong. It was to take a further 20 years to identify Asperger's.

One day I sat in the surgery waiting to see Dr Platt. I was full of dread as appointments with him felt like a battle field. As I went in James, a doctor from the psychiatric hospital, was sitting at the desk. He was filling in as a locum and I could have cried with relief at seeing him. I told him how I felt and he advised me to change doctors. Although the relationship I valued with my GP Dr Hughes had slipped, changing would feel disloyal. As luck would have it, Dr Platt's relationship problems with his colleagues meant that he took up a practice on his own. James joined the surgery and became my new GP.

In order to make sense of my world, the speed of my mind had spilled out into a compulsion to write. I sent my writing to the previous GP and a vicar, to be heard and understood. Far from understanding, I frightened them, reinforcing the psychiatric diagnosis. James agreed to receive my writing and he became my life-line, and no less than a saint. I now had a safe person in the health profession. James was much younger than me, yet I had great fear that he might leave. I reasoned that James would still be there after my death, and my fear was so chronic that I could not even think about leaving the district and losing my only life-line in the medical profession. The worst did happen, and my lovely James took early retirement, due to ill health. I was devastated.

James had total trust in me and because he acted as an interpreter for his colleagues, they became impressed with my insight. My tolerance level with doctors was nil and some time after James left the practice I hit a problem with a prescription for medication, and when I phoned to get it sorted I was told, "Dr Coombs instructed this". This was a critical time for me, in fact the problem happened on my birthday. I sought the advice of the Patients Advocacy Service, as I needed the two GPs to hear me and was calling for a meeting to get aligned with a truer account of my situation. Instead of getting a meeting, it ended in taking a complaint to the top, as they totally refused to meet me together, which was necessary for me to get my records straight and on track.

From there I could not believe the dirty tricks from GPs themselves and the administrators of the health centre. Words used were misleading, such as 'lead doctor' which meant Dr Coombs to me, whereas it wasn't until just before the end they were using 'lead doctor' to mean the doctor leading the investigation. A couple of days before a meeting, I received a message that the doctor had to go to a drugs meeting. What I could see was that the games being played at the health centre were the same as the tactics used by another organisation when I tackled bullying at work.

When challenging organisations, professionals know the game and how to play it, whereas the person hoping for fairness is green by comparison. The complaint process seems a waste of time, as the wrongs of the matter do not get addressed, except for unimportant details such as date of birth.

The good thing that did come from my complaint was that telephone calls are now recorded. People who had been on psychiatric drugs long term got medical checks. Although I wasn't receiving treatment for mental health, I did take something to help with sleep. The result of a health check showed blood in my water, so I had to have a series of tests. Since invasive medical treatment was a trigger for breakdown, I now need safety precautions when having tests or procedures. Luckily major problems were ruled out, but the results of kidney function tests have varied. I had no idea what could be wrong.

My worst experience with the medical profession was when I was well. I worked for a department in the health profession and said to a Chief Executive, "There is nothing to link mental health and spirituality". The reply was that Dr Peacock was a psychiatrist who had a special interest in spirituality. I made an appointment through his secretary to meet him as I wanted to know how spirituality was being merged with mental health and to discuss my own findings.

As we walked through the corridors he asked, "Have you been here before"? I replied, "I have been to a meeting" and by the time we reached the room I had said that I had previously used the service. Dr Peacock sat in a chair with wooden arms; put one of his elbows on an arm of the chair and his chin in his hand. The weary look on his face said, "Oh my God, one of these has got in". He carried on asking about my diagnosis, what medication I was on and how my marriage was going. I was horrified. It was as though history was repeating itself all over again. Doctors were taking it out of my hands and getting it wrong. I explained that I worked for the Chief Executive, to assure him that I was ok. I left and had to see James, my own GP, because the experience had been so traumatic.

When I received my medical records Dr Peacock had written to my surgery. He had sent for my medical notes, which was totally inappropriate as it wasn't a medical appointment and I was not his patient. In his letter he said that I had made an appointment to see him out of the blue to discuss a project I was doing on spirituality in mental health. He continued, "Her ideas were clearly muddled and bizarre, and I felt that she exhibited mild schizophrenic thought disorder. Her mood was mildly elated, with grandiose ideas. Having obtained her old psychiatric notes, I see she has previously received a diagnosis of schizo-affective disorder, and did for some time receive regular depot injections (This was never the case). She could probably do with re-starting her depot (never been on one) and I shall be informing the appropriate team of this".

After a short period, my temporary position with the Chief Executive ended. Rae, my psychologist friend, called him 'a thug'. Doctors have the power to do a lot of damage. What happened to this doctor who I see as unprofessional? He gained promotion and moved into my area. I learned from experience that academia was certainly no measure of intelligence and the incorrectness of being judged 'grandiose' was to me not a diagnosis, but rather a projection.

I believe that for every force for evil, there is a force for good. To balance out the villain of the piece, a Medical Director named Dr Arden Tomison was to be my saint. I met him at a conference and said to him, "You doctors should step up to the plate and take responsibility. Come and listen to my talk". He didn't turn up at the lunch time education meeting, but I saw him at another conference. Again, I said to him, "You doctors should step up to the plate. Come and listen to my talk".

Dr Tomison did come to hear my talk. From there he met me with the head of medical records and looked at my file after listening to me. He smiled and said, "You are more right than they are". It was not possible for anyone to correct anything that was wrong on the file, but Dr Tomison was good enough to write a letter of support and

I copy below some extracts from the letter:

> *"Those who use the information in her health record need to understand that much of the information about her mental health diagnosis and mental health needs is in dispute by Mrs. Jones. If any matters regarding her health need to rely on the mental health information in her record, it will be important to ensure that Mrs. Jones has the opportunity to make her position clear before the information is used or relied on.*
>
> *In that respect, it is important to understand that, having lost trust in the medical profession generally, she now wishes to re-establish that necessary trust. Active listening helps her to know that she has been heard. She is well able to engage in open dialogue, being herself actively involved in teaching medical students and others about mental health issues and the importance of a strong recovery ethos.*
>
> *Finally, any invasive procedures can provoke severe anxiety. At such times she may require sedation. In those situations, and in other contexts when fear and anxiety are paramount, a small dose of (a particular medication) and the restoration of a good sleep pattern has proved the most beneficial treatment over the years".*

I will be forever grateful to Dr Tomison as I take his letter to health appointments and receive protection from invasive treatment that others would take in their stride. Other things that Dr Tomison did for me were to receive my writing in which I tried to make sense of my world and when I asked if he would increase Asperger's awareness, his staff attended an Asperger's Awareness Workshop. I know this because I attended the same course.

Dr Tomison retired and said that, "I will hear of you, as I am keeping an interest in mental health". He expects me to make progress and although a few years have passed, I will prove him right. My friend Tony said, "Arden Tomison is one of the good guys". He certainly is.

Chapter 10

RELATIONSHIPS

Many people on their death bed realise that the most important thing in life are relationships and that no-one wishes they had spent more time at work. When surveys are done on counselling, the prominent topic is relationship.

As a woman with Asperger's, my relationships reached crisis pitch after my mother's death. My family broke down and I became marginalised. To help, Rae advised me to focus on the greater worldwide family and to do good where I could. While this was and is good advice, my heart ached to love my family and be loved by them.

What I have realised is that people who make progress and personal change do lose some people and gain others. I have had some lovely friends over the years, but know that if some were still around I would be doing the same things I did years ago.

When I attended church and went to Evening Prayer I met a group of ladies who are lifelong friends. Jean was old enough to be my mum, a lovely lady with pebble glasses. She was very popular and refused invitations from new people, to stay loyal to the friends and groups she had.

The other ladies were Phyllis, who was of the older generation in the Bunce family; Chris, who was just younger than me and Emma, who was at university studying Politics and Sociology. Emma has a beautiful disposition, with wisdom and common sense far beyond her years. Although I loved everyone in the Bunce family, my greatest support went to Emma, who held up a family so dysfunctional that their life story would be a best seller.

I met the group soon after the man of the house had died. After Evening Prayer we would go back to Jean's house for wine and nibbles.

Jean was a fabulous support to everyone, and it was a shock to open my front door early one morning to see Jean's daughter and hear that Jean had hung herself.

From childhood she had risked losing her eyesight and quite suddenly her peripheral vision had gone. Unable to cope, her worst fear was coming about just as she was distanced from her family because of a contagious bug, plus her phone was out of order. She found a solution by ending her life.

We were all devastated, but what saddened me most was that Jean's daughter said, "You were her best friend. Would you help plan the funeral?" Since Jean had so many friends, I felt humbled and privileged, but very sorry I had not known my standing with her, as I would have taken bolder steps to be there for her.

Christine was to die in her early 50s. Chris had endured her life's difficulties with alcohol and decided to go cold turkey to become sober. Soon after, Chris became psychotic and had another difficulty to overcome. Just as the alcohol and psychosis were coming under control, Chris developed cancer and died on the day of my 25th wedding anniversary, eight years ago. I had gone to pick Chris' mother up to visit. Chris was beautiful and had won a heat in the Miss Pears competition as a child. Chris died at peace with her mother. Chris asked me to be a surrogate mother for Emma. I agreed and will always be there for her.

Another important relationship in my life is Joan. I met her at Bristol Cathedral in 1994. At that time I was a heavy smoker and was outside having a cigarette. Joan stopped to talk and showed such joy at our conversation that she said, "Easter has come early for me". We exchanged phone numbers and Joan and I became lifelong friends. We had so much in common – we both wanted to be nuns, were both manic thinkers, always coming up with high ideas and high ideals. At the same time we both suffered crises of energy and some depression.

Having been traumatised by abuses in life, I was like a stuck record going over and over the hurts I had suffered. Like everyone else, this was difficult for Joan and I was always in her prayers. Twenty-two years on we are still friends. As an English teacher Joan has been helpful in giving me guidance for writing and is incredibly talented in the arts, making fabulous greeting cards, lovely landscape paintings and is yet to publish a children's book she has written. Of late I have become a creative thinker, but I have no talent for the arts and I find it quite incredible that my friends are gifted in a variety of arts. Again, my friendship with Joan will be for life. As we have progressed to follow our paths, Joan spends most of her time between church and encouraging others to develop their creativity, while I have digressed into self-development.

My energy levels were inconsistent, which made life difficult. When I had some energy it was burned up quickly. I compared it to a bank account, which constantly fell short before the next income. It was exhausting, as if I were dragging a huge weight.

Soon after the revelation of having Asperger's I met Bernice, who came in to help me with housework. As usual I blurted out my circumstances, crying as I told her I had Asperger's. The news was trauma on top of trauma for me. Bern also supported me through two freak accidents that were literally disabling. The first was when I was sun bathing in a park with Geoff. I was reading a spirituality book and Geoff was working on a Sudoku puzzle. A van had been parked at the top of an incline and with the hand brake not on, the van crept silently down the incline. My first memory was looking up at the underside of the van, which was crushing me. Luckily it was a hot day with a lot of people around. The van got lifted from me, and Geoff and I were taken to hospital. Geoff had a broken wrist where the wheel had gone over his arm and he had been hit on the head by the bumper. Not that long after, Geoff had a stroke.

Bernice was there for us, coming in to help with housework, taking home ironing and giving lifts to the hospital. She was wonderful. She was also there through the second accident at a local gym, after a strap on the equipment I was using gave way. After suffering concussion, I remember waking up on the floor, having hit my head on a skirting board and again I was taken to hospital as I couldn't remember what month it was. My suffering was typical of spinal injuries.

Bernice is also spiritual, choosing to follow the Buddhist way. I have enjoyed being friends on a spiritual journey and seeing her flower in line with the Louise Hay school of thought. Like Yvonne, Bernice has been a rock in my life.

Another lifelong friend is Tony, whom I met at university. Before service user involvement in health took off, Tony had written on the subject. As we worked together he became my buddy and got me involved in many aspects of university life. For a few years I was the only service user in the mental health team. Like many pioneering projects, Tony was a champion for the cause, while others had varying levels of interest.

Tony took early retirement, which is normal within the teaching profession. At the time he left I had given a talk to *Return to Nursing* and described the medical and psychiatric abuse. A wife of a GP was on the course and put in a complaint. If Tony had been there I would have been defended, but I was taken off lecturing with the mental health team.

At the time the situation was traumatic for me, but I have come to learn that when the way forward is blocked and there seems to be a huge loss, the actual gain in understanding is far greater and meets my need for truth on the situation. I realised that despite tutors having elevated status as university lecturers, their knowledge falls short. I was told that my experience did not exist and that some people would be offended. The kinder version was that the drugs messed with my head. I knew differently and feel that if the consultant knew of the wrong doing in his decision to help me, it was unethical practice. If he was unaware of the consequence of his intervention, it would show that the profession is not fully competent in this area. Doctors have this covered by believing that if things go well it is because of a good doctor or if things go wrong it is because of a bad patient!

Within nursing education, staff members are trained not to have outside relationships with patients. I was meeting Tony as a colleague and it was difficult for him to overcome his nurse training and cross that line by becoming friends.

The most important relationship to get right is the relationship with the self. This means having healthy self-respect and self-love, which makes love and respect for everything else possible. This is where 'authorities' have caused a lot of damage to humanity. We are instructed to be selfless and put focus on other people, but that leaves parched and empty selves at soul level.

In the absence of a healthy self, inflated ego, aka the illusory self, takes over. This happens when people need to look good at the expense of another, and however much they have, it is never enough. People believe those at the top are the most powerful, but psychology has shown that the people at the top are the most insecure. When I first heard this, Bill Clinton was in power as President of the United States. When he was young his mother remarried a man who was an alcoholic and the most powerful person in young Bill's world was a counsellor. What did Bill Clinton become? A world counsellor.

People leave the world to go into monasteries and other religious institutions and I used to think that these people had life all sorted. A psychologist friend said,

"People who remove themselves from the world to live in monasteries do so because they can't survive in the world."

I see humanity as a tree, in that however tall it grows it still needs feeding at the root. I also see that that feed is spirituality, from what is natural and nourishes us from depths of soul.

From my own experience and that of my friends, I can see that our point of view given by the family can hold for a lifetime, unless we stop to review and re-evaluate the journey. My parents called me 'dim and stupid' and this set the bar for my life. Unconsciously I now ask the question, "In this circumstance, what would a dim and stupid person do?" Another thing was that when I challenged my sister for bullying me she replied, "I do this not because of any fault of my own, but because you are a horrible person." I am 69 years old and have lived my whole life with this belief, wondering what's wrong with me so that they treat me this way?

Counselling helped me turn this around and Jackie enabled me to web search 'Cluster B Personality Disorders'. This was apparently in my father, my sister, but most of all my step-mother. Even armed with this new knowledge and lots of psychological facts, e.g. that people project their problems on to others, it has taken an incredible amount of effort to make a shift in the way I see myself after being buried under negativity, as the scapegoat.

My greatest heartbreak has been with my family. I cut off from my father and sister because of their dreadful treatment and betrayal. The tragic thing was that my own children bought into my expulsion. The lowest point of my life was when Geoff went into hospital to have a heart valve replacement. I went to my GP for tranquillisers to get through this period. Geoff's operation went well, but a week later he had a stroke. The shock was so bad, it was as if I had frozen with fear.

Visiting hospital was exhausting, but as fortune would

have it, a new hospital had opened within easy reach and Geoff got transferred closer to home. As Geoff was in hospital, the news came through that my father had died. My son Justin asked if I would go to the funeral and I just didn't know what to do. Part of me wanted to go, but another part of me was frightened that I would have an emotional collapse, or with so much anguish within me I might even have attacked my sister. I could not decide.

The thing I had not expected was for Justin's partner to play the game, 'If she's going I am not going'. They were phoning Geoff at the hospital and I felt further betrayal as he was going behind my back and colluding with very harmful behaviour. I was so distressed by the behaviour that I felt the only way was to divorce Geoff and distance myself from everyone, so I stayed away for a couple of days. The game then came into the hospital, where Justin's partner was called in to visit and again calls were happening behind my back. I tried to stop the foolishness by going in at the same time, but Geoff asked me to take a cup back one day and when I returned he was phoning to warn them I was in the hospital. I was left in total isolation by my family, the people I needed for love and support.

The hospital became aware of the situation and the sister kept saying, "But they are your children," and I kept saying, "Yes, I know." With Geoff as their patient it felt as though I had once again become the villain of the piece.

The hospital wanted to send Geoff home, but I wasn't ready emotionally or physically. It was a year after being crushed under the car and I was still receiving physiotherapy and suffering some post-traumatic stress. No-one checked that I was able to have Geoff home or whether I needed support. Rather than accept the offer for Geoff to go into residential care for a week, he did come home with me. For some reason my family seem to think I am invincible. Support was received from Occupational Therapy and Physiotherapy teams and our friend Bernice called in to help.

The worst part of my own problems was that I carried a guilt complex. I needed to get through to my boys that I hadn't abandoned them as children, but that I had been ill. In common with Asperger's, I tried to explain to them in writing what happened, but was rejected because they thought I was trying to blame others. The role of scapegoat was to stay strictly with me.

For years counsellors had tried to help me stop writing to the boys, but it was as though my survival depended on it. One day Jackie said, "You are feeding the demon". From previous counselling and Professor Walter Wink saying, "Each person and each group has an angelic and demonic spirit", I could relate to that and stopped writing to them immediately. From then on, our relationship started to improve. My first counsellor said, "People are frightened of you because you are intense". I can now see that applied to my daughters-in-law and this has helped me heal hurts through self-acceptance.

Relationship is a critical part of our wellbeing. This starts with self-love that moves out to connect with others. In order to survive the annihilation suffered throughout the years, I have worked to repair the disintegration of who I was. I have spent the summer of my life working to reclaim who I am and what is rightfully mine, and at very long last I can see that I am winning. This is a work in progress!

Chapter 11

INNER CHANGE

Writing about inner change has been like building on shifting sand. Each time I attempted to write, I was in a process of change. As I look back it is clear that I was not merely changing, but going through transformation.

Because of my significant process of change I now feel happy and at peace with myself and the world. All is well and the quality of my relationships is improving. The family has been one of my greatest concerns and is at long last in a good place because relationships have better levels of respect and stability.

Spirituality is my most valued asset in life. Creating theories has not only helped me understand what spirit means for me, but I can now explain our inner workings of subconscious to my friends and associates.

We build our worlds on our beliefs and I can understand the parable of the house built on sand and the house built on rock as it relates to me. Feelings are the result of beliefs, and my beliefs now have a rock-like foundation, whereby I feel secure in my knowledge.

There is a saying 'the girl may have left Lawrence Weston, but Lawrence Weston is still in the girl'. I may have left the church, but church teachings are still within my heart and in the fabric of my being. A significant factor in completing my journey is the support received from Mike Hill, Bishop of Bristol. For years I have taken swipes at the Bishops because I felt let down by the church.

After years of working to combine my understanding of Western psychology with Eastern spirituality, I can now see the difference between religion and spirituality. Most people focus on religion. I find it difficult that spirituality has been marginalised in the church. Religion is born out of spirituality, but the spirit of love gets lost because of academia and the power dynamics of politics within the church and other organisations. I have great respect for multi-faith and for people who are devout in a faith that is lived out in the spirit of love and compassion.

As a lost soul, it was my life or death quest to find my way back to a state of 'true', which to me means a feeling of authenticity. With church teachings as my point of reference, I looked to the Bishop as shepherd. I needed to find my way in as a lost sheep. My language might sound strange to most people, but it feels natural for me to use biblical texts and language. Looking back at this instinctual act, it is now clear that the Bishop was my compass as I sounded out my reasoning to find what rang true.

I was aware that the Bishop was busy and had hundreds of letters from people telling their stories, and I was touched by the speed of his reply. Some of the replies came from Uganda or The House of Lords.

My only difficulty has been that as much as Bishop Mike has been there for me as a person finding my way in, he has been unable to validate my work for spirituality and mental health. This is similar to Dr Tomison who worked in the mental health field. Survival has depended on connecting with people I believed could take my theories through, and it has been hard knocking on doors that would or could not open to accept me, due to my difference and my unusual theories. When desperate and in need, I felt it deeply that the organisations had let me down. From a more secure place within myself I can see a bigger picture that makes better sense.

For 40 years I have been a seeker of truth, trying to make sense of my world. I believe that there is no such thing as absolute truth. What I needed to find was the ring of truth within myself. Since the beliefs of my mind had been completely broken, I could work to 'know' the 'ring of truth'. I was a lost soul because the trauma from medical abuse knocked me off kilter and out of true. After a long and arduous process of making a shift through feelings, from seeing to knowing, I am back to a better state of balance. Each day brings a higher level of understanding and with hindsight I can see that I have lived in a state of panic, which is changing to a newly discovered state of calmness.

Easter was my deadline to stop needing to spew words in writing to Bishop Mike. Since then another significant piece of the puzzle has come through, but in order to be true to my word I have held back from writing to him. The next find was relative to 'big bang theory'. We see pictures of the 'big bang' in the universe as an explosion in space, which is the start of creation. We also see a similar 'big bang' picture in the filming of the creation of a baby. What is unseen is the 'big bang' factor that happens in the far reaches of our mind. This was my entry into psychosis, which is the start of the birth of consciousness process within the inner universe of mind.

Transformation has brought a new level of enlightenment. There are no bells, whistles and mass celebrations. What comes to mind is the expression 'Before enlightenment: chopping wood, carrying water and after enlightenment: chopping wood, carrying water'. There is a paradox of sameness, but difference. For the first time in my life I am feeling safe and secure in my newfound knowledge. I have reclaimed my happiness and can again enjoy the simple things in life. I can now be present in the moment and focus on the task at hand.

As distress leaves me, the quality of my life feels enriched. I have been aware of social anxiety for 40 years and it is not easy for me to be part of a group. For a great many years, I have attended slimming groups with little success. At Slimming World, I found that when I entered the spirit of the group, the spirit entered me and I became part of a team to meet and greet people as they came in and to give support throughout the meeting.

Weight has been an issue for me since my teens. I always felt this would be the last thing I conquered. After years of yoyo dieting, I am now at my chosen weight. In life I have found that there is a vicious circle of bad habits, where I take the easy, comforting way out. On the other hand, I can choose the healthier option in the virtuous circle. I am an emotional eater and feel deeply upset when my husband is in pain or unwell and when I witness suffering in others. I need to remember to resume healthy eating when crisis has passed. The next quest is to learn how to maintain a healthy weight and lifestyle.

Throughout my life I had a weak sense of belonging with ongoing feelings of exclusion. Like my family experience, in which my name as the youngest was 'and Linda', when someone joins a current group, he or she is included and I find I am on the fringe. My need for inclusion in groups has meant that I can see my anxiety as neediness, stemming from my experience with family. Things got worse when I started to think for myself and to ask questions. I got pushed out.

Suffering has led me to dissect and analyse situations in order to understand what has happened. Another source of understanding comes after detaching myself from my emotional state of neediness. From my present standpoint on the journey of discovery, I can see that I have lived with a quiet sense of desperation and sometimes it hasn't been so quiet!

Much of my journey has been looking back into the past. This has been with a view to understanding what went wrong, in order to heal the pain. I now have a sense of going forward and am able to focus on the task. Progress is being made and I am now getting results for my efforts.

The levels of peace and harmony within determine the levels of peace and harmony with the world. My relationships are now better and that gives me a huge sense of relief. I feel aligned and true to my relationship with God and myself. As a result, my relationships with others have improved. I approach life with a greater sense of calmness and less anxiety. Road rage and trolley rage in the supermarket are now in the past.

My relationship with one of my sons was threatened when my late sister's family took my disabled husband's wheelchair for the second time. Rather than contact me, or hire one from my share of the inheritance, they got my son to sneak it out of the garage.

Years ago, when I was in the psychiatric hospital due to a breakdown, two people said I had 'doormat syndrome'. In other words, I allow people to walk over me. I put an end to this by writing to my brother-in-law telling him to keep the wheelchair, as I would rather release my right to my share of the inheritance and let him have the lot rather than risk my relationship with my sons.

The last stage of healing is acceptance. I have reached a place where I can accept all that has happened and move on from it. In dying to the old I am moving into a new way. The most difficult shift has been relative to internalised oppression and finding my place. My need has been to unite spirituality and mental health. In line with my beliefs I have worked to give away my theories, but the authorities would not take them up for me. The world would label me 'grandiose' for having high ideals. Still alone, I am attempting to change the world with my theories. Now I ask myself, "Why me?" The answer that comes back is, "Why not?"

I know from student evaluations that trainee doctors, nurses and occupational therapists have gained from my experience and I help them to see the value of their contribution within the field of health care. One third-year student came up to me after my talk, to share that she was on the verge of giving up her studies, but she found my talk so inspiring that she decided to stay on.

Having gone through the depths of grief and sorrow, I am able to meet others in their depths. When they feel lost and suffer a sense of hopelessness, I can connect with them in empathy and explain what they are going through. Having engaged them at the level of feelings, I can share counter logic based on my findings concerning human nature. Friends have told me that I enable them to gain a sense of seeing, which brings them up from a place of hopelessness. They see for themselves when they re-engage with their own inner resourcefulness, which runs true to who they are. This process often has to run a few times until their state of seeing reaches a state of knowing, which enables them to take control of their emotions in any situation. Everything becomes normal within the circumstances and people do the best they can with the resources available to them at the time. The truth does set people free.

Another improvement in my life is my level of energy, which has been in crisis throughout my adult life. Improvement has come about since working with Nicky Marshall, who devised the Discover Your Bounce Programme. She explained energy to me: how we lose it, and how to protect it. In addition, she showed me the way to take my writing from wishing to reality and included me in her book collaboration, *The Missing Piece in Bouncing Back*. My chapter was called 'Warning, Doctors can Seriously Damage Your Health'.

In addition, Nicky has been instrumental in helping me to turn *Trailblazing the Way From Victim to Victor* into reality. I joined Nicky on a Vision Board Day where we pasted aspects of our wildest dreams on to an A3 sheet of card. My board included pictures and words for:

- Best non-fiction. As the book has progressed, I do see potential for it to reach a wider audience.
- Words of wisdom. As world intelligence is shown to fall short, I see the need to return to wisdom that comes from experience, with respect for elders in society.

- I am energised. Energy levels are much better with improved levels of understanding on how to gain and retain wellbeing.
- Without limits. Awareness has expanded as a result of writing the book. It is in going beyond the limitations of mind that we can see and know boundlessness.
- Healer of the Ages. The process within the story has completed my own journey for healing, shows the wrongs that have happened in the world and opens a way to right the wrongs of the past.

I was blind, but now I can see. With Asperger's I have been aware of my inly blindness, as I could not see at the instinctive level. Effectively, we are all blind because we operate from instinct and are not consciously aware of what we are doing. As I have helped my friends to see, my aim is to help others see. I have been frozen with fear, and again others are frozen with fear when it comes to being up against the system, since we have much to lose by challenging the status quo.

Throughout my journey, my strength has been in my belief in what I am doing. My weakness is that I had no belief in myself. Progress has been made by facing fear after fear, and feeling my pain, in order to heal.

Within dictionary definitions the words 'spirit' and 'genius' are linked. We hear that there is genius in madness and Einstein, who is believed to have had Asperger's, was a living genius. I believe that each of us is a genius in our field and due to psychosis, I found my field. The word 'genius' does nothing for my ego, because within my early psyche are the words 'dim and stupid'. I have dyspraxia and so many things go wrong and are beyond my understanding, so it is difficult to see myself as intelligent. Educationally, I achieved very little. My grandchildren overtake my worldly knowledge in primary school.

Life coaching has been a Godsend in my life. Having

trained with The Coaching Academy I have used trainee life coaches to make progress, while giving them feedback and advice. Each one has been wonderful in their different ways, but my latest is Julie Merrett, who has worked as an Occupational Therapist with people who have Asperger's, but more recently become self-employed as *Thriving Artists*. As Nicky has helped with the bigger picture, Julie has explained Asperger's as it relates to me, and worked to either strengthen my inner resources or to make progress in a given task.

Life is the journey, but I see myself as the vehicle to take things forward. To date more time has been needed on me than on the task. At one level this can feel selfish and counter-productive as regards the task. What comes to mind is the story about the man who sharpened an axe and the moral of the story is that sharpening the axe illustrates the need to work on the self.

Work has been a constant review of where I have been, where I am and where I am going. I was lost, but now I am found. I have reclaimed my life and happiness. I genuinely forgive those who have harmed me, as I can see that all experiences have added to the whole. I am happy to be friends with any who would wish to start anew. The difference now is that I will move towards what feels good and right, but away from what feels bad or wrong.

I still have lengthy telephone conversations with my friend Yvonne. Through the years Yvonne has been able to accept my theories on mental health, but has rejected findings on spirituality. She is now able to agree with the spiritual concepts and I reminded her of this. She said that I was making more sense these days and that I was better able to explain things.

Suffering can lead to understanding and understanding leads to wisdom. Stages of womanhood are maid, woman and crone. The richness of my life is in the crone phase, where I have gained wisdom from my experience. With the emergence of technology all value is ascribed to youth and their abilities. Adults have also become more exploitable. Older age has brought me richness of life, but I find the wisdom of age and experience has been devalued and subject to discrimination.

Through the years, fads and phases are subject to change. It is wisdom that passes the test of time, and wisdom calls from wherever it will. As an older person I feel I have much to contribute to the world, firstly supporting my family in their adult phase of life. From there I am able to give emotional support to others by listening and sharing wisdom gained from my experience throughout the years.

With acceptance as the last stage of healing, I accept Asperger's and what it is to me. I am not wrong, but different. In understanding this difference, I can see how I have been demonised by some people, including family members and in-laws. I can now release from the weight of condemnation placed on me, secure in self-knowledge and my life purpose.

The latest gem in my journey of discovery is in the paradox of moving from seeing to knowing oneness of self as an individual towards the oneness with other people. I now feel that I am an intrinsic part of humanity. I can now see why bullying through exclusion and isolation as a sufferer from Asperger's has been beyond painful and felt like a living death. A sense of connectedness is a vital part of our oneness in humanity – and that goes beyond the divisions in the world.

By going through this journey, I am able to make discoveries from my experience that I can share with others to make the world a better place. For the first time in my life I feel fully alive and have no doubt that this is not just the end of a preparatory phase of life, but the start of better things to come.

Chapter 12

FOR THE GREATER GOOD

Einstein taught that whatever got us to this point will not get us where we need to be. The last step in my journey of discovery is to make the shift from individuality to interdependence in the oneness of our humanity with all its diversity.

The paradox that we are different but the same can be explained in that we all need food, but our preferences vary. Some people show a partiality for certain categories of food. Some types of food can be harmful. Nuts, for example, can cause death if there is an allergic reaction, whilst others benefit from them.

I have made sense of my world by combining Western psychology with Eastern spiritual philosophy in order to find answers. I have progressed to reading some complex professional books to find strands of thought to weave in with my own experiences. The problem is that each school of thought has its own language. I have needed to create my own language in order to communicate with those who support my journey of discovery. Finding such a sounding board has been as confusing as conversing in a mixture of languages, such as English, Welsh and Greek.

Is it appropriate that I take what relates to me and apply it to others? A story comes to mind. A man was busy in his office while looking after his young son. To keep the boy occupied, the father cut up a picture of the world and gave it to the boy to put back together. He was amazed as the boy came back quickly. He asked, "How did you do the puzzle so quickly?" The boy replied, "There was a picture of a man on the back. I put the man together and the world came right." On the basis that we miss every shot we do not try, I put out my findings for the greater good of others.

Humanity is like a tree in that however tall it grows, it still needs feeding at the root. With spirituality out of the equation, many parts of the world are suffering from soul deprivation. Lack of food for the spirit is similar to physical neglect in that we wither or die because we lack important nutrients.

My spiritual model demonstrates that we have poles of consciousness. Sub-conscious needs to be in balance with super-conscious, playing out through consciousness, just as positive and negative energies need to be earthed to provide electricity. Each of us as individuals earth the energies from the spiritual poles.

If we continue to live through the animal side of our nature and neglect the spiritual side, we are acting out the law of the jungle. The world is subject to domination and is under threat of World War III, which could well annihilate life as we know it. We have been subject to corruption as well as to the animalistic side of human nature. Manipulators have by-passed conscience and titivated the demonic spirit within of the seven deadly sins at sub-conscious level.

The deadly sins are:

- *Lust* – at the level of immoral sexual acts.
- *Gluttony* – as overconsumption to the point of waste.
- *Greed* – relative to the pursuit of material possessions.
- *Sloth* – as habitual disinclination to exertion.
- *Wrath* – as uncontrolled feelings of anger, rage or even hatred.
- *Envy* – as the wish to own something belonging to another.
- *Pride* – Vulgar display of self-importance. The deadliest of all sins.

The seven deadly sins can be seen operating

throughout the world on a daily basis. I am sure that, like me, most people have seen each of these sins within their own personalities. The problem occurs when people are driven by the need to dominate and to feel important at the expense of others, thus causing suffering.

I suffer from pride and have been told that I am proud and stubborn. I see myself as too proud to suffer the indignities that I feel have been inflicted on me. When I experience a loss of dignity, I retaliate with pride.

As I looked up the seven deadly sins and saw the old meaning, I had a sense of shock as the significance of my discoveries become clear, just as a fisherman reeling in a fish finds something huge on the end of the line.

I have read sociology and woven strands of thought in with my own. I have read spiritual teachings and combined those in my search for truth. As I read aspects of the seven deadly sins relative to the original meaning of the word, it is clear that the emergence and growth of patriarchal ideology has put the world in an 'anti-God' state. This means in fact that the world is directly opposed to God.

Definitions of 'patriarchy' stem from the word 'father'. Men hold the power and women have been cast as people of lower status. According to the Old Testament the people moved out with the women and chattels. This places women somewhere between persons and possessions, so they are second class people. The result is that men in elite positions have set the norms for all of us to live by in today's world. These rules are grounded in ancient history as well as in the law of the jungle. An assortment of powers are vying to be king of the jungle.

An ideology is defined as 'a system of ideas and ideals, especially the one which forms the basis of economic or political theory and policy'. People, parties and countries base their actions on these beliefs.

In the formation of authorities, people have been

conditioned to look to men and organisations as the fount of all knowledge. My own diagnosis from my suffering is 'Post-traumatic Stress Disorder due to iatrogenic harm'. This means that I got injured by a trusted profession whose role was to heal. Authorities have been given poetic licence as to how they treat people. These authorities also provide a system of cover up when things go wrong. The reality is that, when put to the test, patriarchal ideology does not hold up or produce the goods.

The write up on the seven deadly sins reminds us of the Tower of Babel. This was originally meant to explain the world speaking in different languages. My view is that the authorities have created empires, and the Tower of Babel lives on today in the babel of professional languages that keeps each distinct from the other, and maintains separate empires.

Another aspect of pride is that it puts one's own desires, urges, wants and whims before the welfare of others. There are fractals in life, which are repeating patterns. This can be through time and space, but also throughout groups. Patterns of behaviour happen in families and work places, but there is a mega difference between the elite of society and the rest of us. They have power, possessions and privilege way beyond those whom they are meant to serve.

The theory is that the ego and thus the self are directly opposed to God. An acronym of ego is 'Edge God Out' and that is exactly what has happened. Pride has severed humanity from connection with God and I have been very aware of my own soul deprivation, and so I am on a quest to find nourishment to feed the depths of my being and thus attain that union with God.

Possibly the most significant part of the definition of pride is a 'gross over-estimation of one's abilities'. The great majority of professionals are wonderful people who went in for the right reasons and suffer against the odds for their calling. The result of cultural elitism is a sense of right and privilege that is not only grandiose, but deluded. That is just the helping services!

It is also said that when people are placed in positions of immense power, they seem to become irrationally self-confident in their own abilities, increasingly reluctant to listen to the advice of others, and progressively more impulsive in their actions. Love of self is said to change to hatred and contempt for one's neighbour and this plays out in the news of war between nations.

The most negative outcomes result in aggression and hostility, whereby close relationships can be terminated and conflict is created. In short, patriarchal ideology is not working. It seems that the question is simply: do we want peace or do we want a war to end all wars?

Madness is doing the same thing but expecting different results. Mind control has put humanity in a state of semi-sleep. For entertainment we see hypnotists put people in a trance-like state, during which they act totally out of character and do ridiculous things in line with the hypnotist's command. To come out of the hypnotic state people are told to wake up. We all need to wake up to what is happening. We are either contributing or doing nothing as humanity gets closer to the extinction and death of the world as we know it.

The first step in change is to see, and from that point we can do things differently. As Jackie Clarke put the lights on for me in explaining oppression, it is my aim to put the lights on for others to make sense of how, as part of human evolution, we arrived at this moment in time. If we have lived to what is false, the need is to find what rings true.

When we ask ourselves the question, "Who am I?" how many people can answer this without saying, mother, wife or job title. After years of searching for that answer I can now answer, "I am who I am". I could have said that at any time throughout my life, but the answer did not have the full depth of meaning until I could see and know for myself.

Who we are in the world is a construct fashioned by the family, our place within the social structure and the culture in which we live. This is false self. Deepak Chopra teaches that each of us needs to find who we are and our life purpose, in order to live as we were truly meant to. I am now happy where I am and with what I have. The difference now is that I am running true to who I am and putting out a contribution that would otherwise be blocked.

We have been told that where there is poverty we will find oppression. Wealthy fat cats get richer and fatter, while people in other parts of the world are starving or caught up in wars not of their making. While all sympathy goes to the poor and those who are seen to suffer, I have noticed at the end of the day that some who are the unhappiest are those who have gained at the expense of the 'have nots'. My sister may have hogged the lot, by pushing me out of critical relationships and my father's will, but she was filled with anger and incredibly unhappy in her marriage. She died within two years of taking my share of the inheritance after my father's death.

People who come back from giving aid in deprived countries are amazed at how happy and grateful impoverished people are. In the Western world we see rich and famous people taking drugs because they have found that not all that glitters in life is gold. This realisation leaves them feeling unhappy and unfulfilled.

Wounded leaders have created the way in which the class system operates throughout the world. We live to the way it looks rather than to the way it is. Princes William and Harry are now speaking out, claiming that pretence and a stiff upper lip in life is not working. They are calling for the acknowledgement of emotion. They are getting distress out of their systems as they proclaim the truth.

Prince Harry is a wonderful example of a person who has been set up as a scapegoat by the powers that be, to cover up the insanity of the establishment. News reports refer to Prince Harry's mental health as the problem, but his reaction has not only been normal in the circumstances, but he has also done extremely well to emerge at this stage of his life as a good and caring person.

Most young children would be left emotionally scarred if they lost their mother at an early age. In addition to this, Princes William and Harry would have shared their mother's distress at covert behaviours within the hidden agenda of politics. We cannot abuse the mother without abusing the children.

As the seven deadly sins are in direct opposition to a godly way of life, the move towards God would be through the seven virtues. These are:

- *Humility*
- *Charity*
- *Kindness*
- *Patience*
- *Chastity*
- *Temperance*
- *Diligence*

Humility would be to step down from attitudes of superiority and displays of self-importance. With pride as the deadliest of sins, humility would have a knock-on effect converting other aspects of the sins to the virtues.

The antidote to lust leading to adultery, rape and bestiality is chastity. This is now taken as abstinence from the sexual act, but progress has shown that we give more power to what is repressed. A condition for priests to be accepted into certain religious groups is chastity. We receive constant news of perverted or immoral acts by priests, knowing that many improprieties have been covered up. The sexual act should be grounded in love and I believe the right spirit for love making can be found in the Song of Songs within the Bible.

A new world needs a new way. For me the new way would be through the teachings of Richard Rohr, who is a

Franciscan Monk. We live in a binary world, which means that we are aware of two opposites. A controller can weaken others with a view to gaining power by pitting opposites against each other. This is often seen in the political world. Rohr suggests the power of three, whereby another dimension is added to find a creative solution. Powers of three would include Father, Son and Holy Spirit or mind, body and spirit.

I realise the power of three within my study, which connects with the first two commandments, which are:

- Love God with all your heart
- Love others as you love yourself. This puts love of self in first place in order to give out to others.

To me, love of God is spirituality; love of self is psychology; love of others is sociology where we are all interdependent.

The world has lost its way and we need to find our way back. We have lost all sense of integrity and now live to immoral standards in most, if not all areas of life.

The most important part of the return to a loving world is the integration of the best of female virtues with the best of male virtues. Equality does not mean being the same, but equal in value to the other. Humanity needs to replace what is false with what is natural in nature and nurture. When spiritual and emotional needs are met, greed will fade.

The Telegraph newspaper reported that $1.57 trillion was spent on weapons last year. The turn from war to peace would mean that this huge amount of money could be spent to balance the inequalities, thus creating greater fairness. Through compassion we need to heal and repair health and life that has been damaged by abuse of power.

We hear that the end of the world is nigh. This can either mean the end of the world or the end of the world as we know it. Some aim for a new world order of domination, but with a turn to the holy virtues, we could have a new world order grounded in love and an all-inclusive spirituality.

To date, genius has been rare. I call to mind Roger Bannister in that medics said no-one could run at four miles an hour or the internal organs would burst. Once Roger Bannister beat the record, more and more people broke that record. It is all in the belief.

We live with man-made intelligence that is actually very limited and often foolish. There is more to it than humanity can understand at the present time. We need to look beyond form to the formless for a new dimension in understanding. A good start would be to work with people who are Asperger's or experience psychosis. Beyond that, people would need to work to find their life purpose within true self, which can be found in the heart of each and every one of us.

Good people go through hell because they can't forgive themselves. As for me, I went through hell because it felt as if I had betrayed my young sons by breaking down and so they felt abandoned. I worked out that if I couldn't be with them I would work to make a better place for them. In part, this work is over-compensation. It is my way of telling my family and friends that I love them.

Throughout the world people are suffering and many are going through hell. Who is to blame? No-one, but everyone has some responsibility. We are here as an unbroken line since creation. How fabulous is that? I feel that we are all part of ongoing human evolution and now have had an opportunity to see the foolishness of our ways, whereby our actions are taking us towards World War III and extinction. The words 'darkness' and 'valley of death' need to have meaning in today's world, because unless there is change that is where we are heading.

Humanity is the prodigal son who needs to turn back. Each and every one of us as people and nations has something to give to and receive from the whole. The best in life is yet to come, so instead of leaving our children a poisoned chalice let us point the way towards the land of milk and honey.

Tony De Mello said that if people knew better they would do better and sin is ignorance. We take ourselves too seriously and we should be like Buddha and see the funny side of life. God has given us a sense of humour, and laughter is the best medicine as we turn in the right direction.

At the end of the day life is about relationship. This book has covered how spirituality applies to me but shows the unity of the mind of humanity. Universal truths speak to the soul of each and every one of us. The truth of the theory of relativity within the inner world is not known in the mind, but through the ring of truth in the heart.

CONCLUSION

This book has been difficult to write. Bringing back memories of being a victim has raised a lot of painful emotions. In addition to feeling emotional anguish, my progress has been halted on many occasions because of the fear of putting myself out there. My soul has been bared and there is a sense of vulnerability as I am ultimately saying, "This is me at this moment in time." It is important for me to find some level of balance and I can appreciate that people who victimise others have often been abused themselves, but I am glad that not all people who have been abused go on to abuse.

At the same time, writing my story has been a therapeutic event, as it became a healing process. I have come to learn so much from the experience. The thought at the moment is that actions are prompted by emotion and then justified by logic. In addition, nothing is done for just one reason, and my personal needs in writing have included getting it out of my system, finding a means of being heard and setting the record straight.

Emotion and logic are both valuable, and I have found that stability means living with emotion and logic in balance. Due to problems with my family, the medical profession and the church, I have come to an in-depth understanding of the angelic and demonic spirit that exists within each person and each group. With a more balanced view, I have a great appreciation of each of these groups and feel the world would be a sorry place without them. I am extremely grateful each time the medical profession has helped my husband.

For 40 years I have been facing fears and have experienced painful emotions in order to come out on the other side. The fears I have faced have been huge. My need, rightly or wrongly, has been to gain support in spite of my unconventional way of working. To date, this has not happened.

I am coming to see that each and every one of us is uniquely different. No two pictures or life stories have ever been the same. My story and theories will not be a perfect fit for anyone else, but I go forward for two reasons. Firstly, my story and findings may resonate with people who wish to take what inspires them for their own journey. Secondly, my experience and insights may prove helpful for those in a profession or institution, who wish to understand and help others.

It is part of the human way to accept what fits our beliefs and to reject what contradicts them. My book contradicts convention on many levels. I asked one lovely lady if she would receive my manuscript. Her answer was, "Great to hear you are well and have written a book! However, I might not be the best person to look at it because, if you remember, we have opposing views in this area . My central thesis is about getting away from spatial metaphors and so sub- and super-consciousness are not where I am coming from. I am sure though, that your theories will resonate with many people who do see things in these binary terms. The Asperger's perspective will be particularly valuable and needed - so I wish you all the very best with getting in touch with the right people to help your enterprise forward."

I respect the lady who gave this response and I am grateful she replied by return. The answer to my request was a complete surprise. This gave a quantum shift to my thinking, where I realised I felt alone where convention is concerned. The thing that validates me is that my journey has worked for me. I also know that I have reached friends when they have been in a deep, dark place and they have risen up to be stronger and wiser for the experience. Within the hundreds of evaluations I have received for my talks, which have been tailor made for different groups, the main word used is 'inspiring'. The word most used to describe me is 'courageous'. I have the courage of my convictions and will continue to work on this subject.

Is my fear valid? It most certainly is. Within my experience the psychiatrist with theological experience set out to annihilate me. I was devastated at that time as damaging letters went out to my GP and others saying that I was schizoid. Consequently a job that I was enjoying at the time came to an end.

What is different now? I am in a stronger place and I am more secure in my identity. Beliefs that did not prove true have fallen away and I am stronger because of my revised thinking. What I have come to know is not hard and fast. A concept from someone else can still cause a quantum shift in my understanding, rather like a turn on a kaleidoscope when the whole picture changes.

I am happy to receive different strands of logic because it adds a new dimension to my picture. I hope others can receive my story in the same way. My fear has been that people from alternative schools of thought with different views will set out to trash my work, my identity, or what I bring to the world. There is an upside to everything. If people do set out to trash my work, it will demonstrate the demonic spirit. For the ruling elite to rule, they need conformity from the masses. Free thinking is not welcome.

While I consider spirit greater than ego, each of us has an ego. I have found that as self-respect and self-love improves, I feel better. The levels of love and respect I hold for myself are reflected in the way others treat me.

I am on a journey of transformation and find that not only does suffering lead to understanding, but that the greater the suffering, the greater the understanding. I believe the difference between my sister and I was that my sister was driven by jealousy, greed and revenge, while despite having these traits in myself, I have been driven by the need to love and to be loved. This has helped me to overcome the pain of abuse in myself and in others.

I have now reclaimed the deep love I had for my husband when we were first married and would describe my marriage as happy. I am overjoyed that the difficulties with my sons are over and there is love and warmth from both them and their children. They take care when buying greeting cards, love and appreciation are often expressed in the verses. I have proved that if we want to change the world we have to change ourselves first. It has taken an incredible amount of work, but it has all been well worth it.

The family demon has broken up and I am now careful not to feed it by dropping back into victim mode when I am with my sons. I do have difficult moments when I go to a dark place, but now recognise that some situations trigger fears and feelings of victimisation. These are now further apart and fewer in number and don't last so long. Most memories that were painful now feel as though they are in the distant past, as if I have woken up from a dream.

The vastness of spirit is often referred to as 'the ocean of spirituality'. Spiritual progress towards healing emotional anguish is rather like riding the waves. Sometimes all is calm and at other times waves can come through, from small ripples to larger billows. Recently I told a couple of friends about a small wave I needed to ride when we spent time with Geoff's brother at a family event. Unnoticed by others, Geoff's brother pushed me with an instruction to go and get food. Words alone don't mean much because they are only 7% of the communication with 38% being in the tone of voice and 55% in the body language. One friend congratulated me on my progress and thought I handled the situation well as he was trying to control me. The other friend said that he was a boor and had bad manners.

My journey from victim to victor continues to be a work in progress. I feel like Columbo, the TV detective, who keeps saying, "There is just one more thing".

An incident at church brought painful awareness that

I still feel victimised. The emotional wound became undeniably obvious and ripe for healing. The trigger for painful memories came because I asked for consideration regarding the volume of music, which was loud even before the service began. The trigger initiated a knock-on effect from other heart-felt pains due to previous feelings of victimisation in the church. In addition to that, other painful memories caused by my in-laws and even by my own family were awakened. I have felt unloved and unwanted from the time of my birth.

I was unable to contain the emotional anguish. My Asperger process kicked in. I needed to reduce the anguish I felt through a process of understanding, in order to make sense of my world. I was in a dark place because I was reliving emotions from several time zones simultaneously.

Family and church are the closest to my heart. That is where I feel the greatest levels of love and pain. I have been heartbroken by the treatment I suffered, and all I was doing was working to love and be loved. Courage is also from the heart and it is my love for the greater power, whatever we might wish to call it, that keeps me going forwards.

This is what happened on that day at the church. As I entered the foyer someone commented that the music was loud. I spoke to the appropriate person and asked for the volume to be turned down, explaining that I had Asperger's and the volume was hurting my eardrum. I was met with cold indifference, and this is what triggered feelings caused by unresolved events from the past.

To backtrack: when I asked the vicar for inclusion, he said that it was not for everyone to have a role. Effectively, this is victimisation, because the message I received was that I was unworthy of God's love and a place in God our Father's house. I looked to the church for the power of God's love through the Word. The spirit transforms this to healing of mind and body for me. Instead, I have suffered prejudice and discrimination. My difference is seen as deviation and I have been treated as an undesirable.

As the pain of rejection was re-stimulated, I felt fury towards the vicar who had marginalised me in my church. The force of the fury frightened me, because if it had got out, the power within my rage would have been out of control.

Previous to leaving the church and trying again, I wrote an article on Asperger's, explaining our sensitivities and how noise is difficult for us. After that, I asked the vicar for help with noise during the sermon and he refused. I left the church, because in addition to not getting my special needs met, I was in distress. I once read 'the person who leaves is not necessarily the deserter'. If this was in the world of employment, my departure would be classified as constructive dismissal, because my only option was to leave.

In examining my life, I can see that my reaction and process are typical of a woman who lives with Asperger's. There has been no compassion shown towards me or acceptance of my difference. In my opinion, I have suffered discrimination in the church due to my disability, and the church has failed in its duty of care towards me.

From my perspective, Christianity is not about how priests flatter the bishops. It is not about rewarding people who flatter the ego of the leaders. It is about how they treat the last and the least. Christ's words come to mind, "As you do unto the least of these you do unto me".

What is the duty of priests? I see their role as giving out and living out the love of God. The Word of God, mostly the Gospel teachings, feeds me because it is about humanity living in love with one another. With the right atmosphere and a good sermon, my inner state and life are enriched.

Recently I have been able to feel a lovely sensation as I sit and hear the music and words of beautiful hymns. It is as though my heart is singing. A visual description of my experience would be that of lights emitting on a sound system when music is played. It is a beautiful sensation that brings balm even when I am in the midst of suffering. It also evokes blissful transformation.

I set out as a child to understand what was wanted and to get it right for the people I loved. Instead I have found a huge discrepancy between what is said and what is meant. A line from a childhood poem comes to mind, "Close your eyes my darling, while the gentlemen go by." The thing that puts me in opposition towards the majority who uphold the man-made ideal, is the pretention that the power elite and their followers work to uphold.

Abuse relies on a conspiracy of silence that includes the victim and the rest of us who shut our eyes to the harsh realities in life. No-one suffers in isolation. We are all victims of the system. As I have sought truth to set myself free from victimhood, it is my hope that my work will resonate as truth and people will see what is happening and know it in their hearts.

Healing of my emotional wound is now taking place. Feelings of intimidation and powerlessness are fading, to be replaced by an inner state of balance and steadfastness. I will no longer allow myself to be bullied out of what is mine. My values are truth, integrity and love and my advancement is in line with my values. My mission statement is to end abuse by exposing the domination system and promoting love.

For over 40 years I have been working to understand human nature. It is now time for action and at this moment in time I am waiting to hear from the Disability Adviser who works at the church. At this stage of the journey, I feel sad at the realities that I am exposing. I am not looking for revenge, but pray for illuminated understanding that will bring positive change. It is my hope that I can work with the church and others as an educator on disabilities. Whatever the outcome is, I will work on. Watch this space.

FURTHER READING

Christian Writers

Recovering Your Destiny	Bob Gass
Person-Centred Counselling and Christian Spirituality	Brian Thorne
The Mystical Power of Person-Centred Counselling	Brian Thorne
Develop the Leader Within	John C Maxwell
Immortal Diamond	Richard Rohr
The Powers That Be	Walter Wink
The Shack	Wm Paul Young

Spiritual Writers

Power Vs. Force	David Hawkins
The Power of Now	Eckhart Tolle
A New Earth	Eckhart Tolle
Awaken to Your Life's Purpose	Eckhart Tolle
Mindfulness for a Broken Heart	Jackie Hawken
One Hundred Tips to Love Your Life	Nicky Marshall

The Alchemist	Paulo Coelho
The Monk Who Sold His Ferrari	Robin Sharma
Radical Acceptance	Tara Brach
Change Your Thoughts Change Your Life	Wayne Dyer
Pulling Your Own Strings	Wayne Dyer

Self-Improvement

Cavemen & Polar Bears	Andy Workman
Be Your Own Life Coach	Fiona Harrold
The Miracle Morning	Hal Elrod
The Missing Piece in Self-Love	Kate Gardner
Wounded Leaders	Nick Duffield
The Missing Piece in Bouncing Back	Nicky Marshall
Don't Sweat the Small Stuff	Richard Carlson
7 Habits of Highly Effective People	Stephen Covey
How to Mind Map	Tony Bozan

Academic

Professionalism Reborn	Eliot Freidson
Transactional Therapy in Psychoanalysis	Eric Berne
Games People Play	Eric Berne
Stigma	Erving Goffman
Institutions	Erving Goffman
Gestalt Therapy Verbatim	Frederick Salomon Perls
Re-evaluation Counseling	Harvey Jackins
The Primal Wound	John Firman and Ann Gila
Carl Jung	Saul McLeod

ABOUT THE AUTHOR

Like many others, Lynn slipped the net as a person with Asperger's, which led to the incredible life journey she now shares in her writing. Lynn is a woman of courage, who inspires others and campaigns for change through awareness. Her suffering brought a wealth of understanding on the nature of abuse and the healing power of love.

Through self-directed learning, Lynn works to promote a better and safer way of working for medical students. Through writing and speaking, Lynn works to reduce abuse, promote love and empower people to redress the balance of power. Lynn qualified with distinction at The Coaching Academy as a life coach, helping personal growth and change. She also qualified with the Institute of Supervisory Management and Toastmasters International.

Publications and papers

- *The Missing Piece in Bouncing Back* 'Warning – Doctors Can Seriously Damage Your Health' ISBN 978-1-63452-986-0
- *The Missing Piece in Self Love* 'From Brokenness to Wholeness' ISBN 978-1-5136-0186-1
- Nursing Standards Sept 23-29, 2009 *The Healing Relationship*
- Article for Bristol Disability Equality Forum Autumn/Winter 2015 *Asperger's, From the Inside*
- Regular articles for St Augustine's Church Magazine on social concern and spirituality

- Blog contributor for Spiritually Connecting

Lynn's experiences and suffering have led to a 40-year study to gain understanding and Lynn has produced spiritual theories which have gained validation from:

Validation of theories

- Professor Brian Thorne
- Professor Walter Wink

Previous Speaker Engagements

- In hospitals at doctor's lunch time education meetings
- Student doctors – mental health and Asperger's
- Mental health student nurses
- OT students on psychosis
- Workshops:
    - Asperger's
    - Do Less and Achieve More

In writing this book Lynn hopes to give a unique and alternative view of life that challenges the status quo to create better partnerships working between Experts by Experience and professional workers.

Lynn is available for talks and can be contacted on jones_m_lynn@hotmail.com.

Her website is www.lynnmjones.co.uk.

88171522R00090

Made in the USA
Lexington, KY
09 May 2018